This Victorian Playground

Part I

Policing a Victim Culture in Britain

PC Michael Pinkstone

Published by

MELROSE BOOKS

An Imprint of Melrose Press Limited
St Thomas Place, Ely
Cambridgeshire
CB7 4GG, UK
www.melrosebooks.com

FIRST EDITION

Copyright © PC Michael Pinkstone, 2008

The Author asserts his moral right to
be identified as the author of this work

Cover designed by Richard Chambers

ISBN 978-1-906050-63-4

Printed and bound in Great Britain by:
Biddles, 24 Rollesby Road, Hardwick Industrial Estate
King's Lynn. Norfolk PE30 4LS

For Robyn
my love, my life

Contents

Contents (cont.)

Introduction Part I

Hello. My name is PC Michael Pinkstone. Whether or not I'm a PC by the time you've finished reading this book is another matter, but hey-ho. What matters is that I'm a PC now and I have a warrant card to prove it. I'm a real life, flesh and blood police constable with short brown hair and a cheesy grin. I am also an opinionated little so-and-so. This book is therefore full of my feelings about the current state of play within the police service in Britain, and how fucked up it all really is. For that I remain completely unrepentant. This book is also about attitude and existence. It's about mentality. It's about Britain itself, and where we find ourselves at the moment.

However, please do not expect to find anything libellous, crude or personally offensive on the forthcoming pages. No names are mentioned. No secrets told. This book is not intended in any way to bring the police service into disrepute. The only disreputable behaviour mentioned is political incompetence that leads to quite mind-boggling administrative procedures and organisational antics. Although the police are not completely without fault – they are, for the most part, simply doing what they are instructed to do by the Government. And when I talk about 'The Government' – this applies primarily to the administration at the time of writing this book, but the other political parties shouldn't feel in any way blameless. They are all a part of this shambles too. For in the event of any change of Government, the pressing points raised in this book are valid regardless, and it would be up to any new administration to prove that they are taking serious heed of them – although I don't hold out too much hope. While each political party can poke their fingers at each other concerning the current situation – the point remains the same: we're buggered. In which case, let's do something about it …

No-one is without blame in this life. We are all responsible for our actions and, sometimes, our omissions. We are accountable for everything that we end up doing or neglect to do. Whether we like it or not, we are all a part of this crap and we all have the option of doing something about it. We are all answerable for the journeys we take and the choices we make.

My own current journey began a few years ago when I joined the police service, having spent several years pretending to be a primary school teacher. One day I even got an award for being 'Supply Teacher of the Month'. This basically meant that I was stupid enough to work in schools where all the teachers were having nervous breakdowns and the children threw heavy items of furniture at each other. I once went into a school in Plymouth and introduced myself to the Head, having arrived to teach a Year 5 class. He looked wearily at some blood-stained list and said, 'Oh. You're in Mrs Wilson's class.' I said, 'Oh, OK.' He glanced at me with a mixture of pity and helplessness. 'I'm going to go and fetch Luke,' he said. 'Oh, OK,' I said again, thinking that Luke would show me where the classroom was. Perhaps he was one of those *helpful* children. 'I'm going to fetch Luke,' repeated the Head slowly, 'because if he sees you and doesn't know you, he *will* throw a desk at your face. He did it last week to poor Miss Turner…' At this his eyes wandered back to the tattered and bloody list in his hands. 'Sign here Mr Pinkstone,' he said, holding out the list. 'I'll show you to the classroom …'

Fortunately I left all of that behind. All of that danger and unpredictability. All of that red tape and Government bureaucracy. All of those little swines who wanted to hurt me and blame me and call me nasty names. So I joined the police service instead. I leapt with a kind of blind stupidity from the frying pan into the kiln. I'm not even sure why I joined now, come to think of it. Ah, that's right. I joined to make the world a better place. I joined to lock up the children I had once taught. The children who had once thrown things at me and attacked me with sharpened objects. I joined to kick the shit out of the little bastards because I couldn't do it in the classroom. That's not true by the way. I don't advocate violence. But I do advocate common sense and justice.

I even spent two years teaching in Kuwait. I moved there at the end of August 2001 and then had the added intricacy of being surrounded by Arabs and Asians during September 11th. Surrounded by people who are stereotyped in the West. Although a lot of them seemed particularly cheerful about the incident, not one of them ever said or did anything nasty to me, or my Western colleagues. The majority were horrified, albeit in a somewhat distant kind of way. For most people I met out there were wonderfully kind, hospitable and endearingly friendly, yet clearly cultures apart. An Egyptian taxi driver called Ibrahim picked me up from outside my flat on September 12th and he was beaming all over his face. 'Ibrahim,' I said, 'why are you smiling?' He said, 'America. It's good we got America.' A rather distasteful thing to say considering the monstrous nature of what had happened, yet not said with any malice whatsoever. He just said it, and was quite surprised to find that I didn't agree.

It's a bizarre world we live in. A bizarre world indeed. It's also a dark and suspicious world, filled with clashing convictions and eternal hatreds. Ibrahim was one of the nicest chaps I've met by the way. Just in a completely different place. I mention this because it is relevant and important. Relevant, in part, to some things I raise in my book. It's relevant to race and diversity. It's relevant to Britain today. It's also important because one thing we need above all else is a completely blunt and honest look at the way things are. We need to be quite candid indeed. No holds barred!

So not long after that I returned to England and joined the job. Did my training and went straight to shift as a regular frontline PC. And here I am today. Neither a sinner nor a saint. In fact, I'm a nice guy really. My friends will tell you the same, hopefully. I even think I'm quite good at my job! So far no-one has given me too much of a bollocking about anything. So far everything has been quite satisfactory. So far my Performance Development Review hasn't highlighted any particularly gaping crevices in my ability to police in this super country of ours. So far things are going OK. I even managed to pass my Sergeant Part I Promotion Examination first time in March 2007. (I didn't get above 70%, in case you were wondering. Close though.). So I'm neither a genius nor a thicko. In fact, I think I'm kind of ordinary and should be getting on with my job without moaning. The world is my oyster!

Yet, of late, I have become somewhat downhearted. Somewhat angry even. Elastic limit has been reached and I'm now holding on to the frayed edges of the endmost part of my tether. The simmering, bubbling fury erupts on regular occasions, echoed by many of my friends and colleagues. Such are my outbursts of rage and malcontent that I have earned the rather glitzy – but unofficial – title of 'Shift Morale Officer'. You can count on me to make everything better and boost your happiness and self-esteem! If you're in a world of shit, I'll grab you by the hand and pull you out. Actually, I won't. I'll take a seat next to you, light up a cigarette and agree with every darn word you say. It really is quite naff at the moment.

So why am I writing this book? Surely we all know what it's like in the police service already? Well I think we *do*, and we don't. We certainly know *what* it's like, but we are not entirely sure *why*. We all have some ideas as to the context of this current crappiness, but I'm not sure if many coppers have been daft enough to try and explain it in such viciously opinionated detail. So that's what I've done, or at least tried to do. I've theorised and postulated and criticised and moaned and bitched and been sarcastic and silly and everything else I can think of. Hopefully by the end of the book you'll feel as exhausted as me.

Now as an ex-teacher I'm going to do something a bit teachy. After all, one can't escape the past. I'm going to share with you my objectives. That is to say I'm going to tell you what I aim to do in this book. It's something of a new-fangled teaching method. I never recall it happening when I was at school. Objectives? What the hell are they? I think my teachers all operated in a much less educational environment than they do nowadays. Anyway it's how it is today in schools. We share our lesson objectives with the class. Well, I no longer do such a thing because I escaped. So these are my objectives. At the end of the book you have to look at them again and see if any of them have come true for you.

Objectives

- To examine why the police service is fucked up and how this is mainly the fault of the Government
- To discuss the tragic demise of common sense and explore the scourge of political correctness
- To examine what the hell I mean by 'Victim Culture'
- To inspect the issue of 'Diversity' and beat the stuffing out of it in the process

- To redefine 'Racism' and make some comments that fly in the face of current 'acceptable' behaviours
- To give examples of the prevailing crappiness by telling real-life policing stories and embellishing some of them for fun
- To vociferously argue against the current administrative sludge clogging up the police service
- To try to bring some small measure of reality and context back to life in Britain before I leap off a pier in utter despair

In which case, we'd better get going. We'd better move on to the, er, second part of the Introduction …

Introduction Part II

There's plenty of talk at the moment about 'reducing bureaucracy' in the police service. By the time you read this book it will be a few months since I wrote it. In which case there may very well have been some changes. Certain procedures may have altered and particular policies may have been modified. Concerns raised about specific things may have led to variations here and there. However, you can be sure that where one bureaucratic method is removed, it will be replaced by another. Nothing changes. For the problem is not simply 'bureaucracy.' Rather it is the mindset that creates bureaucracy in the first place. The problem is therefore not a superficial one. It goes extremely deep. It's not so much about what we do – it's about *why* we do it. You can change procedures all you like, but until there are elementary changes at the deepest levels of political thought, attitude and mentality, the police and the country are not going to get any better.

For Britain is in a serious social predicament.[1] The police are running ragged.[2] The Government makes it worse. To say that we

---

1 Basically Britain is fucked.

2 Frontline policing is also fucked. The Home Office is sorting this out by cutting our budget even more and then 'helping' us cope with our lack of funds by sending in teams of 'experts' to offer advice and make suggestions. Very soon we'll have no one and nothing left. Very soon things will disintegrate like vampires in *Blade.*

are caught up in a vicious circle of immense political proportions is to make a rather significant understatement. To say that we are affected by a deleterious cloud of political correctness is to step somewhat short of the mark. To say that the police service is battered, bruised and almost broken, is to appreciate only half the problem. We are in *terminal* decline. We are damaged perhaps beyond repair. We have a one-way ticket to the end of the line. The very end.

We need a wake-up call and we need it now. We need to stop farting around and start addressing problems with real honesty and integrity, not just pretend we do. This book aims to slice directly through all the layers of pink and fluffy bullshit and get as close to the heart of the matter as possible. This book is not so much about what is going on in the police service, but an attempt to explain why things are the way they are. An attempt to put things into context. Although I write from the perspective of a serving police officer, it is not my intention to simply talk about the police and what the police do. However, I hope that even when I do talk about the police, you will note parallels in other organisations or businesses.

We are all puppets of the administration and it is my firm belief that the police clearly represent and reflect the whims and impulses of any Government. Attitudes and priorities change like shifting sands, and the police get given targets in line with whatever the current priorities are. Meeting those targets then becomes *our* priority, and in doing so inspires some of the most bizarre, detrimental and nonsensical organisational behaviour you can imagine.

What has started off as a rather good theory in the halls of power becomes a procedural nightmare and bureaucratic swamp for the police. At present we are wallowing in a quagmire of unnecessary and burdensome administrative sludge. Our role is made all the more arduous by a society that has gradually lost its sense of direction, self-esteem and ability to take responsibility for itself. Over the past several years, and especially of late, the police have moved away from enforcing the law to grovelling in pathetic deference before a socially inept and incontinent nation. Ironically enough, the *true* victims of this nightmare are the people who have always been the victims – those who really don't want to be. But for those people who enjoy being victims, it's a playground.

Now I think it would be somewhat rude of me to present this book to you without acknowledging the fact that others have written about many of the same issues contained within my book. Some of my material echoes what is in those publications, as it is relevant to my overall theme. This will, I trust, only help to prove the points each author makes. So if you have read elsewhere about the administrative nightmare within the police, I do apologise! Any repetition, though, should be seen as necessary and positive, as certain issues are worth reiterating time and again. If we make enough noise perhaps someone in their ivory tower will actually take heed.

With my book, though, I have aimed to be more detailed about certain issues than other publications, and add a level of potency and rage perhaps hitherto unexpressed in print by a police officer. So between the few of us that are stupid enough to write books, or annoyed enough to maintain police 'blogs', perhaps someone, somewhere – at some point – will stop suggesting that we are writing works of 'fiction' and take notice. And then actually do something incisive to sort out a fucked up police service and a fucked up country.

Despite my feelings of ire, however, I have to say that the organisation for which I work is excellent and I am proud to be a part of it. I doubt that I will ever work for a better police service than the one for whom I work now; or be surrounded by such committed and worthy colleagues and superiors.

Like all the other police organisations across the country it is full of hard working and dedicated staff. This book is *not* in any way intended to be purely an indictment of the police itself and in no way an indictment of the behaviour of any of my colleagues. Although I think the police could stand up for itself more against the bureaucratic crap spawning forth on a daily basis from the Government, it is clear that we really have to do as we are told.

I have had to be extremely negative and condemning in this book about a great number of topics, and my disapproval forms the basis of many of my arguments. Basically there is really very little to be cheerful about, so I didn't have much choice. This scepticism, though, does not negate the hard work and positive effort of any member of police staff in the communities they serve. Nor does it undermine any excellent results achieved through skilled investigation and unwavering dedication to the job. Unfortunately, though, we are all pissing against the wind, and despite all our effort, significant change is needed in all areas to ensure that the police service itself can maintain any form of effectiveness in the forthcoming years.

I make no apologies for sounding harsh and for slamming the way things are however. There is a great deal of malcontent simmering away under the surface in the police service, as has already been highlighted in other brave and praiseworthy publications. This malcontent is not without very due cause. Furthermore such ill-feeling is clearly visible in modern British society and I also address potential reasons for this, as well as possible repercussions. I hope you enjoy this book and find it useful and enlightening. I do not bombard you with facts and figures, but with observations and opinions only. You have every right to agree or disagree as you see fit.

PC Michael Pinkstone
June 2007

I do solemnly and sincerely declare and affirm that I will well and truly serve the Queen in the office of constable, with fairness, integrity, diligence and impartiality, upholding fundamental human rights and according equal respect to all people; and that I will, to the best of my power, cause the peace to be kept and preserved and prevent all offences against people and property; and that while I continue to hold the said office I will to the best of my skill and knowledge discharge all the duties thereof faithfully according to law …

… by doing lots of pointless, ineffective things,

… but in a streamlined, efficient and business-like manner.

1. The Victim Culture Part I

We begin this book by examining the current stalemate concerning the police and society – a stalemate wherein everyone blames everyone else, and no-one really accepts responsibility for anything. We are locked in a ceaseless tug-of-war between *trying* to deal with crime and social ignorance and not actually being able to deal with it. Our ability to effectively combat the numerous social and cultural defects present within Britain is persistently undermined by a veritable festival of poo. It's a pageant of dung. A festoon of turds. A carnival of crap. A decorative wreath of doo-doos. We are submerged beneath a cow pat of political and social incompetence so rich and abundant that the baneful fumes emanating from this extensive pile of excrement have radically altered our minds and stripped us of our common sense.

A Government that is both weak and insidious, limited by its own grovelling and spineless incapacity has brought Britain to a shameful and shuddering stand-off. No longer is Britain a nation to be reckoned with. No longer do we stand with our heads held high. Instead, our national pride has been replaced with a national guilt and a national sentiment of paranoia where people of substance, grit and honour are overshadowed and undermined by sycophantic fools in ivory towers.

We've been sold off cheap to the lowest bidder. Abandoned. Deserted. Cast aside. Courage and fortitude rejected in favour of lap-dog drooling and cushion-plumping subservience. A once mighty nation now pimping ourselves out like budget bitches: the tacky lipstick of political correctness and gaudy garlands of so-called human rights doing little to cover up our emaciated and fragile frame. We're grovelling. Bowing down. Craving our next fix. Weak and pathetic and contemptible. Cringing and wheedling. Pleading. Entreating. Honour and valour lying in overgrown graves and lonely cemeteries; the selfless sacrifice of millions engraved on neglected crosses of marble. Streets and pathways where once the feet of our worthy ancestors trod; now littered, filthy; stained with blood and vomit.

Britain has become a whore-house of specious, pandering, political charity. All we do is tease and tickle, without any real satisfaction at the end of it. There's nothing of substance. Nothing of focus. Nothing of permanence or stability. We flit and flirt and fuck around: public urges and national needs met with short-term political fixes. Organisations left blustering, fussing and farting about, chasing pointless targets and seeking irrelevant goals. Promises of social integration and community cohesion, spawned by vague and half-baked policies – insipidly inspired and indifferently implemented.

We're fractured. Dislocated. Disjointed and disengaged. Postmodern values of life and living equating to nothing more than cultural wretchedness. So-called morality and decency little more than scummy, pitiable, disease-ridden ideals, oozing from every pus-filled social pore and orifice. We're encrusted with the filth of self-obsessed, self-conscious political inveigling; creating for ourselves little kingdoms; fiefdoms of municipal glory, yet ignoring the desperate cries of the forsaken and forgotten: those downtrodden souls who truly need a tough and tangible resolve to uphold their rights and liberties – tempered by compassion and humility; to cradle them in secure and steadfast arms when the weight of despair crushes and smothers them, and emotion beleaguers them to the point of untold desolation. For we will be defined by our actions and not our policies, and judged by the worthiness of our deeds in a world screaming out for justice and liberation.

Yet here we are, languishing in our civic citadels; chilling in our sanctimonious sanctuaries: political strongholds built upon insolvent promises and perfidious truths; an absolute abandonment of ethics in professional form. Officialdom, bureaucracy, red tape: the justification for inaction; the pretext for organisational dysfunction. In those distant halls of power, where pitiful political puppets congratulate themselves on their empire-building; on their well developed performance – look at all those ticks in all those boxes! – aspirations of promotion and shoulder-rubbing; well-managed projects and glossy leaflets. Nice, fat bonuses for crap ideas. New conceptions and new spreadsheets. Sterilised morality; whitewashed humanity. A self-perpetuating administrative nightmare, nourished by hapless internal two-stepping, and sustained by graceless acquiescing. A shameful and humiliating defeat. An embarrassing charade of nervous grins and cringing nods.

Where has Britain gone? This once potent and rugged Isle. It lies conquered and wasted, but no Armadas have reached our shores. We have but destroyed ourselves. We are authors of our own demise. We have penned this tragedy; this calamity of nations. Years of striving for intangible dreams and vaporous hopes – visions of oneness and unity supplied by ignorant and disingenuous fools – have left us gasping for reality. Gagging for context. Desperate for common sense. Now we are but a theory; a premise; a 'look good on paper'. No more than a conception. A potential. An insubstantial pledge.

We have laid aside our reason; disregarded our resolve. Anxiety is now our guarantee. Consternation and dismay our token course. Terror of terror our tremulous path. We walk with nothing more than shrouded and muted certainties; aghast at offending or affronting. Repelled by making tough decisions or clear-cut judgements. There's too much to lose. Too much risk. Too much blame. We are tearing ourselves apart through fear. A panic attack on a national scale.

And all the while society crumbles and deteriorates. Imploding in upon itself without a decent focal point. There's nowhere to run. Nowhere to hide. Our desperate pleas for help and frantic appeals for stability met with little more than dismissive shrugs in distant corridors. The foundations have fatigued to the point of teetering collapse: a structural failure – a mangled and twisted framework. Where once were solid girders, are stressed and fractured struts, barely withstanding the pressure; the anatomical integrity worsened by insufficient funding and insufficient willpower.

And while our mental health decomposes with every passing year, and triviality becomes our focus; while families rend themselves apart through lack of substantiality; while debt mounts and stress takes hold; while fear grips us and grinds us down; while everything seems to fall apart around us, we look for an escape route; we desire some form of release – some form of social and emotional compensation for our state. Our befuddled and wrathful minds seeking, searching, soliciting for emancipation. Offended and annoyed and up-tight by the slightest social glitch, we demand some form of recompense. We demand that others do what we no longer have the faculties to accomplish.

But who *can* we turn to? Who can sort us out? Who is there to help us? For we no longer have the ability to deal with our own problems. We can but hold out our hands in the hope that someone will give us what we need. Who can inject us with comfort? Who can supply us with our next social fix? Who can do for us that which we no longer have the will to do for ourselves?

Who, among all organisations, are but a free phone call away, and have a remit that would appear to cover everything we need?

Thus we turn – as has now become the all-consuming trend – to the nearest, the cheapest and the easiest. That organisation that has always been there. That uniformed presence. That reassuring bastion of hope and help. Those whose remit is to solve everything and make it all better. The ones with the sticky plasters and little bottles of sweet tasting medicine. We turn to the police and get fed from a silver spoon while we tuck ourselves up in bed and look ill for the effect. A problem shared is a problem dumped onto someone else. And so we offload it all. Everything. We lay it all at their door. We make it *their* problem in the expectation that *they* will do the business and sort it all out. They are the social overseers. The guardians. The supervisors of life. They'll deal with it. After all, we pay their wages. I want something back! I'm a victim – come and attend to me. Come and attend to me *now!*

* * *

In the midst of this horrific social nightmare the police are therefore confronted with an enormous problem. What exactly *is* our remit nowadays? What, if anything, is the nature of our role? Whatever it is, we can be sure it's all our fault when things go wrong. We have become a buzzword for blame and failure. In a nation desperate for restitution and solidity, it is the police who are more than likely denunciated – we are the ones, apparently, who have to sort everything out, and are wholly responsible for making society a safe, secure and healthy place. Yet, as we will see – and as we probably already know deep down inside – the police are simply not capable of doing this. Not one, tiny little bit.

To attempt to address this complex situation we need to approach it from a particular angle. We have to start somewhere! In which case I have somehow deemed it agreeable to start by focusing on the *victims*. The victims of this social dissolution. I am a police officer after all, and at present it is apparently the *victim* that needs the most attention. The police service is now *victim*-led.[3] So let us continue our journey by examining the basic nature of 'victimness'. (I think I may have just made that word up ...)

In Britain today there are three types of victim:
1. Those who *are* victims
2. Those who *want* to be victims
3. Those who the Government decide are victims

We'll be dissecting these concepts in depth throughout this book, but before we go any further, it would be pertinent to say that where you have a victim, you will most likely have an offender. This is not always the case as we will see, but, for the most part, it is the norm. Day in, day out, the police are dealing with victims and offenders; aggrieved persons and criminals; injured parties and scrotes. It's a never-ending carousel. And the police are particularly good at flushing valuable time succinctly down the toilet dealing with people who want to be victims. If you've just had your house burgled, you clearly didn't *want* to be a victim, so this section isn't about people like you. I'll deal with you later. The people who *want* to be victims represent a significant percentage of society and demand a lot of time, attention and mollycoddling. These are the people who can't seem to take any responsibility for their own lives whatsoever. These are the socially inept victims of nonsense and trivia who keep the police on their toes 24/7. And while such people may not believe they *want* to be victims – but

---

3 Another well-used phrase is *'citizen focussed'*. It all means the same old thing.

rather feel overshadowed by circumstances beyond their apparent control – it is their lack of desire to turn their own lives around that demarcates them as the socially and morally incapable. Yet this incapacity is in itself fuelled by weak political role models who nourish society with false ideals and tainted covenants. A lack of desire, decency and stability from every angle resulting in a social degeneration of vast proportions, and a vicious circle that would appear to have no end.

For a mentally decaying nation has produced a lot of needy and bewildered people, yet even those who do not call the police are affected by the problems. The predicament Britain faces – in terms of its policing capacity – is not simply concerning idiots who call the police when they don't need to and subsequently waste their time, true though this is! The whole nation is swallowed up in this shameful pantomime of cultural chaos – people of every class, caste, race, religion and colour. We are all victims in some shape or form.

For we live in what could be described as a victim culture and the police, unfortunately, help perpetuate this through Government induced bureaucracy and a general remit of paranoia. Citizens are positively encouraged to be victims. If they are the social casualties of anything that could possibly be construed as a crime,[4] then ring the police and get a crime report – hey presto! You're a victim! It doesn't actually matter what's happened. Context appears to be entirely irrelevant these days. Mind-boggling triviality is treated with as much earnest thoroughness as grim and serious happenstance.

In fact, the Government doesn't really care what's happened – so long as it's all recorded properly and your ethnic details are correctly inserted into the relevant ticky box. Assuming that the

---

4   Of course, people don't have to be victims of crime. They could be victims of anything. So people end up suing each other and blaming each other and not really accepting any responsibility. It's always the fault of someone else. Living in Britain nowadays is all about pointing the finger.

current standards of computer based monitoring are adhered to, the circumstances have become irrelevant: I've had two text messages from my ex-boyfriend. *Victim!* Somebody in Woolworth's swore near me. *Victim!* My brother is pissed and won't go home. *Victim!* My children are arguing over the remote control. *Victim!* Someone bumped into me in a queue. *Victim!* I've lost my mobile phone. *Robbery victim!* I've just been robbed by two giraffes and a male I know called 'Tricks'. *Victim!* Nothing whatsoever has happened, but I'm going to call the police anyway. *Victim!* I made it all up just to get a crime report. *Victim!* No, honestly I made it up. *Victim!* No, you really aren't listening to me officer, I MADE IT UP. *Victim!* Sod off, I don't want the police. *Victim!* No, really, sod off. I called you because I was pissed. I hate you. I don't want you here and I'm not going to tell you anything whatsoever. Now piss off ... Filth. *Victim!* I didn't call you. I have no idea why you're here and you've woken me up. I live on my own and have never had a relationship with anyone, at any point ... *Domestic victim!*

In the end, anyone who calls the police about anything will automatically be a victim. It's already reaching that stage. Such is this bizarre and uncommon focus at the moment. There is absolutely no differentiation with anything any more. As soon as you imply that you might, possibly, be the victim of some sort of crime, you become the most important thing in the world. I wish that I was exaggerating here, but as you will discover – I'm not. All of the above examples, with the exception of the giraffes, are based on real life frivolity that frontline police have to deal with every single day.[5]

At this point I could insert hundreds of stories from the front line of policing concerning such trivial and inconsequential crap. Believe me when I say that the utter absurdity of some incidents

---

5   Mind you, the police do get a lot of calls from mad people, so the giraffe example may not be too far removed from reality.

we *have* to attend leaves me, at times, completely speechless. Any police officer reading this book will have in the back of their minds numerous situations where they have been expected to deal with the uttermost dregs of social fucked-up-ness – and treat the situation as a crime worthy of investigation. It's a travesty that we even have to use the word 'investigation' in relation to some of the trivial shit we deal with, but that's what we have to do. For there's murder investigations and there's investigations into triangular teenage love arguments involving the sending of several bitchy text messages and the odd playground squabble. Unfortunately, the police get requested to deal with stuff like the latter far, far too often. It is pertinent to point out now, however, that police officers really don't mind attending triviality. We're just not allowed to treat it as such any more. This is one of the main problems of policing within the victim culture. Throughout this book we will look at real examples of how stupid it has all become.

In fact, let's start now. This story is an example of a typical modern-day victim who allowed himself the pleasure of consuming a huge amount of police attention and resources over something that was *his* fault and *his* problem. It should never have been anyone else's.

Not long ago, we received a phone call from a chap reporting that someone had robbed him of his car keys and walked off with them. Robbery victim! All systems go! All units to make! Except for my colleague and myself. We held back because everyone else was already on the way. We had to leave at least one unit free to cover the rest of the town.[6] Now, me being the cynical little git that I am, had already decided it all sounded rather dodgy anyway. Been robbed of his car keys? My arse. So we floated close by, to coin an official police phrase.

---

6 A 'unit' means an available police vehicle containing an officer or two, or an officer or two utilising other forms of locomotion, such as their feet. Or hoverboards.

When such jobs come in, the police get updated en route to an incident as to anything else they might need to know, like whether the victim is lying through their teeth, or whether they are just using us to sort out every shitty little problem for them. Of course, this doesn't really happen. We never get told such things. We have to treat every report as fact until proven otherwise, which in many cases is still irrelevant, as we will discover in this book. Truth and lies get treated as the same thing so that the police can cover their arses, just in case they are interchangeable, or might become interchangeable in the future.

In this instance, the report came in and units began to zoom towards the area to safeguard the welfare of the poor person calling us and perhaps find the baddy in the process – treat it all as genuine until the real facts present themselves through investigation. Often in these situations, though, we have immense difficulty in locating the victim. I once spent all night looking for someone who had phoned us reporting he had been robbed. The following day he was circulated as being missing. The day after that he was circulated as being Wanted, which was the case all along. Little swine. In this instance, however, it was likely the victim would be quite easy to locate – he had no car keys, after all. So this incident wasn't any different to most robbery reports in its early stages. After about three minutes, the first unit got on scene and found the 'victim'. They calmed, soothed and comforted him in his hour of need. Then they updated over the radio saying that he *might know* who the offender is …

Ah. He *might know* the offender. This might not mean much to someone who isn't in the job, but for the police it's a crucial thing to hear. In our eyes, it usually means that the victim is often nothing of the sort and it's all a load of bollocks, especially when it's concerning a crime like a *robbery.* What kind of moron gets viciously robbed by someone they *know?* Believe it or not, loads of recorded crime happens between people who know each other, and a lot of it is pure crap. So I looked at my colleague and said, 'Drug deal gone wrong.' He looked at me and nodded. After a few minutes, the unit who had located the poor victim further updated via the radio what had happened. The circumstances, it transpired, were that the victim had been in his car with a male he knew only as 'Gooboo' (drug dealer nickname has been changed to protect the non-innocent) and that Gooboo had taken his car keys and walked off with them. The victim *might* know where Gooboo lived, because he was round his house earlier.

Ah, so this isn't really a robbery as suspected. It certainly is a pile of poo. However, we're not allowed to suggest such a thing. The victim comes first! It will be treated as a crime no matter what! At this stage we should have told him to piss off, but can you imagine the police treating our poor victims in such a heinous manner! So my colleagues got him into the police car and drove him around in an effort to locate the house where Gooboo might have gone. As they approached the street where Gooboo may have been lurking – perhaps peeking out from behind the curtains – they called up on the radio to ask for my assistance. That's not because I'm super cop – it was because I was in an unmarked car. In police terms that means a bright red diesel Corsa with bald tyres and lots of warning lights on the dashboard. We'd stolen it from CID. Thanks guys.

So we drove to the relevant location and sat the victim in the back of our car. He was a right twitchy little idiot. He was also nervous about something. Perhaps he was scared of Gooboo. And he'd have every right to be. Poor little mite. We drove him around for ten minutes and pointed out various houses where Gooboo might have gone. Is it this one? *No.* Is it that one? *No.* Are we in the right street? *Don't know.* By this time the victim was really grating my cheese and already I could feel some unprofessional thoughts bubbling away under the surface. After ten minutes of fruitless searching I had a private call from my other colleague to say that the victim did actually know where Gooboo lived but he didn't want to say!

At this point I turned and faced the victim and said, 'Do you know where this chap lives?' I think I may have said it a little too unkindly, because the victim got very irate and started babbling about something and saying 'innit' several times, but didn't answer the question. I then said to my colleague, in a rather irritated voice, 'Stop the car mate – he's wasting our fucking time.' At this point the victim practically exploded in a tirade of abuse and anger. I let him out of the car and he squared right up to me, puffing his chest out and looking like a right pillock in the process, calling me very bad names and saying something like, 'The Feds is racist man.' I recall just shaking my head in sorrow, wishing I was anywhere but there. My other colleagues pulled up behind us and I literally threw the victim in the back of their car saying I'd had enough.

Twenty minutes later, the victim decided that he didn't want police assistance any more and that he felt that he wasn't really the victim of a robbery. He just wanted to find his car keys. In fact, he thought that Gooboo may have even thrown his car keys in the hedge by his car, so a police dog-handler kindly spent half-an-hour looking for them with him. Aren't we nice? We also did a police check on this so-called victim and he was well known to us for a variety of reasons, including violence, drugs and weapons. Furthermore, he had a drug dealer nickname as well. I think it was 'Bugflob', but I can't be sure.

Now I'd like you to hold this story in your mind. Keep the names Gooboo and Bugflob close to hand, because we will be referring to them again later on. Regardless of the circumstances of this incident, Gooboo was an *offender* and Bugflob was a *victim*. Remember that. Remember it well. It's what frontline policing seems to be all about nowadays. In fact, one could write a book about all the Gooboos and Bugflobs the police deal with day in, day out. They represent the majority of the kinds of people we have to police. They represent most of the idiots that float like turds down the cultural river. Yet we have to be so jolly nice to them, even though I wasn't at the time.

I also use this example because it was truly the most hard-nosed I have ever been with anyone purporting to be a victim. It was an epochal moment in my policing career and began the slow but steady process of eroding any hope I had in making a difference. Not that I really expected to. After all, I'd been a teacher. It shocked me, nevertheless. It turned the tide. It broke something. I think it had all been building up for a while, and suddenly it snapped. 'Stop the car mate – he's wasting our fucking time.' He's wasting our fucking time. He's wasting our fucking time. At this point I knew I couldn't do this job for much longer – not without some kind of major changes being made. Not without some context back. Some context, *please.* In many respects it led to the concept of the victim culture and the creation of this book.

You see, we now have to treat the victim as a victim and the offender as an offender, irrespective of any context whatsoever. Lies, truth, folly and madness all rolled into one. We are not allowed to differentiate any more. Discretion? We'll look at that later. Instances of mind-boggling insignificance contributing to crime statistics and national figures. They are allocated crime categories such as 'Criminal Damage' or 'Domestic Harassment' or 'Assault Occasioning No Bodily Harm, Mental Harm, Emotional Harm, Financial Harm, Spiritual Harm, Economic Harm, Educational Harm or any other Harm That I May Have Forgotten, Otherwise Known As Common Assault'.[7]

Occurrences of head-shaking, eye-popping, bin-kicking, desk-slamming, mind-numbing, foot-tapping, fist-clenching complete and utter inconsequential bollocks. Incidents that become

---

7   I made this last one up, of course. But I didn't make up the offence of 'Common Assault'. Some other pillock is responsible for that…

logged, that become crime reports, that become investigations, that become blown out of all proportion to the realm of the ethereal, that simply do not fit under any category at all save one: *Fucking, Fucking Unbelievable.* It's like some kind of crime report acid trip. The whole situation, as will become more and more apparent, is a nightmare of quite substantial proportions. Wrongdoing has been redefined. Criminal activity is now on a completely different plane. It's away with the fairies. Entered a parallel universe. The definition of crime, itself, has changed. Now *anything* is a crime.

There appears to be little or no distinction any more between crime that is clearly a crime and situations involving people not being able to cope with life. It is far easier to expect someone else to sort your life out for you than to take responsibility for it yourself. As soon as things get a little bit difficult then call the police – we are always on hand to give you a crime reference number and all the support possible. We are not allowed to walk away from your mind numbing and, quite frankly, disturbing social incontinence.

So, come on dear Reader, what are you waiting for? There's loads of free crime reports out there for you. You can be a victim. Just think of something completely inane and call the police. You can even make it up if you want. However that's not essential as most of the time you'll get a crime reference number anyway. Just make sure you know what ethnicity you are and when you were born. The Government only cares about those bits. So long as it's recorded properly in line with the current standards – that's the most important part.

Being a victim is extremely easy, you see. If you split up from your partner about thirty-four years ago and they send you two text messages over a period of eight months and those messages are, in fact, quite pleasant – but you didn't want to receive them – then you could be a victim of harassment. In fact, you'll also be a victim of a domestic crime and your ex-partner will be recorded indelibly on a police computer system as an offender. How about that! If you're really, really lucky, then whoever you contact in the police to report this monstrous and soul destroying situation, will record it as full scale, no-holds-barred domestic harassment. Then your ex-partner might even be arrested. That really improves your victim status!

In fact, being a victim of harassment is, perhaps, the easiest way to get yourself on the police computer systems and initiate the process of investigation into your trivial little affairs. So, *become* a victim of harassment – it's as easy as pie. All you need is two occasions where something has happened to you that you didn't favour and you can be a victim. Fandabbydozy! It doesn't even matter if what happened to you *isn't* nasty by the standards of ordinary people. It also doesn't matter what the police think either, probably because we're not allowed to think any more.

So you can have a person smile at you twice in an evening, and if you feel harassed by that – guess what? Victim! The milkman puts your bottles down on the wrong step twice in the same century? Victim! Your partner splashed two drops of wee on the toilet seat? Domestic victim! It's all about how *you* perceive it to be. There's nothing objective about crime any more. If you *feel* you're a victim, irrespective of the facts, then you *are* a victim. Basically, you can be a victim whenever you want, and for the most pathetically unimpressive reasons. The police are duty bound to assist you, because we *must* focus on the victim.

For in a wishy-washy environment devoid of reason and common sense, it is the 'feelings' of the person that take precedence. How are you feeling? Do you need some welfare? Do you need our help? What can we do for you? You poor, poor victim. Let me just wrap you up in cotton wool and nurse your existence back to the level of acceptability that you desire. Let me be your crutch, because you are clearly incapable of doing anything for yourself.

The police cannot turn you away, because that is simply *mean.* Goodness me, we can't do that! We can't be anything but *nice.* We don't want to hurt your feelings even more, because then you could be even more of a victim! So it really and truly doesn't matter if nothing has happened, or if something so trivial has happened it makes the police shake their heads in wonder, because we simply have to assist you sort it all out. And we won't shake our heads in wonder anywhere near you, because we wouldn't want to upset you, or cause this victim culture to be exposed for the fucking shambles it is. Owing to this and a plethora of other issues, the police spend less time dealing with 'real' crime and 'real' victims and spend most of their time dealing with the weakness and feebleness of society.

Of course, there may actually be situations where a *real* crime would appear to have taken place. If you're the tenant of some stinking pit in the deepest recesses of some filthy part of town and your landlord has served you with a thousand eviction notices because you have refused to pay rent for three months, shit on the sofa and had lots of drug-taking skanks round on a nightly basis, but get pushed out of the door by said landlord in his final, desperate bid to get rid of you from his life and his property – then yes, victim it is! I've been assaulted! I'm a victim! Police! Police! And we'll turn up and arrest the landlord. Believe me, we've done it.

So don't worry too much about the circumstances or the context of the incident – because the police aren't. We lost sight of context ages ago. There's no common sense left in our role. If you report a crime – we *have* to record it and we *have* to deal with it. We can't tell you to get stuffed and get a life. It's got to the stage where you can be a victim even if no-one else on earth would consider you to be one – it is *your* perception of what someone says or does that matters. It is also clearly a very dangerous world out there because there's lots and lots of victims. There's also lots of people who are just waiting in the wings to kill you. If someone says something to you that you don't like, or find threatening, then that's fine because they have most likely threatened to kill you – so call the police.

If anyone ever says to you 'You're dead', or infers something vague about your forthcoming demise, or says 'I'm gonna get you' or 'Watch out', then this is clearly a *threat to kill* and you would have every right to feel completely and utterly terrified. It doesn't matter if you've really pissed someone off, or are part of a violent gang, or owe some drug money, or are just a non tax-paying layabout, time-wasting, pissed-up little toad – there's no room for context. Please don't take any responsibility for your life at all. Everyone is out to get you, but, believe it or not, a threat to kill doesn't actually have to contain any sort of threat whatsoever – that would be far too sensible.

It's all as simple as that. You don't even need an address to be a victim. In fact, you don't even need to *exist* to be a victim. The police are good at recording 'crimes' when nothing has happened to anyone or anything, but we record them anyway, just in case. We can create victims out of thin air. But most importantly, we can make you a victim whenever and however you want. It's your choice. It's your call. Don't worry if it's all a load of bollocks, because apparently we don't either.

* * *

Of course, the dear Government would love to step in at this point and tell me that I'm talking nonsense. It will tell me that I'm either making things up, or delusional. It will tell me that there *is* no victim culture. It will tell me that trivial crap *isn't* treated like crime. It will tell me to be quiet you silly little boy. Been robbed by two giraffes indeed! PC Pinkstone, have you ever worked on the front line? I put it to you officer that you have no idea what you are talking about. (I put it to you in return that you are ignorant imbeciles of gargantuan proportions.)

So come with me, dear Government, in the top pocket of my stab vest cover to the police station at 6.45am on any given morning. Peek out through the Velcro at the faces of my colleagues sitting around waiting for the 7.00am briefing meeting to commence the start of shift. Look at them studying their emails with frowns of bewilderment and perplexity, at the plethora of bullshit raining down upon them with remorseless constancy. Now see some of them get up and walk with shuffling steps to the briefing room. They're already exhausted. It's only 6.58am and there are at least five or six 'essential' things that they need to do immediately in relation to their morning inbox. But there's already an infinite amount of other enquiries to do relating to their outstanding investigations. Do I need to go into those? Well, not really. In that respect they are no different to anyone else who has a busy job with lots of bureaucracy. Too much to do, and not nearly enough time to do it. Such is life. They just have to get on with it.

So they sit down at about 6.59am and wait for the Sergeants to come in clutching the morning briefing papers. Aha! The good bit. The crewing information comes first. Crewmates and call signs allocated. No-one wants to be with the crap officers, of course, so it's a bit pot luck. Bollocks, I'm with Bob. What a cock. Anyway, that's just team dynamics. It's like that in all organisations. Pretty realistic so far. So they've got themselves to work, read their emails, walked into a meeting and realised they are crewed with the naffest copper ever to wear a uniform.[8] Nothing ethereal about this.

So the Sergeants go through the briefing papers. Few stolen cars. Few thefts. A few robberies. Look out for so and so – they're out of prison and believed to be criminally active again. Criminally

---

8   The police recruitment process doesn't always work particularly well.

active? You mean prison hasn't worked? Bugger me. And what do you mean he's out of prison? It was only last month when we sent him down for twelve burglaries with elderly victims. Still, I suppose he's served a few days. Better than no result at all. Better than a kick in the happy sacks with a hob-nailed boot.

Still realistic though, wouldn't you say? I see no sign of giraffes just yet. Right, this crewing can take a look for that high risk missing person, and this crewing can deal with this overnight burglary. All very well. Jobs allocated. Crewings complete. Information passed. Briefing over. So get your car keys and get out there. Go and keep the streets safe. Go and turn people over. Go and be proactive. Go and be visible. Go and patrol. Go and fly the flag of justice. Go and deal with those burglaries and robberies; those reports of serious anti-social behaviour; those nasty domestic assaults. Go and support those victims of crime and show them all the professional courtesy expected from a highly trained officer of the law. Go and save the day.

Then the radio crackles. You can't hear it in my pocket as I have my earpiece in. You wouldn't want to hear it anyway. It's the controller. She sounds harangued. She's calling the shift Sergeant by his call sign. It's the usual story. She's got over fifty outstanding jobs. Can she allocate units? Loads of domestics, thefts and criminal damages. Robberies, burglaries, assaults. Frauds, drugs and miscellaneous. Traffic problems. Breaches of the peace. All logged and graded. Many of them already on the database with their crime reference numbers designated. Dozens and dozens of alleged victims ... and about eight officers to deal with them.

OK, so we're busy. What's special about that? We all know that frontline policing is a stressful and challenging thing. It's exciting, cutting edge, dangerous. It's manic. I couldn't do your job, officer! Is it dangerous? Have you ever used your baton? My cousin, Emma, wants to be a copper ... Does she? Does she *really?* Perhaps she'd like to jump into my pocket along with the Government and sit there while I take my earpiece out so you can listen to the radio. It's the controller again. She's handing out jobs like sweets. There are crime reports flying over the airwaves like Red Devils. It's like *Top Gun* – with allegations instead of planes.

The first job we get is a domestic harassment. Sounds pretty nasty. A couple have split up and, er, they've been harassing each other. It looks like the bloke has been sending her some rather nasty text messages. He's also left a few voicemail messages. It's been logged and a crime report for harassment has been started. The victim is available to be seen any time after 7.30am. She's very upset. She's already complained that nothing has been done about her situation. So leave behind everything else that you planned on doing before it got too busy. Leave behind your breakfast. Leave behind all hope of actually policing this town of yours and go and deal with this poor victim. Get your bulging folder of paperwork and get in the car.

Yeah, show me en route. Show me arrived. Show me walking in through the front door. Show me greeting a female in her twenties and sitting down on her sofa. Show me asking her what's happened. Show me wishing I was dead. Show me listening to a tale of utter woe. Show me demonstrating the utmost professional sympathy to my poor aggrieved. Show me thinking that I will do all I can to assist her in her victim status. Show me getting my pen out. Show me getting my statement paper out. Show me getting my Domestic Risk Assessment (All Relationships are Murders Waiting to Happen) Form out. Show me taking the statement. Show me filling out the form. Show me doing something-or-the-other to do with the Victims Code of Practice. Show me leaving the house an hour or so later. Show me heading back to the police station to update the crime report on the computer system and complete the Risk Assessment. Show me now nearly three hours into my shift. Show me reading the statement again and frowning at it whilst shaking my head in wonder.

My victim has just split up with her boyfriend. He called her a *slut,* by the way. She then sent him a text message to say that she'd slept with his best friend. He then sent her another text back saying she was a slut, *again.* Ouch! He went round to her house and she told him it really was over. He left. He then called her a few times, but she didn't answer. So he called her a few times again and left her some voicemail messages telling her that she could come and pick her stuff up from his house. He also told her that he was upset and was going to put a picture of her on the internet. She got upset and text him back … Blah, blah, blah and more fucking blah.

The Sergeant looks over my shoulder. The offender has *got* to be arrested. The victim *has* to be supported. So, you may want to get out of my pocket now, dear Government, and random cousin called Emma who wants to be a copper. I have to go round to some bloke's house and arrest him for sending two text messages and for leaving a couple of voicemail messages. I have to arrest him, handcuff him and take him down the police station. I have to interview him. Challenge him. If possible, sanction him. I reckon by 4pm he and I will both be ready to go home. What an incredibly efficient service I'll give to my poor victim. For the victim must win at all costs. They must be assisted no matter what. There is no room for reality or context. You *must* support the victim.

I wish that this wasn't a true story, but of course, it is. Not the bit about the Government being in my pocket, or that rather bizarre addition of someone's cousin (just think of her as a ride-along), but the part about the domestic 'harassment' and the manner in which it was expected to be dealt with. I use this example because I fear it epitomises what policing has become. As you read further and further into this book, you will begin to see just *why* the victim had to be supported, and *why* the offender had to be arrested. You will begin to get a fuller and further understanding of how silly it has all become. You will see just how painfully real the decontextualisation of life *itself* has become in the world of policing. You will realise just how possible it is for you to be *arrested* for sending *two text messages.* Let me say that again. It is possible for you to be *arrested* for sending *two text messages.*[9] So if you've reported a real crime and have been waiting two days for the police to turn up – this is one of the many reasons why: we're completely swamped by shit. Your burglary will just have to wait in line behind the tit-for-tat, fucked up bollocks of the socially and morally incapable.

Of course, we wouldn't really treat someone saying that they'd been robbed by two giraffes as a crime, but should we treat a situation involving the sending of two text messages as a crime? Is this in any way a sane thing to do? Both situations are just about as bizarre as each other, and both worthy of immediate dismissal. Unfortunately nowadays, the victim is allowed to dictate whether something is worthy of investigating, and the average police officer is a mere automaton, tasked with dealing with it in a prescribed way. It would appear that the nature of the incident no longer bears relevance to the manner in which it must be dealt.

Last year my highlight was 'Theft of Sandwich'. Just imagine, if you will, the context in which a sandwich could be thieved. Perhaps some scallywag has gone into a supermarket and run out of the door with a BLT. Perhaps there's been a hijacking of a catering van. Perhaps someone stole some bread, butter and a packet of ham from their local grocery store, in which case it would have been 'Theft of Items Concerned in the Production of Sandwiches', but you get my point. Now once you've imagined

---

9   I honestly can't think of anything less trivial than receiving a couple of unwanted text messages, but I'm sure that police officers have been pressured to make arrests concerning even more trifling things.

all of that, try to imagine this: You're knocking on the door of a grubby first floor flat in a rather unpleasant tenement block. You already know what's inside. You can smell it. You don't even need a sixth sense to tell you. Your other four senses are already agitated beyond belief. The sight, the sound, the touch. Let's not even think about the taste.

The door opens. You are greeted all at once by a blast of hot air and a rancid smell so mighty it knocks you three feet backwards. Your eyes water and you put out your hand to steady yourself on the doorframe. It sticks. You look with dismay at the goo on your palm, and then turn your gaze to the apparition in the doorway. Is it a man? A beast? Fuck knows. It could be anything. What's more, it's wearing a shirt with two buttons and it's covered in ... what the fuck is *that*? You stare at the shirt. You can't even begin to look at the face. It's just *covered* in egg. Your mind whirls. Your brain falters. Egg? Is that ... is that *egg*? Why am I standing here in this pit, surrounded by a smell so pungent it would frighten a corpse, looking at someone who is covered in egg? What's going on here? Who have I upset? You look at the face. You wish you hadn't. Whatever it is, it's smiling. You hear the words that make you wince like a twisted nipple ... Come in officer, come *in*.

You look beyond the humanoid form into the hallway. The damp rising up the walls – the spores are visible and *enormous*. They're floating around like golf balls in space. You steady your nerves and stay put. What's happened, sir? He smiles again. My friend stole a sandwich from my fridge. Long pause. He did what? He stole a sandwich from my fridge. A sandwich from your fridge? Yes, my fridge. A sandwich. We were all getting drunk last night, and this morning I've noticed that my sandwich is missing ... I think it was egg but I'm not sure ...

I'm not sure either. I'm not quite sure what a police officer was doing responding to a theft of an egg sandwich by a drunken friend. I think at that point I entered the Twilight Zone and, to be quite frank, I haven't exited. There was only one victim in that story and it was me. Those spores have given me nightmares. I see egg people. My brain hurts. Did I really join this job to arrest people for sending two text messages and treat as victims those who've had sandwiches removed from their fridge? Whether or not I joined for these reasons is now immaterial. It's what I do.[10]

It's what frontline police do. We are but cleaners of social piss and shit. It's endless. Ceaseless. Infinitely depressing. A merry-go-round without the merry. A stalemate. A dead heat. If we blame them, they blame us. If they blame us, we blame them. We replace it, and they remove it. We remove it, and they replace it. To and fro. Up and down. Push and pull. Call and respond. Victim, offender. Offender, victim. On and on, and round and round. No end in sight. A deadlock. A draw. No winners, no losers. Two steps forwards, two steps back … It's hopeless. It's *utterly hopeless.*

Every day at work, police officers face the most extraordinary amount of crap. It's like King Kong's first dump of the day. A mind-boggling pile of poo so monstrous it cannot be concealed or controlled. It spreads itself out where it wants, when it wants, and our remit is to clear it up. It rules our working lives and dictates our every action. We have no choice but to shovel shit day in, day out. It's like the whole of society has suddenly become incompetent. No one seems to be able to have any control over their own lives any more. We're encouraged to be weak. Encouraged to call the police. They deal with shit! Let's give them some more to shovel! Suddenly everyone becomes a victim, or perceive themselves to be one. They took a look at their lives and think, 'Hey, I deserve better than this. I want someone to sort it all out for me!'

---

10 Police in Brazil have been known to cull street children by shooting them, while police in Britain deal with thefts of egg sandwiches. Is this world not a fucked up place?

Now police officers are tasked with attending incidents of such utter inanity that no amount of true story-telling or fictionalising could ever demonstrate the absurdity of it all. We have to deal with banality beyond comprehension and show the kind of top-quality professional behaviour expected of an officer of the law. We have to sit in houses so squalid they make you twitch, and write down in statement form the frivolities of an inept, ill-educated and irresponsible nation. We also have to sit in slightly more salubrious conditions and deal with the unfortunate deterioration of youth behaviour unconnected with social deprivation or bad schooling, yet be expected to deal with it in unrealistic and burdensome ways.

We have to pretend we are concerned when someone has had their doorframe slightly damaged by their drunken ex-partner who they haven't really split up with, but may have split up with, and who has a drug problem, like them, but they want something done about it, even though the house itself is an utter shambles, and paid for by other people anyway. We have to trouble ourselves with squabbles and bitching and teenage strife, mostly via mobile communication, and treat it all as serious criminal investigation. We have to constantly try to get a grip on the corrupting mental state of the nation, whilst appearing keen and fair and dedicated. We have to treat everyone as that all-important victim, if that is what they have decided to be. We have to wallow in the mire of mismanagement and Governmental misdirection until we collapse with exhaustion. It really is utterly hopeless.

How on earth did we get to this stage. Where do we start? How did the police service in Britain become a dumping ground for such mindless, inane and trivial bullshit? How did society become so weak, irresponsible, dependent and desperate to be victims? How do you even begin to answer that question? Thus what follows is an attempt to address this situation and perhaps add some small measure of context to something that has gone, quite simply, beyond the pale.

* * *

So, where does this victim culture come from? Where can we trace it back to? How far do we go? How deep? Perhaps a good place to start would be in our lifetime. Our relatively recent lifetime. To me the victim culture seems a natural progression from the 'rage culture' that seemed to abound in the early 90s. Everything was about rage then. Road rage, air rage, parking rage, supermarket trolley rage. It was all the rage to rage. You couldn't turn on the news without hearing about some new manifestation of rage. It was all getting rather out of hand, and then it all but disappeared. Not overnight, but suddenly enough. The rage was distracted. Deflected. Ignored for want of something new. Something better. And so the country waited with baited breath as to the new direction we would go. Where would we be led now? What's the plan? The vacuum created by our apparent cessation of rage needed to be filled with something.

Into this void stepped the Government. Mid to late 90s. Shiny new and striding towards the Millennium with a jaunty gait and confident air. Young, fresh and inspirational. Still wearing the tags. Promises of challenge and change. The dusty, musty, seedy, sleazy, stale and lethargic have no more place in politics. Been here long enough. People getting pissed off. People getting angry. Got nasty in the end. Need a change. No more of this fuming nation. No more of this anger. No more of this rage.

Suddenly – like a bolt out of the blue and with repercussions that cannot ever truly be measured – the police became branded as nasty, untrustworthy, ineffectual and raging too. We became *institutionally racist* – a comprehensive reason for major changes to be brought about. No more of this nastiness. No more of this cold-hearted racism. No more of this evil beast. We don't want that kind of society and we certainly don't want that kind of police force. Shock waves were sent reverberating around every police organisation in the country. My God, we're racist! We're nasty! We're really, really bad! Blimey, that was a punch in the guts and no mistake. What on earth are we going to do about that?

And while the police were reeling from this stunning and sensational blow, the Government made its move. It spread out its motherly arms and cooed to us poor, distressed victims of crime and disorder; us victims of heinous domestic abuse; us victims of evil, nasty racism. Come to us you poor, poor citizens the Government cried! Well, don't come directly to us, because we don't really give a shit. Come to the police! We will turn that evil, nasty, unapproachable, racist beast of an organisation into something soft and pink and fluffy, for you to use as a societal crutch and expect nice, pleasant, all-inclusive help in return. They will be a *service*, not a force, and they will mother you and protect you and help you and give you love and peace and joy. See, all the rage has gone! We are a respectful, diverse, cohesive community, bound together by service and support. This, of course, is utter bollocks.

One thing the Government has failed to realise is that because of this, and many other reasons, this country has gone to the dogs. We are in serious and terminal social decline. We are rotting from the core. Although I write from the perspective of a police officer, it is very clear that other agencies and organisations that deal with social, economic, educational and health issues are also reeling from the stench of decay in so many areas of life in Britain. A nation falling into rack and ruin. A nation reaching elastic limit. A country on the brink of total disintegration.

Crime – including a serious escalation in firearms offences – terrorism, obesity, alcoholism, drug use, anti-social behaviour, racial tension, teen pregnancies, immigration strife, overcrowding, a general decline of mental health – you name it, we've got it in abundance. We've got it in untold copiousness. Any organisation that picks up the pieces of this social collapse know it only too well. Yet we are powerless. The police, amongst these organisations, no longer have any affect. We are impotent. Paralysed. We are crippled by an inordinate excess of unnecessary bureaucracy and mind-boggling policies. We have had the wind knocked out of us. We've been completely neutered.

If Britain wasn't knackered in bygone days, it certainly is now. The already fragile backbone of Britain has been well and truly shattered by an administration that has choked all the common sense out of policing, replacing it with theoretical values and ideals several decades out of date. We're living in a Victorian playground. We're living in a pink and fluffy paradise. The Government tells us we're fine. It tells us we're moving on up and advancing. When the shit seems to hit the fan, it soothes us and comforts us and gives us nice little treats. There there, there there. It'll all be fine. Just call the police. Just call anyone. You can get all the help you need. Don't worry, we'll sort everything out for you. Come to nanny.

Instead of facing up to the harsh realities of life and all its imperfections, the Government simply began to paint over the cracks with a smooth and shiny gloss. Made us think we deserved more and deserved better. Hey, I want my life to be shiny and glossy! What about me! Me! *ME!* It gave us perceived human rights and workplace entitlements. Empowered us to make things better. Empowered us to change. Empowered us to take offence at anything we didn't like. Made us all selfish, introspective and hoity-toity. Made us demand a seemingly better life.

Made us all into victims. Made us all weak and dependent. Made us wish for more and wish for better. Made us tiptoe around the gaping crevasse of serious social breakdown, mental ineptitude and cultural degeneration, and focus on all the things that were irrelevant and false. Made us ignore the issues and deny the facts. It perverted our priorities and twisted our outlook. Fogged our minds and clouded our judgements. Turned us into squabbling, bitching children who need constant care and attention. Turned us into grovelling, self-serving, brown-nosing twerps. Stripped us of our identity and gave us a graceless, nameless and faceless 'oneness' – put us all in the melting pot together and stirred vigorously until we blended and mixed and absorbed each other. Tried its very best to keep us nice and united and cohesive.

This kind of mentality was further enhanced by the whole issue of *political correctness.* What better way to numb us even further than to embrace this particular mode of language and behaviour? Political correctness as a notion and a concept had been developing for a while, yet it appeared to solidify as a recognised term in Britain during the early 90s. By the time the new Government came to power it was already being bandied around as a term worthy of debate and academic analysis. Many intelligent studies and theories on the issue were produced by men and women in all areas of life: politicians, linguists, social commentators. Today people are *still* writing about it, discussing it, and giving it plenty of attention. Although these debates are not uniform, and people hold different views on the issue, it is clear that political correctness is significant enough to warrant a goodly amount of attention.

Such debates, though, are often a bit too academic and cerebral. If you were to do your own research you may come across phrases such as 'Marxist-Leninist' or the 'Sapir-Whorf hypothesis.' You'd read about 'grammatical categories' and 'acceptable descriptors' and 'marginalising attitudes through the instrumentation of public disesteem.' While these phrases may be apt and well thought out, they are all a bit too distant and intellectual for my liking. We need to approach the issue from a more basic and realistic perspective. We need to discuss in quite blunt and pragmatic terms the onset of political correctness and the overall effect it has had.

So, by the mid to late 90s it was firmly cemented in our minds and we could at least demonstrate we knew something about it and could somehow relate it to our everyday existence, whether at home or at work. Already people could recognise the potential damage caused by political correctness and this inspired numerous popular culture reactions in music, documentary, satire, drama, film, books, TV, poetry – basically any arena for expression or exercising some form of free speech. Unfortunately, though, we were unable to stem the flow. We were being gently suffocated.

For we could see the negative effect it was having, but could only manage to shake our heads numbly, as slowly but surely we were dragged even further and deeper into this mental sludge. We were helpless against the all-pervading noxious fumes while they gradually overwhelmed us and overcame us. One by one business, organisations, schools, the Forces, the NHS, the police – all of us became contaminated and defiled, and slid limply into the mire. Heavy-limbed and foggy-minded we began to crawl around in grotesque subservience. Yet from the beginning the warning signs appeared to be ignored and the new Government did nothing to stem the rising tide of this debilitating, all-consuming trend. In fact the Government *promoted* it. Weak, insidious and subversive, it welcomed the idea of political correctness and the power it held, and ensured its policies and procedures fell in line with it. Political correctness would ensure these policies would work.

Above all, the Government knew that a subservient and grovelling country, afraid to speak with honesty and expression, with restricted language and behaviour, would be far easier to force to toe the party line. We would be far easier to manipulate and control. Far easier to moan at and malign. Far easier to treat like the puppets we have truly become. Against this backdrop of ideological insidiousness the Government began its campaign of nullifying certain organisational behaviours and bringing to the fore its own impotent and fawning policies. Slowly the police began to lose a grip on pretty much everything and became pathetic, political and pandering. In the midst of this choking change and with the full backing of political correctness the Government could further promote their victim culture.

It seemed that if we were to become a victim culture, we would therefore need to ensure that our language could not possibly offend anyone or anything. We needed a language of unity. An all-embracing rhetoric. So we ensured we stopped saying what we actually meant and instead replaced real words with meaningless drivel. A sterile, inert and dispassionate language. An all-inclusive, neutral language. Words of nothingness. Words of barrenness. This affected all areas of society and especially institutions of all kinds, not least the police.

Digitally under-represented, vertically challenged, cuddly, outgoing female seeks male. (Or, short fat slapper with three fingers wants a shag ...)

In place of true verbal or written meaning came bizarre 'non-speak' such as the above. This later paved the way for a far more insidious version of political correctness firmly cemented in place in recent years (see next chapter), but at the offset it was designed to be an all inclusive, nice, warm and soft language that couldn't possibly create victims, or draw attention to the fact that you already were a victim. So if you were in a wheelchair, for example, you were clearly a victim of something or the other, so you could be described as *physically challenged.* The word *disabled* became a big no-no as that was far too harsh and victim-unfriendly. If you were obese you could be *horizontally challenged,* or if you were as thick as two short planks you could be *mentally disadvantaged.* And on and on it went. Gradually society stopped saying what it meant to the extent that it didn't really know what it meant when it said what it did. It all became a big farce.

It started working though. Organisations such as the police had to take note of the new taboo words and phrases. God forbid you should now say *half-caste* for example. I don't need to explain what half-caste means as the majority of people should already know, but there are some that would frown in confusion at the completely ridiculous phrases *mixed heritage* or *mixed parentage*. I really don't see how the word *mixed* could be any the less insulting than half-caste – if half-caste is insulting at all. The word *mixed* makes you sound like a bit of a mistake – implying you've got a bit of something in you that you shouldn't have. Sorry, I got a bit mixed up. Yeah, my mum accidentally got knocked up by a chap who was a different colour to her. She got a bit mixed up too. It was dark. Yeah man it sucks.

Non-white became another no-no. If you are going to separate people into two categories, then non-white is actually quite effective, because at a very basic level you are either white or you're not (assuming we know what we mean by *white* and I think we pretty much do know.) However it was deemed to be derogatory to people who weren't white and was subsequently discarded as a description. On some police paperwork dating back several years you can still see a ticky box for the 'non-white' but this has been pretty much outmoded by a more inclusive (but crap) system of ethnic classification which we will examine later on.

Of course, it wasn't just the police that were affected by this 'non-speak'. Many teachers, for example, had to stop saying *blackboard* and replace it with *chalkboard*. Clearly the board is black but it would be inappropriate to say that for fear of offence. *Whiteboard* became *markerboard* and children were no longer lazy, thick or annoying little shits. They had this syndrome or that syndrome, or ADHD… (actually, I don't think I've met a child, or teenager, this year who *hasn't* got ADHD …) So, you could be a lazy, obnoxious and a badly raised little shite, but still claim victim status as you clearly had some form of syndrome.

But the police seemed to be quite seriously affected by this whole debacle. For example we can get into hot water for asking for a *black coffee.* It's *coffee without milk,* in case you were wondering, as black coffee is apparently highly insulting and damaging to black people – almost on a par with the slave trade. We had to start to take stock of absolutely everything that we said or did on the off-chance that it might be insulting, racist or generally upsetting, irrespective of our intentions. Not meaning to be nasty was no longer an excuse. And being firmly in the public eye meant being well and truly accountable and transparent and open to as much criticism as possible, and the Government would be the first to slam the police for any breach of this new organisational behavioural code. I hold the belief that the police is the manifestation of any current Government's paranoia – we represent it on every level. We are quite simply puppets of the administration.

So, into this melting pot of goodwill to all men and women, where the rage was apparently left behind and replaced by an all-inclusive niceness, was poured lots of juicy Governmental anxiety. The plan had to work, at any cost. Now that the police had a major reason to change (we were *all* institutionally racist apparently), the Government would ensure that we certainly *would* change. It was the perfect excuse to make us behave in a new, much softer way. There would be no room for dinosaurs any more. No room for people who didn't toe the party line. No room for anything old-school. No room for this canteen culture. Police officers joining the service would be force-fed a diet of pink and fluffy ideals and values. The law itself would take a back seat and be overshadowed by diversity training, victim training and how to be a robot training. You will think what we tell you to think and say what we tell you to say. You will *not* be prejudiced. You will *not* discriminate. You will bend over and be smacked if you even *think* something that you shouldn't. We've got our eye on you and don't you forget it. Nothing is allowed to undermine this victim culture. Especially not the police.

To assist in this freakish control of police behaviour, the Government would eventually change police training even more. *The Secret Policeman* clearly demonstrated that police training centres were dens of racist iniquity and therefore it decided to put an end to this once and for all. It also determined that this attitude clearly carried over into police stations, wherein teams or groups of police officers exercised this kind of awful canteen culture type behaviour on a regular basis. To facilitate the destruction of such nasty police conduct, the Government would now start to send police probationers to college in plain clothes and give them an NVQ in policing. It would call them 'student officers'. Give them rights and entitlements. Empower them. Rid them of marching, saluting and parading. Rid them of this stuffy and outdated discipline. Make them socially conscious and much sweeter and softer and politically correct. Encourage them to challenge *any* form of perceived inappropriate behaviour and rid the force of evil, nasty racists and discriminators. Turn the tide of this woeful workplace demeanour and make everything nice and kind and clean and precious.

Assuming, therefore, that the police were getting nearly everything wrong, it would be interesting to look briefly at the wider picture in society at the time. It was almost as if someone was saying to the whole of the country, 'Look ... you don't want to do it like that ... you want to do it like this.' And suddenly we all needed showing what to do and how to do it. For example, pretty much every television programme became a bit more motherly and instructive. Look folks, you're not cutting the mustard ... this is how to do it. This is how to raise your children. This is how to run your family. This is how to train your dog. This is how to cook. This is how to move house. This is how to make your garden better. This is how to buy something. This is how to sell something. This is how to dress. This is how to look. This is how to eat.

This is how to live. This is how we want you to live … Over the past decade there have been literally hundreds of programmes dedicated solely to teaching us how to live properly. Such programmes have existed for years of course, but in recent times they exploded and expanded to the extent that you couldn't turn the television on without being told how to do something – e.g. how to run your life. You don't want to be a victim of your own incompetence! The constant bombarding of our lives with demonstrations of our own inadequacy ensures that we never end up believing we can accomplish anything, because there's always more to achieve and better ways of doing things just around the corner. So we end up living vicariously through the lives of others and slowly, bit by bit, become to rely on them for everything.

Thus, in all areas of life, we constantly have to learn how to live. We have to be guided in the best way of doing things. We have to be led. Nurtured. We need daily demonstrations on how to conduct our lives, as clearly we have no idea. But of course it's all done in a very nice, agreeable way. Television delivers it with a smile and training environments are now soft and full of plump armchairs. The old fashioned ways of *do as I say, chalk and talk* – or being told firmly how to do something as opposed to having it demonstrated pleasantly for you – are no longer the preferred method. Not pink and fluffy enough. It's much better to experience it. After all, no-one likes being told what to do, surely?

We don't need telling – we need showing. We need it to be touchy-feely. Interactive. The best way of becoming better is by *pretending* to do it. Experiencing it. Have a go. Play with it. Live the dream. Think this way. Talk this way. So every day we have to learn. Improve. Reach for the stars. But there's no end to it all. Self-illumination doesn't really exist. The cycle never ends. The learning never stops. You will not achieve your goal, because there isn't one any more. And we rely on this ideology so much that we forget how to do anything for ourselves, because we're not actually doing anything – we're just experiencing it. We're playing a game. We're living in a playground. It's all one big façade.

Instructing gives way to mentoring; instrumental gives way to experiential; telling gives way to cajoling; self-sufficiency gives way to dependency, and responsibility for one's own life becomes the remit of others. We become socially inept and incompetent. Old fashioned values perish. Common sense falters and gives up. And other issues, such as the rise of mobile phones, ensure that we no longer know how to talk to each other face to face. Basic life skills of communication and human interaction dwindle and get swept under the carpet, along with all else imaginative, creative and aesthetic. People forget how to deal with each other and deal with life.

We begin to shun doing things for ourselves and demand that others take on our responsibilities. We think that the world owes us a living. We can sit back in our chairs, reach for our phones, and make the world come to us. It's all so convenient. Help is also just a point and a click away. We hardly have to trouble ourselves. It's all there on one screen. Even when we leave the house we can find everything under one roof. We can get all that we need in one place. Huge, sanitary supermarkets selling our lives under the bright glare of neon lights. The personable interaction of the small and the friendly replaced by the mass-market monster. We feel it's the way forward. We believe the change is necessary. We want it bigger, better, faster and we want it *now.* A nation of greedy, selfish, wasteful consumers demanding far more time and attention than we deserve. Demanding more and more and *more.*

Satisfaction or acceptance is, therefore, a thing of the past. We demand more and we demand better. We are not content with our lot. In this world, other people exist to help us. They are there at our disposal. If they don't help us how we want, when we want – guess what? Victim! We are a nation of helpless, hopeless victims. Like hatchlings with our mouths open waiting for a morsel of food from the one who feeds us. We've forgotten who we are and where we came from, and have absolutely no idea where we're going. Gone are the days of the stiff upper lip. Gone is the era of making do and mending. Gone is the self-sufficiency and robustness of character. We're all encouraged to be a bunch of wet lettuces. And the police service became damp and floppy too.

Discipline perished along with the marching and parading. Orders are no longer barked. Rules are no longer imposed with such strict adherence to tradition or method. Creases lost their razor sharpness and boots lost their mirror-like gleam. No more starch in the shirt collars. No more crispness. No more defined edges. No more old-fashioned sense of rank or role. It all became fuzzy and foggy and muggy. The tide turned in favour of false smiles and empowered ranks. Respect and integrity through political pandering. No more bullying. No more character building. No more practical jokes. No more station piss-ups and no more inappropriate behaviour. One by one police stations lost their bars and gyms. Lost their smoky, dusty, lived-in atmospheres. Even in very recent times this has happened. Even in my few years in the job. It all became very sterile and varnished over with a smooth and sanitary veneer. Sprayed with the disinfectant of political correctness to rid us of those outmoded nicotine stains and good-old-boy coffee mug rings. In with the new and out with the old. Reformed and reviewed and renewed, with toothy grins and promises of advancement.

We left behind the old style methods. We turned our backs on the dinosaurs. Their ways were no longer considered appropriate in this new, young and socially aware organisation. Their primal, intuitive, bone-crunching and flesh-tearing instincts no longer toed the party line. They had no place in this dampened down and politically managed organisation. This organisation with a procedure for everything. A policy for everything. A neatly compartmentalised and 'by-the-book' approach to ensure fairness, integrity and quality of service. A transparent and accountable organisation. A clean and sterile, forward-thinking and dynamic workforce, comprised of clean and sterile people with better attitudes than before. Young, fresh and keen to fly the flag in a new Britain. A model Britain. A changing Britain. A Britain already in the vice-like grip of political correctness and on its way, inexorably, to complete self-destruction.

No longer would the 'old ways' be considered acceptable in the new methodology. No longer would a hunch or some old fashioned detective work be the favourable procedure. Need to use your investigative powers? That's right – don't actually go and use them. Here, fill in a form the size of Yellow Pages, and maybe we'll do something about the problem in a few weeks when we've managed to read it and check it and stamp it and sign it. Want to talk to someone on the street? OK, but don't forget to fill in this lengthy form. Fill it out in triplicate. In quadruplicate. Fill this out and that out. Update this and update that. Don't actually go outside and police anymore. Don't follow leads or act on premonitions. Don't be silly. There's a form for everything. A procedure. A paper trail.

Slowly and surely the police sunk ever deeper into the mire of burdensome political administration. Their limbs became heavier and their breath became more laboured. Like poor animals caught in quicksand, they eventually succumbed to their fate. The crushing weight of bureaucracy, paperwork and mind-numbing policies overcame them and debilitated them to the point of stupefaction. To the point of paralysis. To the point of disaster. Meanwhile, the nation slid ever deeper into the mire of selfishness, senselessness and inability. With no-one policing them anymore, they became weak and demanding. They became obnoxious and ill-informed. Gangs and groups formed without fear of interference. Yobs began to lay claim to the streets, and anti-social behaviour became completely out of control. Lives were ruled by trivia and frivolity with no standard by which it could be measured.

The gritty, honest, decent and hard-nosed people became overshadowed by fools with beaming smiles speaking bewildering political jargon. Language itself became dispassionate and torpid, bearing all the hallmarks of this insipid new organisational behaviour. Real standards of life and living became marred and blurred and furry, and people with no concept of decency, honesty or value began to rule the roost. Their lives and their twisted ideals became paramount. Mass-market and pre-packaged. Microwaved and tasteless. 'Responsibility' was no longer a word in their vocabulary. The value of life itself became cheaper and weaker and muddied. A post-modern nightmare of truly national dimensions.

A melting pot of fucked up values and contorted morals. With no one allowed to say what was right or wrong, the country became further gripped by its own debased ideologies. The police had buckled. The Government had backed off. The justice system couldn't cope and couldn't care less. It, too, became soft and squelchy to the point of madness – spending more time and effort protecting and safeguarding criminals than delivering justice and recompense. It all went pear-shaped. Tits up. Fucked up. Went to the dogs. No longer did anyone have a grip on anything anymore. They lost the will. Lost the nerve. Lost direction in the fog.

Where were we? What had we become? Who am I? We realised we had nothing of substance left any more. We stood, holding pieces of paper and mobile phones, all pointing in opposite directions at other people. There were no landmarks. No boundaries. No place names and no demarcations. It was pass

the buck. Pass the parcel. Pass wind and pass time. We didn't
know where we were and what we were doing. We hadn't got a
clue. If someone asked a question we could look at our policies
and check our procedures, but if that failed, what then? What if
the answer wasn't in front of our noses? What if our action plans
and computer system databases didn't provide the exact solution
to the problem? That's right – more policies and procedures.
More action plans. We couldn't really move because we were
lost, and we had no idea which way was which anyway, so we
stayed put and implemented policies on the spot. We began to
contradict each other because the left hand didn't know what the
right hand was doing. All too often our procedures undercut each
other or counteracted each other. When that happened – what
then? Nothing. People became lost in the system. Lost in the inner
machinations of organisational incompetence. Passed from pillar
to post. Transferred and re-routed and led on a bewildering trail,
often right back to where they started.

And this is where we are today. Stranded in the fog
clutching our forms and phones. Delegating and designating and
re-directing. Promising and not delivering. Acting according to
policy and not according to common sense. Yet desperate to be
liked. Desperate to appear nice. Desperate not to offend and not
to harass. Desperate to toe the party line and do the politically
correct thing. Far keener to be pink and fluffy and stay put than
grab a stick and strike out for higher ground. Far easier to give in
and give up than find a way out of the mire. Far easier to say what
people want to hear than what they need to hear. Far easier to sit
back and let it all happen. In the end, far easier not to do anything
of substance at all. Easier to be stranded. More comfortable to be
stationary. Better off being solitary. Turn your back on the world
and look at a computer screen. Ignore the woes and defend the
foes. It's easier. Much easier. In the end we all became completely
and utterly helpless against the rising tide of calamity already

washing Britain steadily away. The sad thing is – it was almost effortless.

* * *

There is nothing especially conspiratorial about any of this – it simply reflected a changing attitude in society, but it would be interesting to consider how much of this change was echoed by the particular pink and fluffy direction the Government was taking in the first place. My feeling about the administration of this country over the past several years is that it has been overwhelmingly weak. There is a definite air of wishy-washy-ness about the running of the country that has been evident in a number of arenas, such as the European Union and criminal justice. I don't feel too ill-informed saying that a hallmark of the current administration has been that of ineffectual and sycophantic policy-making, ensuring that society has no real sense of direction, identity or self-esteem. And every day the police are mopping up the spillage from this social disaster.

Now whether society affects the Government or viceversa is something that depends on the circumstances leading to any change, but I would consider it a pertinent suggestion that the Government wished for a major shift in attitude and outlook, and achieved this. However, I do feel that this shift in attitude desired by the Government has now become something of a horse that's bolted. This will be further examined in later chapters, especially concerning diversity and racism. For such issues are still at the very forefront of policing, affecting pretty much everything we do. They affect everything from our targets to our own professional development, and the horse that bolted will unlikely be caught for quite a number of years yet.

So not only were television programmes – and, of course, all manner of media – ensuring that we knew how to do stuff and were getting our lives right and bringing our children up properly, but schools also reflected this general shift in attitude. Schools had to start teaching about *citizenship.* How to be a good citizen of this country. How to have respect for race, culture and difference. How to toe the party line and not rock the boat. There is nothing intrinsically wrong with promoting such attitudes towards being a good citizen. Who could argue that teaching children respect, integrity and valuing diversity could ever be wrong? Unfortunately, the overriding factor in this educational shift in emphasis was one of knee-jerk paranoia and graceless deference.

Children were to become the new model citizens in this all-inclusive, cohesive British community. Trouble was, it left them with very little sense of their *own* identity, because they were far too busy trying to appreciate everybody else's. Now many children don't know who they are supposed to be, what they are supposed to believe, or how they are supposed to think. What they *do* know, however, is that whatever path they choose to walk in their lives, they mustn't tread on the toes of others who are different to them. It would be far safer *not* to do something that upsets or offends anyone else than go ahead and do it, even if it's a good idea in the first place. In fact, it is even more preferable to decide on behalf of other people what may upset them and therefore negate any chance of this happening. The gist is, therefore, one of personal weakness and an evasive attitude to honesty and truth; culminating in a dismal failure to be able to address serious social or cultural issues for fear of consequence, because we're all to busy trying to be falsely nice and accepting. In other words, it's best to just bury your head in the sand.

So, the police were effectively policing a nation that gradually began to lose a substantial grip on reality, identity and common sense; a nation that preferably didn't say what it meant and preferably didn't rock the boat. A nation that was encouraged to take less responsibility for its own actions and instead rely on others (e.g. the police) to sort everything out for them. A nation subversively encouraged to be weak and clingy and contact the police – or anyone else for that matter – at the earliest possible opportunity regarding anything that upset them. A nation that didn't actually know what it wanted, or what was going on. I know, let's call the police – they deal with everything.

Gradually, the phrase *not a police matter* ceased to exist. Gradually *everything* became a police matter. The victims were queuing up to report everything and the police duly responded by recording everything that was reported. Shift officers got passed incidents to deal with that not only could have been resolved over the phone, but should never have been reported in the first place. And this is how it is today. The problem is much deeper than simply how the police deal with things – it is more of a social problem than an administrative one, but is certainly perpetuated by how we do things in the police. We now cannot turn round to people and say 'Sorry, not a police matter.' It would confuse the hell out of them because they genuinely feel we are some kind of surrogate parent, and what decent parent would tell their poor, confused and hurting child, 'Sorry, it's not a parenting matter. Now bugger off and play.'

To be firm and decisive does not fit in with the victim culture and the police mustn't undermine society. We police by the consent of the public and, therefore, we will deal with whatever they want us to deal with. The Government agrees and encourages society to be weak, dependant and in need of constant mothering. We are a *service*, not a *force*, and we certainly do not enforce the law. Not any more.

The remit of the police is therefore so broad as to be incomprehensible. On a day-to-day basis, I really have no idea what my role is supposed to be – am I a social worker? Teacher? Counsellor? And where, exactly, does the Government want me

– behind a desk updating a computer system? On the streets? Half the time I don't know where I should be. I get told off for being indoors doing paperwork because I should be outdoors, and then get maligned for being outdoors when I should be indoors. I spend more time updating a computer system (to the effect that I haven't had time to update it) than actually doing whatever it is I need to do that would lead me to updating it in the first place. And overriding it all I must give everybody I meet a truly quality and professional service, even though I don't really know what service I am supposed to be providing exactly. Most of the time I'm doing people a disservice, because I can't really sort their lives out in the way they want or expect me to. I can't nanny everyone, even though it's my remit.

Certainly, this leads some people to recognising that the Government is an overly obsessive and nannying bunch of imbeciles. This promotes various contemporary outcries and cultural debates wherein words such as 'nanny state', 'Big Brother', 'CCTV', and other examples of a close political eye on our existence, are banded around by people feeling ill at ease with current social trends. In this climate the police, in many respects, help to perpetuate the Government's fawning policies on mollycoddling and mothering the nation, to the detriment of social responsibility and stability. Thus, I think the phrase *nanny state* is an entirely appropriate and fitting description of what Britain has become. The Government wants to take care of every aspect of our lives and uses the police to partly manage this. We are the bastion of hope for a poor, quivering nation that cannot possibly do anything for themselves.

Because of this, I tend to ask most of the people I deal with a very simple question. 'What are you expecting from us?' In other words, you've called the police, what do you think we can do for you? People then either shrug, because they haven't actually thought about it, or come up with something ludicrous and unrealistic, or often say they expect nothing – they just wanted to 'report' it. The trouble is that once something is 'reported' it starts a chain of events that is something akin to an avalanche – of paperwork and procedural bollocks that is. Later on, we'll see just how bad its got, but for the moment it is fair to say that the expectations of the police from the Government, the nation and the police themselves, are all really quite different. Perhaps the greatest irony of this state of affairs is that we *should* feel somewhat aggrieved by it. Guess what ... I'm a victim!

* * *

In the following chapters we will be looking at several pertinent issues pertaining to the current state of play within the police service and how this is relevant to society in general. How the police, sadly, help perpetuate this victim focussed nannying. I trust you will find parallels with other organisations and make links to your role if you do not work for the police. In the final chapter, we will wrap everything up and take a look at the future and what this may entail. Thus, without any further hesitation or beating around the bush, let us initially examine the most important thing in the world at the moment ...

2. Diversity

Worth repeating again. *Diversity*. A very familiar word to a police officer. A very familiar word indeed. A word that inspires moans and groans of despair! I'm not going to treat the issue of diversity like an ancient and dusty volume to be handled by trained professionals in special gloves. No. The gloves are coming off. There *are* no gloves. I am going to drag diversity away from its obsequiously appointed throne and strip it of all the gaudy political embellishments and festoons of specious organisational nicety. It needs to be shaken, woken and beaten. Flung against every wall and bounced off every surface. Put through the mangle and hung out to dry. Disrobed and decorticated. Shaved. Peeled. Exposed and revealed. Tossed, turned and unveiled. I want to take it, break it and remake it. Leave it trembling in fear of what it has become, and force it to take an honest and unadorned look at where it's going in the future. By the end of this chapter, I want to leave it quivering naked in the dark. By the end of the book I will re-clothe it and put it back in its truly rightful place, which isn't where it sits at the minute.

Now if you've ever seen the classic film *The Cook, The Thief, His Wife and Her Lover,* then you will know that 'the Lover' comes to a rather unpleasant end at the hands of the Thief and his cronies. He'd been caught doing rather saucy things with the Thief's wife – played by an ever glorious Helen Mirren – and ends up being cooked and almost eaten by the Thief, played with vile gusto by Michael Gambon. Then, the Thief gets shot in the head. Pretty 'in your face' stuff, as it were. Now, the way that the Lover is killed is particularly gruesome. He is basically force fed pages torn from books, which are shoved down his throat with a wooden spoon, until he comes to a bloody, choking and juddering end.

This is akin to how the police have received their diversity training. It has been rammed down our throats with a kind of detached, unstoppable savageness. Now when I hear the word *diversity* mentioned, in the context of more training and even more input, I want to run screaming like a banshee and fling myself with reckless abandon off the nearest bridge. To say that the Government is obsessed (and I mean *obsessed*) with diversity is to make one of the biggest understatements possible. To fully understand why this is the case, we need to start discussing diversity at such an early stage in the book and revisit it again in the final chapter. To begin with, let us consider an example of this obsession in practice.

Not long ago, my own dear father had an interview for a police position. A civil engineer by trade, he had been involved in a variety of work, from designing drains to managing recycling projects. The position he was applying for was a civilian role – that of a Scenes of Crime property officer. Responsibilities included all manner of paperwork and other desk-related tasks, as well as essential exhibit management. Particular attention to detail was required, as exhibits used in criminal proceedings must be correctly logged and maintained. The paper trail for an exhibit is extremely important. Now you would have thought that in an interview lasting an hour and ten minutes, my father would have been asked to describe his previous experience and how this would relate to the job for which he was applying, amongst other relevant things. No. This would be far too sensible. Instead, he had to spend the first fifty minutes of the interview explaining his understanding of diversity, and what he understood diversity to mean in practice, and how he had demonstrated a keen understanding of diversity in his previous jobs. He came out of the interview in complete bewilderment and, needless to say, was not particularly impressed.

For the past several years, diversity has been at the very forefront of policing. You first come into contact with it during your preparation to become a police officer, then during your interview and then get blasted by it from all angles during your initial training. You continue to complete online training packages about it and attend workshops and seminars throughout your career, just in case you forget what it's all about. Ever since the police were labelled 'institutionally racist', the Government has done its utmost to stamp out anything that may confirm this label, and enforces diversity training in all levels of policing. Anomalies such as *The Secret Policeman* appeared to confirm the Government's suspicion that the police service really *was* a racist beast, and thus empowered them to choke us even further with more and more diversity training, targets and policies.

The last diversity training I had was not long ago, and I sat there with my colleagues – in a hotel conference room, no less – trying to determine whether I was a *non-prejudiced discriminator,* a *prejudiced non-discriminator,* a *prejudiced discriminator* or a *non-prejudiced non-discriminator.* Talk about tying yourself up in knots with psycho-babble bullshit. What point, exactly, were they trying to get across? I think they were trying to make me decide that I was a *non-prejudiced non-discriminator* (e.g. a robot), but there was a pretty good argument coming from Row 3 that we could be *prejudiced non-discriminators* (e.g. we *can* have – indeed, we *do* have – prejudices, but so long as they didn't affect how we dealt with people). The trainer smiled patiently and then pointed to the *non-prejudiced non-discriminator* box and said that really we should all be in there. Row 3 then tried to say something else realistic, but was soon squashed by the trainer and no-one else could be bothered to say anything because we all wanted to go for lunch. After that, we looked at how we might end up killing someone if we were racist, which made us feel even more happy and special, and then mercifully, the overhead projector exploded and we all went home. Actually it didn't explode. We just went home. I think the gist of the final session was that the police are basically all racists, and without diversity training, we'd be cold-blooded killers of anyone different to us.

So, if we were racist, then we were also clearly homophobic, sexist and ageist too. We didn't respect other people's religion. We clearly had no regard whatsoever for difference. We were prejudiced and discriminatory. We were very, very bad. Diversity training was, therefore, the best way of sorting us all out and ensuring that never again would we dare behave in such an awful way. The training enabled us to see where we were blatantly going wrong and allow us to become much more inclusive, ecumenical and holistic. And *nice*. The thought that the police service had such a bad attitude – and that this attitude was *institutional* – freaked the Government out completely. This clearly was not compatible with the new model Britain – a nation to be mothered and mollycoddled, not abused and shit on by its own police. How could the nation respect a police service that didn't respect them? It would not be possible.

So we had to learn how to behave. How to treat everyone equally and not discriminate. Motivated partly by an almost unearthly desire to rid us of anything that could upset anyone, and driven partly by an inclination to be seen to do the 'right' thing, the Government would teach us how to get on down and groove with *The Six Strands*.

Race
Religion
Gender
Age
Sexuality
Disability

Now what could possibly be wrong with an inherent respect for these things? Well, absolutely nothing at all. I entirely agree that everyone should treat other people well. Be good to your fellow man. No-one likes a bastard.

So why do I detest diversity training so much? Probably because it assumes that *I'm* a bastard. It assumes that I'm racist, sexist and homophobic. It assumes that, without being led in the right direction, I'm going to neglect one race at the expense of another, or give people with different sexual preferences a different kind of treatment. It suggests that, without Governmental direction, I'm going to be entirely prejudiced and discriminate whenever and wherever possible. It assumes that the Government needs to tell me how to live.

One huge problem with training me to become a robot is that it grates with human nature and fails to comprehend that, despite the odd joke I may make here and there, or the odd comment I may let slip regarding certain topical things, I'm really not that bad. And nor are 99.99% of my colleagues. Did the Government ever stop and think that diversity training would actually prevent bastards from being bastards? That it would somehow weed out the tiny percentage of truly nasty idiots that did end up wearing the uniform? Of course not. That would be far too sensible. *The Secret Policeman* proved that very point. It's the kind of mentality that leads interviewers to ask potential police officers the daftest questions. A colleague of mine was asked this very question during his initial interview: 'How do I know you're not a racist?' And his reply? 'How do I know *you're* not a racist?!' What a fucking debacle.

Despite all the training that has been shoved down my throat with the Governmental wooden spoon, I haven't changed one bit. Actually, that's not true. I have changed. I've become a lot more pissed off than I used to be. I've become a lot more paranoid about things I'm 'not allowed' to say or do. I'm much more aware of things that might 'upset' people, even if I would have no intention of upsetting them by saying or doing those things in the first place. But that's just it, you see – intention no longer appears to be relevant. We shall examine this in a lot more detail later in the next chapter on racism, but for now, it would be fair to say that *perception now overrides intention*, which for me, is one of the most dangerous concepts of recent years.

Every day police officers now walk around on eggshells, terrified that one small slip-up will cost them their jobs. And that 'slip-up' will not necessarily be something bad like selling drugs, or beating an innocent person up, or otherwise being a bent copper. It would most likely be something like a comment that someone else perceived to be homophobic or racist. Nothing objective of course. And on an even more insidious level, police officers are positively encouraged to rat on their colleagues – and the criteria for ratting? Well that would be any behaviour of a racist, sexist or homophobic nature. Any behaviour that does not conform to the total and utter robotic nature of being a true modern copper. Plus, in all other areas of society, people are treading on eggshells, terrified that an innocent comment will be construed as something noxious that will land them in trouble.

So, if I make a joke that some would construe to be racist, then I'm clearly not fit for the uniform. And the victim? Well, there doesn't have to be one. We've already seen that a victim doesn't need to exist – there are theoretical victims everywhere. Victims created ethereally by nasty comments made by nasty people. And then there's the victim created by perception. If you perceive it to be a crime, it therefore is a crime. So how on earth am I still wearing the uniform and doing the job? I guess the diversity training must be working. It must be keeping me on track and stopping me from being the bastard that I obviously am deep inside. What a load of old bollocks.

In a nutshell, diversity training doesn't work. In fact, I'd rather call it paranoia training, as that is what inspires it and drives it forwards. It doesn't work and it hasn't worked. It has achieved the square root of diddly squat – in terms of what it aimed to do. The only thing it has done is instil paranoia and a general feeling of apprehension about getting into trouble for the most minor and meaningless things. It has created a climate of cringing submission. It is as if the Government determined on behalf of everyone who was 'different' that they deserved far more than they already had. That they were automatically victims of discrimination and prejudice and, therefore, automatically entitled to extra special care and attention. It's this kind of mentality that inspired what is known as *positive discrimination.*

Part of the trouble now, is that people can take full advantage of this sycophantic environment. People who embody any part of the six strands can use their difference to create a false sense of their own value and importance. And so we pander to people. Where before people were valued according to their skills or abilities, or whether they were in fact decent people, they are now valued *automatically* for their diversity. We now have to appreciate people's difference not because it is valuable, but simply *because* they are different. The facts become meaningless. Someone can be a right arsehole, or completely crap at their job, but if they represent that six strand minority then it's very difficult – nigh on impossible – to have anything done about it. On a positive note though, I've met very few colleagues who represent any of the six strands who use their 'difference' for their own advantage. Rather, any unfair or unwarranted advantage gained is perpetuated by those in authority who dare not do anything to undermine those people. They are too scared to say or do anything that might upset someone from a minority background for example, or a homosexual, regardless of whether that person is good, bad or indifferent. As such, merit can be falsely gained by difference and is falsely maintained by toadying deference. It's all very superficial and shallow.

The outcome of all this feeble fawning around is the exultation of 'difference' on a kind of freak-show level. Where the police employ anyone who is from an ethnic background for example, such as a Sikh, or black person, then they are paraded in an almost sickeningly flattering manner. The really annoying thing about this is the fact that the difference *itself* is so superficial. So what if someone is black or homosexual? It's only a very small part of who that person is, so why exult it so much? Why place so much emphasis on it? Why elevate it to an unrealistic level? Why even describe a homosexual as a homosexual? I'm heterosexual, but I'm hardly ever described as such. If someone is a Sikh then great, but don't put a Sikh on a pedestal for that reason alone. If I was blind I wouldn't be able to see what a black person looked like, in which case I would not have to trouble myself with worrying about that external demarcation. It's so pathetic.

The things I appreciate about people are far, far different to what the Government wants me to appreciate. For the Government wishes me to appreciate things for the sake of it, for the sake of difference. Therefore, the Government is hardly promoting an appreciation of worthy human values or behaviours. Instead, it is forcing us to appreciate what marks us out as different, as opposed to what marks as out as good human beings. But that is wrong. So wrong. To appreciate someone just because they are demarcated by their colour, religion or sexuality is so extraordinarily hollow, which makes the whole thing even worse. Therefore, I will appreciate what I want to appreciate in a person, so long as I don't treat that person badly if there is something that I *don't* appreciate about them. And ironically enough, it is almost 100% certain that the things I might not appreciate about people would not have anything to do with their ethnicity, sexuality or religion anyway.

If I work with someone, or deal with someone, who is an arsehole, then that's what I'll think of them, whatever their ethnic or sexual differences. I've worked with some black and Asian colleagues who I either like or I don't. I work with some white people who piss me off more than anything else in the world. However, this does not presume that I would mistreat anyone based on a personality clash. It's just life. We all share this world and make of it what we will. So long as our actions make us worthy citizens of life. For example, the males who killed innocent people in the 7th July 2005 London bombings were evil scum, with twisted and debased ideologies far removed from the religion they purported to follow. It is as simple as that. I lived and worked in an Islamic country for two years, and while there was a significant amount of the culture that I really couldn't appreciate, not once did I feel unwelcome, unwanted or unsafe. There are some right shits in this world and they come from every race and religion, and they do horrific things at times.

Unfortunately, in the police, we tend to see the worst of whatever race or culture crosses our path. I've seen the dregs of white British society and a huge amount of them are plain awful. I've dealt with Asian males who have massive chips on their shoulders and who really do need a kick up the arse. I've dealt with black males who you simply want to scream at due to their hard-done-by attitude. I've dealt with dozens and dozens of Eastern European males who are frustrating beyond words because they seem not to have any inclination about how to conduct themselves in line with the law, or within other acceptable social parameters. I've seen other Europeans who come to this country just to steal and then drive back home – taking full advantage of their EU status for ease of passage. They know what they are doing and are simply taking the piss.

Every town and city in this nation will have its own share of problems relating to the specific behaviour or particular racial and cultural groups. Yet covering all of this, like some noxious blanket, is this culture of 'niceness' and inclusiveness: of not saying anything to upset anyone, and above all, valuing and appreciating other people's difference. Believe me when I say that I don't value some aspects of some cultures at all. Not one little bit. But I'm damned if I say anything to the contrary as I'd be branded a racist! We mustn't malign *anyone*, especially in a racial context, irrespective of the facts and circumstances. The facts may be staring you in the face – in fact, slapping you across the cheek[11] – but you mustn't dare say anything for fear of appearing racist, nasty or unprofessional. In fact, it would be wise if you didn't say anything at all.

And of course, I can't really say that someone is a thieving little shit, or a drug dealing swine as that clearly doesn't fit in with the current softly-softly mentality. And I really, really can't say that many of the people I deal with on a daily basis are time-wasting, annoying and pathetic little twits. If I said those things to any citizen, I'd be hauled over the coals and then most likely disciplined or fired. In fact, I'm pretty much damned if I say anything at all. The boat must not be rocked. The Government would rather I buried my head in the sand just like they do.

This, of course, is where it's all gone horribly wrong. This is where political correctness has foreshortened common sense to the point of disaster. This is that insidious issue I mentioned in the first chapter. We now live in a time where people are afraid to say

---

11 In some cases the facts may very well be kicking you in the bollocks, to take the metaphor slightly further. If you're a female, I'm sure you could think of something excruciating to apply to your own metaphor …

something sensible in case they are branded something toxic like a racist, but deep down we all know that something needs to be said. The climate of not saying what we mean, coupled with not being allowed to say what we think for fear of reprisal, married to the issue of being forced to appreciate what we don't need to, has reinforced this weak, sycophantic and dependent society. A society tiptoeing on the edge of reason and yet still parading itself as cohesive, inclusive and community minded. Look at us! Aren't we great! We have this person in that role and that person in this role, we all love each other and value each other, and we all treat each other equally and with respect. It's all nice and happy and cosy and perfect. It's not. It's a Victorian playground. It doesn't really exist. And as soon as anything impinges a teeny weeny bit on our playground – as soon as something spoils our game or ruins this charade – ouch! Victim! We can't cope with it. We can't cope with anything anymore.

And one of the most sickening things about the whole debacle is that the Government wishes us to constantly appreciate what makes people different. I think it's about time we appreciated what makes people the *same*. In that respect you will find far more community cohesion and human integrity than can ever be found in the current sycophantic nightmare.

3. Racism

Racism. Another word worth mentioning again. *Racism.* Doesn't slip off the tongue too easily does it? Some rather aggressive syllables. A rather aggressive word.

So what is racism exactly? Well that depends on a lot of things. It depends where you are and who you're dealing with. It also depends on perception.

In 1986, The Association of Chief Police Officers (ACPO) established a definition of racism that referred to *'any incident in which it appeared to the reporting or investigating officer that the complaint involves an element of racial motivation or any incident which includes an allegation of racial motivation made by any person,'* as being one that should be regarded as a racist incident.

In 1999, following the Lawrence Inquiry, recommendation 12 of the Macpherson Report stated that the definition of a racist incident should be *'any incident that is perceived to be racist by the victim or any other person'.* (This was later agreed and put into practice by ACPO.)

My own definition of a racist incident is *'when wrong is caused to another based on their race'.* This can be as minor as name-calling to as horrific as murder, as Stephen Lawrence found out to his desperate, brutal and tragic demise. You will see from my definition that there is no mention of perception. Instead, it would appear to focus more heavily on *intention*. If I say or do something wrong to someone else *because* of their race, then this is racist. In other words, it's all about my intention.

If you were to pick up a law book and peruse it for a while, you will notice that English law is liberally smattered with words such as *intent*. You will unlikely find the word *perception* in many places. The Latin phrase *mens rea* is also used commonly in the application of English law. It means, literally, the *guilty state of mind*. If I hit you, intent on hurting you in the first place, then I have a guilty state of mind. If I enter your house intending to steal from you, I have a guilty state of mind. And if I throw litter in your garden because you are Asian and I intend to cause you distress, then I have a guilty state of mind. It's as simple as that.

However, you will see from the latest ACPO definition of a racist incident, as recommended by Macpherson, that perception is the key principle in defining what is racist. It is highly subjective. Perception has overridden intention to become the foundation of race crime.

So what is race crime? In simple terms, racist incidents are divided into two categories: racist crime and racist non-crime (e.g. a racist incident that is not necessarily criminal). The term 'race crime' is applied to a specific number of offences that can be aggravated by racism. For example, you can have racially motivated criminal damage, assault, harassment or public order offences. If such crimes are found to be racially motivated they are recorded as racially motivated, and carry a higher penalty upon conviction.

This is all fair enough. I entirely agree that true race crime is heinous, obnoxious, uneducated and particularly shit. Assaulting someone is bad enough, but doing it simply because they hail from a different racial background is entirely reprehensible. Damaging someone's property on the basis of their ethnic background alone is plain nasty and without excuse. Persistently hurling racial abuse at someone, and making their lives a misery because of it, is just awful. As a serving police officer, it would give me great pleasure to successfully charge and prosecute someone who committed true race crimes such as these. And I'm sure the real victim of these crimes would appreciate any effort on their behalf.

Racist non-crime is a slightly different kettle of fish. For there are some incidents that may have a racial element (e.g. depends entirely on perception) but do not constitute a specific criminal offence. Yet they still have to be logged, monitored, recorded, acted on, analysed and generally consume as much time as possible.

Not long ago, I was making my merry way to deal with a burglary. Now please bear in mind that burglary is a priority crime, a particularly nasty crime, and one that should carry a pretty hefty sentence upon conviction (haha). And the incident I was going to was quite unpleasant. Upon returning from his holiday, some poor chap had discovered a breeze block through his patio door, muddy footprints across his lounge carpet and his laptop and other possessions missing. The suspect or suspects had also kindly rifled through most of his drawers, broken several other items and generally treated his house with the measure of disdain common to filthy, thieving little shits.

Anyway, I wasn't too far from his house when I was dramatically re-deployed by the control room to an urgent 'racist incident'. There was a definite tinge of panic in the radio controller's voice. This was after the control room had made the shift Sergeants aware that there was a racist incident to deal with: the shift Inspector had been notified; and presumably, the Chief had been paged and the Red Devils had swooped across the sky announcing it with smoke trails to the whooping crowd below …

so I turned my car around and headed three miles in the opposite direction. I think, by the time I arrived at the location, everyone in the station knew where I was going, and so they waited in tense and nervous expectation for the outcome.

The only information I had been passed was that the incident was racist, it needed to be dealt with and that it was racist. And something else about it being racist, or something. I really can't remember. I don't think that whoever had taken the call from the 'victim' had asked too many questions. As soon as the word *racist* was mentioned, it set off all the alarms. People started panicking. Systems crashed. Kings abdicated. Businesses went into liquidation and cows mooed in terror. Soldiers abseiled down the sides of buildings and, somewhere in the distance, a lonely bell tolled. Ships foundered and baby birds fell from their nests. Hedgehogs flung themselves in front of cars and a thick, dense fog covered every major city. Flowers withered and light bulbs exploded. It was chaos.

Actually, it was a dispute over a parking space. The gentleman who'd called us was annoyed that his neighbour had parked in his space and they'd subsequently had an argument about it. No words of a racist kind were exchanged. I asked the gentleman if he felt the parking violation was racially motivated, he shrugged his shoulders and said, 'Don't know. Could be. I think so.' So I covered my arse and spent half-an-hour completing some racial incident non-crime paperwork. Then I made a phone call to get the incident recorded. Then I rang the race-crime unit to make them aware. Then I made sure the 'victim' was OK and then I left. I never did get to the burglary victim. I was re-deployed somewhere else. To something equally as inane. All in all a perfect example of the Government deciding who is a victim irrespective of the context.

We've already established that there is no common sense left in policing. Therefore, it is highly unlikely, nay *impossible*, that you will find any common sense when it comes to the whole issue of the racist incident. This is rather silly but I don't care:

Ring, ring. Ring, ring.

Hello, police, can I help?

Yes. I want to report nothing.

I'm sorry?

I want to report nothing.

Sorry, you want to report nothing?

Yes. Nothing.

I'm sorry, I really don't follow.

Nothing's happened.

OK, so what exactly do you want to report?

That nothing has happened.

Nothing?

Yes, nothing. Nothing has happened and it's upsetting me.

Nothing has happened and it's upsetting you?

Yes, I'm finding it all a bit upsetting.

Why is that?

Because something usually happens.

I see. So nothing has happened and you're upset?

Yes.

So why do you think that nothing has happened?

I don't really know.

So nothing has happened, and you don't know why it hasn't happened and you're upset?

Yes. And I perceive it to be racist.

I see. So you're the victim of a racially aggravated non-event?

Yes.

OK. That's fine. What we'll do is record it as a racist incident non-recordable. Then we'll send some officers round to speak to you while they are on the way to somewhere more important. Then we'll spend at least an hour with you and after that we'll send you a letter offering you all the support possible. And after that, we'll

*probably ask you to take part in a survey to measure your victim
satisfaction in line with the Police Performance Assessment
Framework requirements for statutory performance indicator
data on satisfaction with racist incidents' response ...*

Thank you ...

That part about performance indicator stuff is all real, by
the way.[12] Hopefully, it gives you a small insight into the treacly
and turgid bureaucracy that surrounds dealing with anything –
literally *anything* – that has even the remotest chance of being
racist.

And what is the fallout because of this state of affairs? Well,
you could say that the police – one among many organisations
– epitomise this acute Government-induced paranoia. We have
already seen in previous chapters that we are not allowed to say
certain things – or even think certain things – and we have to jump
through a million hoops every time the word *racist* crops up in our
daily duties. Furthermore, the recording and managing of racist
incidents in the police service requires whole new departments
to be established, with whole new departments to monitor those
departments, and auditors to audit the monitors and so on ...

It's reached the level of the ludicrous. And it's not just
the police who are suffering because of it. Schools face the
same bureaucracy, along with plenty of other businesses and
organisations. I can only write from a police perspective, but I'm
sure any reader of this book from a different organisation could
find parallels.

The public are also bewildered and confused by it all. They
have no idea where they stand. The amount of times I've been
taking a statement from someone, for example, and have asked

12 The phrase '*Police Performance Assessment Framework requirements for
statutory performance indicator data on satisfaction with racist incidents'
response*' can be found in Paragraph 3, Section 5 of *Home Office Online
Report 42/05: Racist incidents: progress since the Lawrence Inquiry.*

a person to describe someone else, and they say something like, 'Well, he was a black male.' Then they look at me with a kind of scared look and say something else like, 'Sorry, am I allowed to say that?' And my reply is something like, 'Sorry, not allowed to say what?' And they say something back like, 'Sorry, I wasn't sure if I could say the word *black*. I thought it might be racist ... I don't actually know what I'm allowed to say ...'

I have had this conversation in its various forms, describing all different people, dozens and dozens of times since becoming a police officer. Of course, you get some people who come out with some phrases which are quite close to the line, and there are undoubtedly people who describe other races in a particularly derogatory way, but this does not presume they would commit criminal offences against them.

However, there is an even more sinister side to the current pre-occupation with racism. I have heard it echoed by many people – friends, colleagues and members of the public I have dealt with. Basically, the whole concept of what constitutes racism in Britain is extremely – and I mean *extremely* – narrow-minded, one-sided, blinkered and skewed completely off course.

For example, the Brits, for many years, have had a kind of semi good-humoured history of slagging off the French. I've done it and I guess you have too. *Bloody French!* If I was to walk into any office in any part of England, whether in a police station or not, and whether in the presence of the odd French person or not, say the phrase *Bloody French!* I know that hardly anyone would bat an eyelid. I could even say *Bloody Frogs!* And who would give a shit? Not many people, if any at all.

I could also walk into any office in any part of England and say *Bloody Yanks!* And who in their right mind would have a go at me? No-one. *Bloody Germans!* (Especially after a penalty shoot-out.) Would I get into trouble? Hardly. And if I was to walk into any office in any part of England, whether in a police station or not, and start to talk with a Scottish accent, no once would bat an eyelid – even if they knew I had an English accent and was therefore doing an impression. In fact I was doing this today with my colleague. I spoke with a Scottish accent and she spoke with an Irish accent, while on the radio another colleague spoke with a Geordie accent, but it came out a bit Welsh for some reason, even though he's from Plymouth. Who cares?

And if we were all to do the same thing, but talk with an American accent, German accent, Australian accent, Polish accent … no one would give a monkeys. We certainly wouldn't get into trouble. However, if I was to walk into an office and say *Bloody Asians!* whilst adopting a mock Indian accent for effect … I'd get fired. Somewhere, somehow, we determined that racism only applied to certain races and to certain groups. We left out a huge percentage of ethnic backgrounds and worried ourselves mainly with Asians and black people. For most of us don't seem to be overly concerned about ripping the shit out of other races, but if it concerns Asians and black people, then we immediately put on our pinkest and fluffiest boots and tread with ever nervous delicacy over the carpet of eggshells.

And this paranoia was pretty much exclusively created by white British people. There is no way on earth that Asians or black people deserve any blame whatsoever for this situation. The insecurity is, for the majority, a white person problem. I've no doubt that people from different racial backgrounds may have contributed in some way to this neurosis, because there are idiots from every ethnic group, but I'm going to chalk this crap down to W1 – white British.

Surely racism is racism and it doesn't matter where you are from. *Bloody French* should be as dangerously insulting as *Bloody Asians*, but it clearly isn't. And if it isn't then there's got to be another reason for the paranoia. There has to be another motive. And it's that other reason we will look at in the final chapter. You're going to have to wait for that one – it's pretty hefty. So, how can I justify saying that this paranoia was almost entirely induced by white people? Well one thing that really grates my cheese more than anything else is a group of mainly white people deciding what would upset a group of Asian people, for example.

We already know we live in a pathetically weak, dependent and neurotic society, so it should be no surprise when you hear on the news things like the word *Christmas* being banned because it *might upset* people from other faiths. Banning this and restricting that, for fear of upsetting somebody else. Of course this all fits in very well with the victim culture. If you've been watching the news for the past few years you will have noticed more and more this kind of attitude. It wasn't long ago when I read that Christmas cards had been banned in one office for fear of upsetting the Asians in the office. Of course the Asians in the office had *not* been asked if they would be upset by Christmas cards, and they even later said that they wouldn't be upset, but it didn't matter. A group of white people had already decided what was best for the Asian people.

Now there didn't appear to be any similar trouble in Kuwait. This was a country with Islamic laws and Islamic banks. Islamic schools and plenty of mosques. There was a sizeable Christian population also in the country, but the country was Islamic. It had its identity well and truly established and there were no issues about 'upsetting' each other. There were churches for Christians and provision for Christians in other areas where appropriate. Not once did I feel that any Christians were being sidelined or mistreated by the Muslims. And at Christmas time, in this Islamic country, there were Christmas decorations available in shops. Christmas carols. Mince pies. Christmas cards. Santas, reindeer and other festive reminders everywhere. I went to a large, extremely popular carol service that was advertised widely across the country. No-one minded me going.

So why on earth do people in Britain, who really haven't got a clue about anything at all, make decisions about communities they know nothing about? They clearly *think* they have a clue but they clearly don't. This sycophantic, wishy-washy, ill-informed behaviour damages everybody from every community because it perpetuates a weak society that has no identity or self-esteem. I had a more 'Christmassy' Christmas in an Islamic country than I did in England. How the hell did that happen?

Of course, this isn't just about Christmas – it's about the attitudes and behaviours behind this façade of inclusiveness. Because if it's not Christmas, it's something else. Of course it doesn't have to relate to any racial group either – this paranoia affects everyone. Let's ban Mother's Day in schools for example, because it might upset children who don't have mothers. I read that in a paper recently. It's political correctness gone more than mad. It's gone way beyond common sense. It's bloody light years away from sanity.

It is also extremely obvious there is a particular focus on not wanting to upset particular racial groups. This has been evident in many areas. And in my opinion I believe that we have pandered to certain racial groups so much and with such obsequiousness that many people from those groups don't know where they stand either. They are not sure of their boundaries, or the appropriate scope of their influence. They have been so encouraged to be victims, and put on a pedestal, that their bewilderment leads to an often disproportionate expectation of service from others, including the police. Some people take advantage of it – not many, but some. This leads a few idiots to attempt to use their ethnic background for their advantage, or cry racism when something doesn't go their way. And they know that organisations, especially the police, will grovel in fawning apology.

When I say this country has gone to the dogs, it has nothing specifically to do with anyone who lives here, or moved here from elsewhere. It has everything to do with a weak Government and poor policies on protecting our sovereignty, culture and heritage. It's about maintaining identity (if the British are still allowed to have one ...) It's what we do to ensure that Britain remains British, and if we want to live here then we will appreciate and recognise what is British. If we do that, we can quite happily be identified by our own culture if we so desire, so long as it conforms to the laws of the land, and then we will be able to identify our boundaries and the limit of our influence. At the moment, it's a melting pot of cultures not knowing what country they live in because it has no identity left.

The country must be allowed to preserve its cultural heritage, to maintain its Britishness. Most people don't care where others are from so long as they speak the language, want to join in, obey the law, work hard, pay tax and otherwise contribute to the welfare of the nation. The baddies are those that take the piss, and there are lots of them, and they are of all different races. In the final chapter, we will examine in much more detail the concept of 'Britishness' but for the meanwhile let us be rather basic.

If you consider yourself to be important because you are a 'native' – e.g. if you think you're extra special because you're white British, or black British, or from any other background but born here, then you're not. You have to treat this country like home. You don't get treated any differently. You get benefits because you need them, not because you want them or think you deserve them. You will also work hard, appreciate the culture, obey the law, pay your taxes and contribute. Otherwise, you are as undeserving as anyone.

The people who annoy me hugely are the white, non tax-paying, layabout scum who persistently commit petty crime and disorder and then moan about 'immigration' and 'Asians' and 'blacks'. And the other people who annoy me are some of the

Asian displaced and confused individuals who seem to want the best of everything, but the responsibility of nothing. They don't appear to know what their identity is, but have every idea of what they *don't* like about their background. Good idea would be to start to take some responsibility; start to appreciate where they live and stop moaning about why being Asian is screwing them up. It's not an excuse. And how about the black teenage gangs running rife in certain parts of the country, shooting and stabbing each other? How about you stop doing that. Your lives aren't that bad. Take a look at where you live and if you don't like it then do your very best to move, or do your best to make it better. Social deprivation is real, of course it is, but you are more real. You live and you breathe. Therefore you live and you breathe restoration. Love your country, not your gangs and your guns. Most people don't really have a problem with 'blacks', they have a problem with people like you, and you just happen to be black.

So Britain will remain British so long as people living in it respect, value and appreciate Britishness, and want to preserve its traditions and legacies; learn its laws and take heed of its customs; protect its environment and follow its social etiquette. You don't have to appreciate *everything* about Britain – but if you want to be a valuable citizen, then do your bit for the country. This means being British, and if you're not British, then it means being proud to be part of the British culture. It also means being proud to live in this country. Pride for the country you live in should come first and foremost, and then we can all get on with appreciating the other cultures that exist within it. If you switch that priority around like the Government did then you screw up the country… which is what the Government did.

Racism is one race thinking they are better, or more deserving, than another. And the more different races you have crammed into one small space, then the more racist incidents you are going to have. Over the past few decades, Britain has seen a dramatic influx of peoples from all different races trying to make this country their home. Trouble is, quite a few of them have no idea how to behave and instead, try to live the way they did elsewhere. This creates a shed load of problems and then more established citizens of the country take offence.

If people move to one country from another country, then what they should be doing is looking away from their own race for a moment and adjusting themselves to the country in which they have chosen to live. Once they have adjusted themselves and realised where they are and what is expected of them socially, environmentally and professionally, they can start to live as part of that culture, but still maintain their difference. Other cultures within Britain can, and should, be appreciated (the good parts!) but never at the expense of the nation as a whole. Yes we are a nation of all ethnic backgrounds, indeed a multicultural society, but we are British first and foremost. The Government should make every effort to ensure this is the case. Not pay lip service to it, but enforce it. This is Britain.

People who live in this country, and who continue to maintain aspects of their own cultural identity, must be made aware that if those cultural aspects clash significantly with the law, then they will face the consequences. This should be enforced at the earliest possible opportunity (e.g. the immigration process itself). Here I am talking about *serious* things. Heinous and evil practices such as honour killings, forced marriages[13] and female genital mutilation, which are hallmarks of certain countries and cultures, are a grim problem in Britain at present. And any other practice or custom of a particular country that is so abusive as to be a breach of the most basic of human rights must be considered as detrimental to the health and welfare of the nation as a whole, not least the poor victim.

Unfortunately, we are at the stage where such issues are

13 Please note that a forced marriage is not the same as an arranged marriage.

being discovered far too late and we are merely picking up the pieces. A weak Government and a pathetically inadequate immigration system, and I use the word 'system' in its loosest possible term, has allowed despicable practices to take place in this country because we have been far too soft and unclear about the social, civil, cultural and professional expectations of this country.

As well as extremely noxious cultural practices, other less serious practices must also be considered if they too clash in any way with the law or general well-being of this country. There is nothing wrong with some flexibility and latitude when it comes to the wider issues of diversity and immigration, but this country (Government) has been so flexible as to be ineffectual and, subsequently, there are very sobering problems in many inner city areas regarding certain cultural groups.

Unfortunately, many people from all backgrounds treat this country and its laws with disdain. They do not pay heed to their social environment and are, perhaps, in the country because of other benefits. Often people who were born in Britain are just as lax and selfish. These are people who claim far more than they need and take far more than they give. People of all different cultures are ripping the living shit out of the welfare state. Bleeding it dry. Taking the piss with utter disdain. Day in, day out, I deal with people who don't give a damn about this country, and it's a tragic shame. People who exist to serve themselves and get what they can from life without giving anything back. People who tread on others in order to shirk responsibility and elude hard work. People with absolutely no respect for anything, or anyone, whatsoever.

This country will only survive if people respect where they live. If they don't, then I perceive this to be racist. And I'm sure that by going on about Britain somebody will call *me* racist anyway ...

4. Taking Offence

We have examined in part that race crime is a crime of perception. It depends on how the victim feels. However, if there is so much evidence as to suggest that the crime itself was racially motivated, irrespective of the feelings of the victim, then it would be treated as such. If I posted a letter through someone's letterbox, which abused them, specifically, for being from a different race, then this is clearly a racially aggravated crime and would not necessarily need any element of perception. However, if I posted a letter through that same letterbox demanding that they stop playing music in the small hours, I am clearly intending no racial aggravation. But that person could still perceive it to be racist and, therefore, it becomes a race crime regardless of my intentions.[14]

Recently, a colleague of mine was allocated an incident to deal with, and I recall him sitting there numbly shaking his head at the computer in the office. A female had called us stating that her neighbour had knocked on the wall loudly several times. This knocking was not persistent, nor was it linked to any other kind of behaviour that could be perceived (by police) as harassing, offensive or upsetting. Obviously it matters not what the police think anymore, and the female who called us reported that she felt

---

14 Pretty stupid huh?

the knocking to be 'racially aggravated' and part of a sustained and deliberate campaign of harassment due to her race. Her feelings were paramount in this situation. In this scenario the racial element played a crucial part, yet we now live in a world where people are ready to take offence at anything and everything and find themselves 'upset' over completely pointless things. The purpose of any action carried out by so-called offenders is overshadowed by the effect it has on other people and, unfortunately, the effect is far too often completely disproportionate to the action in the first place.

We therefore have a situation where in some cases the element of perception overrides the intent. We also have situations where the perception or feelings of the victim are the outcome of the offence itself. For many years the police have been dealing with certain crimes where the only result of the crime is one of 'offence'. And for the sake of argument I will also widen the scope of this discussion to include crimes where the result of the crime is *harassment, alarm or distress.* In other words, someone's been upset. In recent years such 'offences' have taken on dramatic new meanings. As we saw in the first chapter it is extremely easy to be harassed these days. It's very easy to be alarmed by a couple of text messages. Every day the police have to attempt to wade through the mire of what is, or what is not, offensive behaviour. How do we ascertain if people are truly 'upset' and even if they are, can we or should we do anything about it? For to be offended, harassed, alarmed, distressed or upset is very difficult to quantify or 'prove' and, as such, how do police begin to deal with victims who feel this way?

First of all, I think it would be pertinent to say that the context of this chapter is *not* concerning situations where a person has been subjected to such sustained or heinous abuse or harassment, or been the victim of such an horrific incident that they have been psychologically distressed to the point of mental or emotional breakdown. This has happened in many situations and I would not presume to suggest that some people are not truly distressed by certain behaviours, so my context is less grave. I am also not talking about anti-social behaviour, where large groups of youths in hoodies congregate on street corners, for example. Such behaviour can be inherently alarming and is an issue worthy of serious attention.

Rather, my context is single incidents, or persistent incidents that are of such a low level and insignificant nature as to be singularly unimportant. My context is throwaway remarks, or people momentarily in a strop. In other words, *life*. For life is full of annoyances, little grievances, set-backs, hold-ups, problems and above all, idiots. People aren't nice to each other and there's some very unpleasant people out there. However, just because someone has 'had a go' at someone else, does not presume that they would want to hurt that person physically or emotionally. There are plenty of people that *do* want to hurt others, but for the moment we will content ourselves with looking at the 'average' person. The person who gets up, goes to work, comes home, goes out for a beer, has a laugh and goes home again. Neither a criminal nor a saint. Just your average person. And certainly not someone who would ever commit a heinous crime or wish someone dead, or want to abuse or harass someone persistently and with malice aforethought. I would place myself in this bracket. I'm certainly not a criminal, but I'm also not a saint. I've had a go at people. I've said plenty of things I shouldn't. I've upset people. It's life. But how much of this life should really involve the police?

Owing to the fact that we live in a victim culture, the police are now dealing with an incredible amount of low-level incidents where someone has been 'upset'. They've been offended. Distressed. They want something done about it. They want someone else charged. They want the police to *have a word with them.* They want to report it. Get it logged. Make the police aware. And because of our infatuation with recording everything (and often turning the most insignificant things into hot-blooded crimes) and owing to the fact that we *must* focus on the victim, we end up dealing with minor incidents on a very officious and unrealistic level.

So we can't say *not a police matter.* We've already seen that this is the case, so we have to have some involvement. We *have* to deal with whatever is reported. And behind the scenes, the police policy-makers and bureaucrats are recording, measuring, assessing, compiling, checking and auditing. There's targets to be met and ticky boxes to tick, so if someone reports that they've been sworn at in a supermarket, the pieces are set in motion for an incredibly over the top reaction.

First of all, you have the social factor that someone can't cope with being sworn at. It's upset them. Then you have the administrative factor that the police have to deal with such things. Then you have the bureaucratic factor of incident logging, criming, paperwork and job allocation. Ticky boxes, Drop down menus. Ethnic details. And above all, *Think Victim!* And overseeing all of this like Big Brother is the Government who has established all of this nonsense in the first place.

Now, being sworn at is not particularly pleasant. I was sworn at the other day in a road rage incident. I was off duty and driving round a roundabout, and for some reason, a smartly dressed gentleman in a nice car took offence at me driving. He pulled out in front of me, shouted 'You fucking cock', and sped off in a right strop. Perhaps he thought he had right of way. Perhaps he was having a bad day. Perhaps he was plain grumpy all the time. But I've not seen him again and I don't care. At the time, I just ignored it and drove on.

However, the police get a lot of calls regarding a lot of things of this level. In this case, the 'offender' was unknown to me, but he could very well have been someone I know. It doesn't really matter either way. Now the questions I want to ask are these: Was I offended? What is offence anyway? How is it measured? How is it proved? Is it a mental feeling or a physical one? I have to say that I didn't particularly enjoy being sworn at. It wasn't the sort of thing I'd celebrate with a nice slice of Victoria sponge and a cup of tea. But neither is it the sort of thing that would make me ill or lose sleep. How on earth does one deal with such a thing? I know. Call the police. Let them deal with it.

There have long been offences, mostly in the area of public order, that involve an element of perception. Sections 5 and 4A of the Public Order Act 1986, for example, relate to incidents that result in harassment, alarm or distress, or were likely to result as such. They also relate to incidents that someone may find threatening, abusive or insulting. And to feel threatened, abused or insulted is also a matter of perception.

Nowadays, people are very aware of what they find insulting or offensive. They have such an acute awareness, however, that they find it very difficult to deal with situations when they arise. Because society has been mollycoddled to such an extent that we are incapable of dealing with anything ourselves any more, we need a crutch. And this crutch is more often than not the police. Unfortunately the police perpetuate the problem by not being firm with people because we are not allowed to be. So the cycle continues day in, day out, but very few people seem to be addressing the crucial issue of what exactly is offence?

How long does the feeling of being offended actually last for? It's an entirely subjective issue and perhaps best left for other people to discuss, but I hope it has raised a couple of interesting thoughts. For if the police get told by someone that they have been offended, upset, distressed or whatever, then we usually pick and choose a crime that best fits their story and deal with it as such. It often ends up being one of the lower level public order incidents, or an harassment, but it is clear that the objectiveness, the common sense, has all but gone.

The spirit of the law and of certain Acts of Parliament is not being recognised in many cases. The Protection from Harassment Act 1997, for example, is designed to protect people from serious stalking. However, it is now mainly used for people who have received a couple of text messages they didn't particularly favour. It is being abused by the police who are applying it to incidents of utter inanity in their effort to do things 'by the book' in terms of criming, recording and logging everything.

I wonder how on earth people coped several years ago when the police simply didn't deal with things to such an over-the-top degree. Sure, people have always reported crap to the police, but in many cases, it was dealt with there and then with some stern words, or we didn't waste our time with it. We should be enforcing the law, not babysitting. However, because we are living in a Victorian playground we are the teachers called in to split up the petty squabbles. Years ago, police might be called to an incident of disorder or very low level harassment style behaviour and would tell each party to go their own way and leave each other alone. It was much more gritty and realistic. Go away and get a life. Now we have to pander to everyone. We also have to criminalise people who don't deserve to be, but that's an entirely different story. We'll have a look at this issue briefly later on.

So how did people survive when they couldn't get a crime report and have the police sort everything out for them? Was society such an awful place to be? I think the answer to that must be 'No'. We were a lot more hard nosed and self-sufficient years ago. We were able to deal with things better. In fact, we *had* to deal with things, because the 'support' industry wasn't quite as prolific as it is nowadays.

Now, we are just itching to take offence at everything. We demand that our lives be perfect. Any small glitch and we can't cope. The generation that lived through World War II must be baffled by this social incompetence. I'm almost inclined to believe that evolution has started working backwards. Very soon we'll be amoebas again. It's a rather pathetic state of affairs. It is a rather calamitous hallmark of the victim culture and applies to everyone of every race and walk of life.

For this state of affairs involves a very large portion of society – far more than those who report things to police. We see and deal with the worst of it, but this social ineptitude goes much further and deeper than what the police have to deal with. It's endemic. We've become a bunch of wishy-washy wet lettuces in all areas of our lives. We have a pre-packaged, convenience, paper and plastic, disposable existence. There is nothing of substance any more. I find myself gazing at buildings made of stone; looking longingly at things that have stood the test of time – things that haven't yielded to the elements or the changing whims of mankind. Now all we can manage is a small whimper when something upsets us or doesn't go our way. All the fight has gone. The spine has been removed. We are nondescript, jelly-like organisms slithering around being weak and wretched. Apologies if you took offence to that …

* * *

Against this backdrop of social ineptitude, the police are now rather stuck in the mud. To fully appreciate this nightmare, we now have to take a look at some administrative actions the police employ. The next few chapters are thus clearly about how the police deal with things, but it is necessary to go into such detail as the subject matter is indicative of much wider professional and organisational issues in these overly bureaucratic days. For anyone who is used to mind-numbing bureaucracy, red tape and bewildering decision making processes, you will certainly understand just how bad it has all become.

5. Crime and Recording (... everything)

There are standards for recording crime, apparently. And you can find all you need to know about the regulations surrounding crime accountancy in a saucy little document entitled the *National Crime Recording Standard* (NCRS). Introduced in 2002, it aimed to promote greater consistency in recording practices between different police forces. It tied in with other Government initiatives concerning an improvement in quality of service, especially for victims. I first became aware of the NCRS several months ago. Being a frontline shift officer meant that I didn't really need to know too much about it, but I steadied my nerves and read the document. Afterwards, I hit the bottle. Hard.

It's one of those things that seems exceptionally good in theory, but in practice has become a raging, out of control beast. What started off as a rather good idea in principle has been somewhat blown out of all proportion by paranoia in practical application. Like many ideas that come from an ivory tower, it has probably earned someone a pat on the back and a tick in the promotional box, but in reality, has led to some of the most bizarre and frustrating organisational behaviour on the face of the planet.

To appreciate a little where we have gone slightly askew, we need to take a brief look at the NCRS, or rather the spirit of the standards.[15] Now there are three basic principles to the NCRS and they are as follows.

1. All incidents reported to the police shall lead to the creation of an incident report.[16]

2. Incidents will be recorded as a crime if, on the balance of probability, it is more likely than not that a crime has occurred.

3. Once a crime has been recorded it will stay recorded, unless it is proven that there was no crime.

Now these are the bare bones of the NCRS. I am inclined to think that they are pretty sound and sensible principles in their most hypothetical form. I'm sure that whoever dreamed them up thought the same thing. If someone calls the police to report something, we make an initial note of it. Nothing wrong with that. If the reported incident is a crime then we investigate it. Should that crime have occurred, we record it indelibly as a crime unless it is proven otherwise. Fairly simple and straightforward.

You can probably guess though that it's all gone a wee bit pear shaped. The Government is completely obsessed with recording everything and every day the police spend a huge percentage of their time doing just that – recording everything. Collecting information. Compiling statistics. All we do is monitor – we don't actually have much time to do anything of any substance. Certainly not as much as we used to. The reason behind all of this, I believe, is that the police service is supposed to be intelligence-led. By recording anything and everything we supposedly gain a better and bigger picture of what is happening

---

15 There's a 'hidden' standard to the NCRS, but we'll take a look at that in the final chapter.

16 Different police forces call their 'incident reports' different things. They may be referred to as *Logs, CADs, URNs* or whatever. They are, quite simply, the initial details of the reported incident logged onto a computer system.

in any given area. Unfortunately, a large percentage of what is recorded is completely useless information. It's not intelligence, it's bollocks. It reflects the lowest level of social incompetence. As such we have very little time to spend trying to obtain *real* intelligence because we're too preoccupied with dealing with trivia, and ensuring that all the ticky boxes have been ticked. The 'standard' has actually ended up *lowering* standards and leading to a plethora of shit.

The Government is very keen to ensure that the police are recording everything properly. They want to make sure that we are *NCRS Compliant.* Basically, the facts of any reported incident appear to be totally irrelevant – it's all about how we record it and whether or not we've ticked the right boxes. More often than not, this has led the police to creating crimes out of nothing, or making certain crimes fit certain incidents. There is another angle to this regarding the role of civilian employees, but it is fair to say that whoever records the details of the reported incident is following orders from above. And those orders come from Government.

There are also time limits on the recording of a crime from the time a crime is reported to us. In a nutshell we have seventy-two hours to record a crime if someone has reported it. I find this rather ridiculous as it shouldn't make any difference, but I think the spirit of this restriction is to ensure the police attend reported incidents as soon as practicable. After all, we don't want to keep the poor victims waiting …

I have had comprehensive arguments with people much higher up the food chain than me about the NCRS. Unfortunately, the basis of my argument doesn't wash well with some of my superiors. While my police service correctly records crime according to the standard, I would like to suggest that the standard itself is insane. So while my employers can turn around and say that they are correctly following procedure, it is the procedure itself that is bollocks. The principles are sound but they are missing a crucial caveat – i.e. if it's a load of crap, we shouldn't bother recording it. But as you can imagine, this isn't going to happen! Although the standard states that crimes are recorded on the *balance of probabilities*, this is simply not so. Firstly, the police do most things to cover their arse and therefore err succinctly on the side of caution, to the point of madness. Secondly, your average frontline police officer no longer appears able to determine whether a crime has occurred or not – such decisions are made by people sitting in offices sipping mochaccinos and applying rigid and unrealistic principles. Thirdly, in a decontexualised, imbalanced and generally paranoid organisational environment, we will tend to record most things anyway – just in case, irrespective of the facts and common sense. The NCRS is, therefore, unable to differentiate between what is shit and what is not.

This leads the police to dealing with utter trivia because it has been raised up to the level of the important, simply due to the process by which it is recorded. Talk about being slaves to the system! Anything important is therefore lumped in with all the crap and priorities get confused and twisted. This levelling of the playing field or standardisation – under the guise of promoting consistency – has in effect, ruined any dwindling hopes of encouraging common sense or social responsibility. It forces the police to deal with things by rote and advocates ill-informed decisions and bewildering methods of criminal justice.

The NCRS has therefore, quite literally ravaged any remaining shreds of discretion that may have been clinging on with desperate hope to the methodology of the police service. It is a complete and utter nightmare. The NCRS is fucking awful.

* * *

A pertinent issue to consider now would be the amount of crime that is *not* reported to police. For example, in the past ten years I've had my car damaged on at least eight or nine different occasions, where the damage has been wanton and deliberate, including smashed windows and stolen radio. Several years ago, I was assaulted on the street with some friends by a gang of drunken yobs, and at university I had personal effects stolen. None of these incidents I reported to police, mainly because I knew there was nothing the police could do about it! I didn't need a crime reference number for anything and I didn't particularly need any emotional support. However, I was in effect a real victim of criminal damage, assault (which was a clear ABH) and theft. I should have contacted the police in retrospect, but like a lot of people, I didn't want to waste police time! Some of the nicest and most decent people I meet at work are real victims of crime who endlessly apologise for 'wasting my time,' which wrenches my heart on every occasion they say this. If only they knew!

I'm sure the same sort of thing is happening day in, day out across the country. And I know that some people don't report crime to the police for a number of other reasons:

a) They hate police.
b) They don't think it's worth it as the police can't really do much.
c) They would prefer to sort it out themselves.
d) They don't care.
e) They're wanted by police.

In other words, there could be a number of different reasons why actual crimes do not end up being reported and recorded, which means crime figures are a complete misnomer anyway. So not only do we have crime figures that are affected by paranoia and mis-criming (i.e. it's entirely subjective), but also by the fact that a hell of a lot of crime goes unreported anyway. Bringing in a 'standard' for crime recording is all very well, but it hasn't made any difference whatsoever, except to increase bureaucracy and stress levels.

To massage crime figures, all you need to do is tweak the system here, or add a little ticky box there, or merge a few related crimes together and Bob's your Auntie. The whole system is a joke. Any Government can parade crime figures to their advantage if they so wish and any Opposition can parade crime figures to make their opponents look crap. We all know that statistics prove that statistics prove nothing, and this is highly evident in the arena of crime recording. So while there *should* be some form of standard, you cannot ever really ascertain whether crime is increasing, decreasing, staying the same, or whatever. It is not possible to get a handle on it.

But the crime recording analysts and Home Office auditors do their very hardest to get some kind of grip on the slippery mass that is crime accountancy and it's a never ending process of changing policies, altered procedures, counting rules and other statistical methods that bear little relevance to the police officer on the street, or the person who has reported the incident in the first place. The Government is concerned with recording and figures, and *pretends* it is concerned with the victims, while the police officers are concerned with the victims (the real ones of course) and not too fussed about recording and figures. This of course creates a conflict of interest and everyone ends up paying the price.

Living in a victim culture has also ensured that a lot of alleged crime ends up being treated as crime. Allegation and fact are not to be confused. We have already seen that feeling and perception can falsely alter fact, and pandering to people perpetuates the cycle. As I write this very paragraph, across the country the police have probably just created several hundred crime reports – a huge percentage of which are most likely complete and utter nonsense. Mixed in, there will be the real victims somewhere – probably at the bottom of the pile, but they will be hugely overshadowed by time-wasting idiots and those who cannot take any form of responsibility for their own existence. And while it seems I am blaming such people, I am also apportioning plenty of that blame to the Government that encourages this state of affairs in the first place. It is extremely frustrating to have to deal with the same kind of people day in, day out when most of them should be told, in no uncertain terms, to grow up, get a life and stop being so pathetic. This frustration isn't really directed *at* those people – after all, we all share this world and I'm no more important or deserving than anyone – it's rather annoyance at a system that perpetuates weakness of character, social ineptitude and non responsibility, and sidelines those who are truly affected by criminal conduct.

So, the Government, and therefore the police, content themselves with their ever changing methods of crime recording, analysing, counting, checking, auditing and measuring, and the average police officer spends most of his or her time driving between allegations of crap in order to update a computer system later on with irrelevant details, and the nation continues to be socially incontinent, misguided and in bewilderment as to what is really going on.

In my particular police force (sorry, *service*) I cannot 'file' one of my crime reports until there has been a thorough and sensitive investigation, utilising specialist departments and external agencies, and employing an array of dynamic and office based methods of inquiry to ensure that the victim receives the best possible service and any potential offender is brought to swift and appropriate justice. This investigation is overseen by a Sergeant, an Inspector and Investigation Managers to ensure that no stone is left unturned and there are no further possible avenues to explore.

Actually, this isn't quite true. For me to 'file' a crime report I just need to know someone's ethnic details and their date of birth, and ensure it is recorded properly. If I don't have this information to hand then, regardless of the investigation itself, I cannot show that crime report as being dealt with. You see there's priorities and there's priorities. The Government cares about recording 'properly'. It's obsessed with it to the point of madness. And my priorities? Well, I didn't join this job to tick boxes ...

6. Facts, Figures and Targets

… But I might as well have done.

Now I suppose I could spend the next few pages bitching on about paperwork, but I really don't have the energy or inclination. It's no secret that the police are constantly submerged under a huge amount of paper and files, with the odd staple sticking out here and there, so I don't really need to repeat what is already known. I *will* say, however, that having a comprehensive computer database for the recording of crime has made absolutely no difference to the amount of paperwork. Also, any other online system we employ to assist us in our daily role, such as finding missing people or compiling other information, does not negate the use of paper. The trees are not safe just yet.

This chapter isn't about paperwork anyway, but I just thought I'd mention it for the sake of it. Instead, the spirit of this chapter is about the office based monitoring that goes on behind the scenes. The facts, figures and performance targets that malign my role. Ever wanted to know what is up on the walls of a police station office? Then read on.

Yes, police work in an office. It pains me somewhat to use that word, because I still can't quite accept that far too much of my time is spent in one. However, I am in reality a shift officer, which means

I leave the station when and where practicable. Now being a shift officer means my targets are somewhat different to that of an officer who doesn't leave the station. And across the country, by and large, shift officers are measured on a specific number of things.

Of course, it is not quantifiable to measure my performance in terms of how professionally and appropriately I have dealt with people. Neither is it really practicable to measure any of us on the *prevention* of crime. After all, we can't effectively record how many crimes *haven't* happened. That's just daft.

Instead, we are measured on how many crimes we have dealt with (preferably *detected*), how many people we arrest and how much useful information about our manor that we pass to the people behind the scenes.[17] These things are about the only bits of our role that can be effectively compiled and monitored. In other words, you can create a pie chart with this information. If you can create a pie chart with such material, then you can justify having a whole department to create the pie charts and tell the shift officers where they are going wrong. But surely this is internal politics? I hear you cry. What of the victim culture? Well, let's start with *detections.*

A detection occurs when a crime has been recorded and the offender has been either cautioned, charged or fined for the offence in question (*please note that a crime only needs to have been recorded – it doesn't actually need to have occurred ...*). There are other forms of detections, but those are the main three: caution, charge or fine.[18] When someone has received this kind of

---

17 If I hit lots of pointless targets then I'm demonstrating 'effective performance in the workplace.' Perhaps that means I'll get a financial bonus. Thankyou Home Secretary!

18 Fines from the police mainly come in the form of a *Penalty Notice for Disorder (PND)* which can be issued for offences such as Section 5 of the Public Order Act 1986 (disorderly behaviour), shoplifting or criminal damage. The fines are £80 and a huge percentage of people don't end up paying them.

sanction, a virtual update is made and we have a 'detection'. In effect, a detection is an administrative and computer-based tick in a box relating to someone either admitting an offence or having so much evidence weighed against them that they receive a sanction for it anyway. These administrative ticks are therefore referred to, commonly, as '*sanction-based detections*'.

The more detections the better. Oh yes. Oh yes *indeedy*. We want detections! Detections are very good for the police, and even better for the Government. They provide a means to an end, whatever that end may be. I suppose the end should be something to do with justice, but that's such a rookie thing to say. I rather think that detections are all about favourable crime figures, but that's just a cynical thing to say.

The police are limited in the sanctions they can impose without the case going through the courts.[19] In cases involving adult offenders, we can caution or fine them. With juveniles we can do the same, but they can also receive reprimands and warnings. All other forms of police 'sanctions', such as issuing traffic related fines, closing down crack houses, issuing ASBO's, seizing cars – and much else besides – do not result in the obtaining of a 'detection'. Whilst those things are measured and recorded (of course), they tend not to be the remit of the everyday shift officer like myself. Such things are also being sidelined at the expense of the all-important, golden child of the detection.

Of course, to make it all seem worthwhile we are encouraged to believe that detections actually make victims happy. In fact, I have been known for the phrase *victim-based detections* to be banded around occasionally. How lovely. *Victim-based detections*. I just love this Victorian playground. Anyone for a nice cup of tea and a lump of sand to bury your head in? The next time

---

19 If a case goes to court, the Crown Prosecution Service will most likely have played a part in this. In most cases they let criminals walk away scott free. Or bail them so that they can fail to appear at a later date.

an important police officer says to me the phrase *victim-based detections,* I may very well just tell them that the development of some vertebrae wouldn't go amiss.

Victims couldn't give a monkeys whether or not we've got a detection. Rather, they want some form of justice or compensation. For detections do not automatically amount to rectitude or recompense. They are not one and the same thing. This has to be the most frustrating thing about the whole debacle. Detections are simply the Government saying, 'Look, the police have solved this crime and an offender has been given some form of sanction … wow, aren't we great?'

Er, no. the offender hasn't. If a sanction is a fine then that is some rather distilled form of justice, but most offences can't be dealt with by means of a fine from the police. If the sanction is a caution or going to court, then what follows is another book. We all know the so-called criminal justice system is awful and that the Crown Prosecution Service exists to protect criminals, so the least said the better for the moment.

Detections are, therefore, a completely false statistic from the word go. They mean absolutely nothing. I feel that this is such an important thing to say that I'm going to repeat myself: Detections mean *absolutely nothing.* The real issue (or rather what *should* be the real issue) is what happens to the offenders, and what compensation and support is passed to the real victims. In most cases, detections do not enter this arena at all. I despise the word, the concept and the fact we are measured on them.

So much division and ill-feeling is caused by the constant nagging to obtain detections. Talk about being blown out of all proportion to the extent of bewilderment. Not long ago in my police area, a two-year-old child tragically drowned in a stream. His parents were in bits as you can imagine. They were completely and utterly beside themselves. An horrific and awful thing to happen. Obviously the police were involved and several officers spent long hours dealing as best they could with the situation. The following day, those officers may have got a quick word of thanks for their effort and life goes on. However, while those officers were dealing with that tragedy, other officers may have made some poxy arrest and got a crappy caution for some minor and trivial offence. They would have been applauded as heroes, and their personal statistics would show such hard work and effort. The Chiefs would beam down at them in admiration. The officers dealing with the dead child would not have got anything out of it at all, if you follow my meaning. No ticks in any boxes. Nothing to put in a pie chart. Nothing to send to the Government.

True policing is not being appreciated any more. It has been sidelined by performance related targets. The reasons why most police officers joined the job no longer seem to exist. The worthiness and professionalism of our role has been overshadowed by a bitchy squabbling over statistics. Sickening or what. Sickening because most police officers joined to deal with tough situations and assist people with real problems. They joined knowing that life is hard and they will face extreme stress. Now, the only true stress comes from not meeting a detection target or not having a good set of figures. It is a complete and utter travesty.

A lot of police detections don't come from worthwhile investigations anyway. Forgive me for sounding crass, but we deal with a lot of *Shit on Shit* crime. This is basically one scumbag committing an offence against another scumbag. We make arrests and we get detections. So what. Whoopy do. Other detections come from making unnecessary arrests. Because we live in a victim culture, we need to do our very best for the victims and as such, we are encouraged to criminalise people who don't deserve it. Actually, that's perhaps a bit harsh. We're not necessarily *encouraged* per se, but it's the end result. So if you get recorded as an *offender*, then you need to be a little bit concerned. You may only have committed a very low level offence and you will most likely get yourself a low-level sanction, such as a caution or fine, but it's all good for our figures! The fact that the matter could have been resolved without the need for a specific sanction, or even resolved without police attendance, only goes to show what a victim culture has created: lots more 'victims' and *lots* more 'criminals'.

Another rather important area is that of 'detectable crime', for not every criminal offence results in a detection. If I arrest someone for criminal damage and that person is later charged to court then I have a detection and a tick in the box for my personal set of statistics. But, if I arrest a drink-driver and charge them to court I do not get a detection. That's because drink-driving is not 'detectable'.

Now here it would be pertinent to say that the word *detections* hasn't really got anything to do with detecting crime. It's just a word we've employed to mean that we've 'cleared-up' a specific crime by means of a sanction. In fact, I'm not even sure if it *is* a word. Real *detection* doesn't have much to do with anything. I can't remember the last time I actually did some detecting. But I don't need to worry about that as it isn't my remit. I'm just a dogsbody. The Government wants me to get detections so that's what I've got to do.

So, if you're going to court for committing criminal damage you should know that the police officer who charged you has got a tick in the box, a pat on the back and is doing exactly what the Government wants him to do ... at the moment.[20] It could all change of course. But if you're going to court for drink driving, the police officer who charged you hasn't really got much out of it. The difference between criminal damage and drink driving aside,

---

20 If, by some extraordinary miracle, by the time you read this book the police are no longer measured on detections – just think of something else completely fucking stupid and measure us on that instead. How about bogey texture? The crustier the better for the victim. *Crusty-bogey-based victim support.*

the clear issue is why should some crime be detectable and some not? It's all it bit lopsided. In which case, this makes detections themselves seem even more false.

Then there's arresting people. Police powers of arrest were amended recently by the Serious Organised Crime and Police Act 2005 (SOCAP). The spirit of the new powers is that all offences, in theory, could lead you to being arrested, so long as the necessity criteria are satisfied. The criteria are quite broad and allow for a certain latitude which was already the case with the old Section 25 of the Police and Criminal Evidence Act 1984. Even with the new powers in place, it hasn't really made too much difference, except that you might find yourself locked in a cell for a really poxy offence like common assault, whereas before, you might have just been reported. Or, the person who reported it might have been told to get lost. Either way, you're more likely to be nicked for crap these days. The obvious reason for this is that we need detections. Shift officers also need to arrest people. This isn't one of the necessity criteria by the way, but it might as well be:

So, officer, why have you arrested this person? Well, Sarge, he committed criminal damage and I want to interview him about it. Also, I've only had one arrest this month and the Guv is getting on my back about it ... Every time I arrest someone it creates an arrest statistic. Well done, officer, you've had seven arrests this month. Whoopy do. A trained monkey could arrest someone. What should count is arresting the right people for the right reasons at the right time. Arresting real criminals for committing real crimes. Sometimes these crimes might actually be very low level, but in certain cases the necessity criteria could be well satisfied. Unfortunately, the context, seriousness or facts of individual cases are completely overshadowed by the fiendish desire to get a tick in the right box. Therefore it's not about justice or supporting people, it's about targets. With this skewed mentality, we are not truly assisting real victims of crime. We arrest people on the off-chance there might be a tick in the box at the end of it. We arrest people to keep the figures up. We prefer to deal with detectable crime. We pick and choose jobs that will make us look favourable. In the end everyone suffers.

Also, we have to spend much of our time dealing with *Shit on Shit* crime as mentioned before. People who take no responsibility for themselves. People who epitomise this victim culture. Most of our arrests and detections, therefore, come from such people. It's like a conveyor belt. The same people and the same crappy problems. The incontinence of society. They are always getting arrested.

As an aside, one of the most annoying things about arrests within this current climate is that the victim is usually allowed to dictate whether or not someone gets nicked. *I want him arrested.* I really hate that phrase. Whose decision is it to arrest someone anyway? I don't recall reading anywhere in SOCAP that a criteria for arresting someone concerns the wishes of the victim, however upset they might feel. If it's justified, it's justified. If not, the police officer should be allowed to say so. Unfortunately, at the moment, the victim is calling the shots. We just have to do as they wish because we don't have any discretion and we have to deal with things by rote. Also, we have our minds plagued by things like detections.

At the moment we arrest people, and either they receive a sanction or they don't. Of course, it is the much preferred option to have that tick in the box, so every effort is made to ensure that all those 'named offenders' are arrested as soon as possible. Not to ensure justice. Not to help the victim. Not to promote a healthy society. No. The only reason is to hopefully get a detection. If you are not a police officer, dear Reader, I hope you can appreciate the utter disgracefulness of all of this. It is truly a travesty beyond words.

I couldn't care less whether a crime is detected, as we have already seen that detections do not necessarily equate to justice or recompense. What I do care about is whether the real victim is indemnified once their case has trawled its way through the machinations of the justice system. Arresting is simply a means to an end. Unfortunately at the moment, the end is all too often confused with statistics rather than justice; figures rather than fairness; targets rather than the welfare of society. Of course I will continue to make arrests as and when necessary, but it's rather a shame that I'm measured on them and even more of a shame that the system doesn't care either way.

Not long ago, I turned up for an early shift along with the rest of the team and sat in the briefing meeting at 7.05am awaiting to hear who I would be crewed with and what other depressing stuff was going on in the town, when I was deployed straight out of the meeting to deal with a drunken customer at a local hotel. Drunken at 7.05am? Yeah, that sounds about right. So PC Oscar (I've changed her name, of course) and I made our way to the hotel in order to sort the situation out.

When we arrived, a gentleman was standing in the Reception area being a pain in the arse. He was accusing the Receptionist of stealing his laptop and generally acting in an annoying manner. He smelled of alcohol, but owing to his demeanour it was clear that he was probably on something else he shouldn't have been.

A hotel worker then walked through the door and spoke to me. He told me that the gentleman had been causing problems all night with noise and erratic behaviour. Furthermore, when the hotel worker had tried to calm him down and asked him to wind his neck in, he'd been grabbed maliciously by his own neck and thrust against the wall, causing injury.

At this, I arrested the gentleman for assault and had him taken to the local police station to be booked into custody. On the way there, his behaviour was extremely up-and-down and there was something not quite right about him. Of course, he gave us false details. This proved to be quite enjoyable, because he had a suitcase with him that contained his wallet, which in itself contained his *real* details. He turned out to be Wanted by another police service for traffic offences. So he was beginning to dig himself into a hole. Not only was he trying to pervert the course of justice, but he had also assaulted someone and was already Wanted by police.

PC Oscar and I then went back to the hotel to take statements, whereupon we were informed that the gentleman had trashed his hotel room. This wasn't known to the hotel staff at the time we arrived – it had been discovered after we'd arrested him for assault, so we now had quite a serious criminal damage to add to the list of offences.

I walked into the hotel room and 'trashed' barely covers it. The room had been completely demolished. Almost everything made of glass was shattered. The bed and all the chairs were broken. The bathroom needed a new shower and the toilet had to be professionally unblocked. There were large dents in the wall that would need filling in and repainting. All the other sundry equipment like the kettle, phone and ashtrays – all of them were smashed up.

There was a soiled condom leaking onto the floor and a broken laptop underneath the bed, which was covered in a sticky substance I really hoped was beer. The room was a complete tip and the estimated damage and costs of repair for the hotel were about £1000.

I then went into the bathroom again and looked on the shelf behind the toilet. It was a shiny blue surface and ideal for doing something naughty with a white powdery substance. Ah, yes. What a surprise. A white powdery substance. So that got scraped into a drugs bag and two hours later, PC Oscar and I left the hotel with several statements and a bag with a Class A drug in it. I left the condom where it was. A Scenes of Crime officer had also turned up to take photographs of the hotel room – always good to have such evidence for court. All in all, it was looking pretty good for a conviction and pretty bad for the naughty gentleman.

An hour after we left the hotel we had all the paperwork ready. It was now well past lunchtime and we had three offences to be dealing with. Assault, criminal damage and possession of a Class A drug. All of these *detectable.*

Of course, this was the most important thing. Sod everything else. Sod the victims. Sod compensation. Sod real justice. In the end, the gentleman turned out to be so high on drugs that he wasn't interviewed until 10pm that same day. PC Oscar and I had finished long before that time. Someone else had to deal with him.

The following day I turned up at work to discover that the gentleman had received a caution for all of these offences. This gentleman (who was not only a lying, Wanted fraud with a string of criminal convictions dating back for the last eleven years, but also a violent, drug taking scum) had received a *caution.*

A caution is about the equivalent of an official slap on the wrist. A slap on the wrist with a sponge. He walked away scot-free, pretty much, and would not have to pay any compensation whatsoever. He got away with causing hundreds of pounds worth of damage, taking a Class A drug and then grabbing someone viciously by the neck.

In the meantime, my police service had got *three* detections. Excellent result! And the officer who got the detections would get a huge pat on the back and a beaming smile from one of the Chiefs.

Because we are measured on detections, we will do anything in our power to get them. The circumstances leading up to that all-important tick in the box, and the aftermath, are apparently unimportant. It's a fucking joke.

We're also measured on other areas, such as how much information we can pass on to the police behind the scenes about the manor we patrol. Gathering intelligence is obviously quite important and shift officers are checked on how many reports they submit, or documents they forward to relevant departments. Suffice to say there are only a certain number of hours in a day and because most shift officers aren't omnipotent, and because shift numbers are being depleted to feed other areas of policing, then there's only a certain amount of stuff we can actually do. Most of that stuff is bureaucratic but we're still expected to 'perform'. And who suffers as a result of all this? Everyone.

So now do you want to know what's on the wall in the office at my police station? Clearly you would expect something useful, like a large map of our patrol area, or pictures of who and what to look out for: anything that might lend some assistance to real police doing real work with real people. I can placate you by saying that there is a tiny bit of useful stuff on the walls at the moment, but a large portion of our bulwarks are taken up by performance figures.

From a distance, it looks like a collection of heart-rate monitor print-outs. Upon closer inspection it turns out to be a collection of beautifully produced little graphs about how the Borough is performing. A little peak here, a little trough there. Looks good on the old detection front this week. Not so good last week. Chief's not happy. We're under performing. Got to hit our weekly detection target or ...

... Or what? I must have missed that part of training. What happens if we don't get our ninety-six detections a week, or whatever the current target is? Do we all get fired? Do limbs start being amputated? It's all a bit bizarre. You can't walk past any wall without being blasted by some performance related graph or chart. We all have targets and we're all expected to meet them. It's the current paranoia. Therefore, we'll advertise it to all the exhausted and under-manned shifts by having their weekly statistics in full view. Aha, Team 3 – you were particularly crap last week. But well done Team 4, superb arrest rate. Team 1 –

good work with that murder job, but you didn't hit your detection rate. Then next week it all changes. Well done Team 3 – awesome amount of detections. Team 4 – I know your shift wasn't actually at work, but we'll still demonstrate how crap you were on this graph. Here, look! And Teams 2 and 5 – good, solid results. Nice all round figures.

This beguiling obsession with facts, figures and targets has made this Government inspire some of the most calamitous organisational behaviour imaginable, wherein the police are no exception as we have seen. Worthwhile criminal investigation has given way to chasing after pathetic and worthless ticks in boxes – a performance-related political debacle of truly immense proportions. In some police organisations various teams have been established for the *sole* purpose of getting detections. I have also heard stories of crime investigation units being disbanded and its officers sent out on the streets to literally *find* detections, while leaving behind worthy investigations of real crimes. I cannot begin to stress enough how bad it has become. The focus on so-called performance has truly, truly meant that this job has completely and utterly gone to the dogs.

Furthermore, the important police officers (those without numbers on their epaulettes) have to attend constant performance meetings where they either get blasted because their statistics are crap or fawned to because they are excellent. Highly trained, highly ranked and respected police officers are reduced to whipping boys if their figures don't cut the mustard. Chiefs who I have a great deal of respect for, seem to spend all their time urging their frontline staff to meet targets and get ticks in boxes. Emails fly all over the place, clogging up our inboxes, with daily updates on detections being down by 1.2% and crime being up by 0.3%. Then as we reach the end of the week the important people start to panic, because the figures aren't quite good enough. Threats and bribes are made; bounties offered. Smiley faces for 'good' performance. All I now associate with the senior management in this job is performance-related bullshit, and for that I am really disappointed. The sad thing is, that it's all so false.

For example, if detections are down on criminal damage then that becomes the flavour of the day. If we've had good results on drug detections then we can leave that aside for the moment. It's not really about solving or investigating crime. These facts and figures are never, ever a true indication of what is happening on the streets. I could arrest someone for smashing the wing mirrors from fifteen cars in one street and, therefore, have fifteen detections for criminal damage. This would inflate the figures dramatically and favourably, but the context would not be looked at by the number crunchers. This is because everyday reality is not an issue when it comes to analysing data.

Therefore, it's not really about what we do, it's about the way that we measure it and the so-called 'results' that are obtained, irrespective of the context. Policing has become a bureaucratic swamp. It's like wading through treacle in flippers. Facts, figures and targets are quite simply the most important thing going. Sod everything else. Frontline policing could be falling apart round your ears and the country going to the dogs, but so long as we can still crunch numbers, tick boxes and analyse data, that's all that matters. In my opinion, it's a travesty of everything that is sagacious. It's an indictment of common sense and reason. It's a pathetic, spineless, debilitating and sycophantic pile of hogwash. Put that in your pie chart and eat it.

7. CRAPPIES

This 'computer system' I keep mentioning has a name. In my police service it's called CRAPPIES, which stands for the *Crime Recording and Analysis Portal: Police Investigation and Evaluation System.* Or CRAP for short. Actually that's a bit unfair. It's not CRAP, it's called something else. So CRAPPIES is a pseudonym, but the real system sounds something like that. I've used a pseudonym for various reasons, including the fact that it would be unprofessional of me to say what the *real* system is called, but also due to the fact that different police organisations use different systems to record and investigate crime.

In my organisation we use CRAPPIES. Just got to update CRAPPIES. Have you updated CRAPPIES? I need to check CRAPPIES for something. It's all on CRAPPIES. How many jobs have you got on CRAPPIES? I need to do a CRAPPIES non-update. Sorry, that update was more of a backdate. Didn't have time to check CRAPPIES today, I was too busy not doing something else. CRAPPIES review. Supervisor input. Your jobs are twenty-eight days old.[21] CRAPPIES, CRAPPIES, CRAPPIES. It's all about CRAPPIES.

---

21 A twenty-eight day old investigation isn't quite as bad as a fifty-six day old investigation. When it reaches that age, the big Chiefs tell you off. When it gets to ninety days old there's nowhere to run and nowhere to hide. However, I prefer to let my investigations mature like a fine wine or cheese.

The most important bits of CRAPPIES, however, are the ticky boxes and fields that contain your ethnic details and date of birth. The criminal investigation tools appear somewhat irrelevant. So is the context of the crime itself. The tools are there so that we can *pretend* we've investigated a crime, but the most important part is getting all the details on the system and getting everyone's ethnicity on there. Otherwise, the system abuses you and refuses to let crime reports be shown as complete. The rest of the information is neither here nor there.

For CRAPPIES doesn't really mind what's actually happened, so long as it can record the incident, and preferably as soon as possible. Let's get it recorded on CRAPPIES straight away, just in case. Let's follow procedure. Let's follow the NCRS. Let's lose all sense of proportion, perspective and common sense. Remember Gooboo and Bugflob? Who could forget them! Well, they ended up on CRAPPIES. The incident was given a crime reference number for robbery as police were making their way to the victim – while they were en-route to sort out Bugflob. I think in the end, it may have been allocated to one of those officers to deal with,[22] which actually meant spending a lot of time trying to file it away forever. This, in itself, was a hassle of immense proportions. CRAPPIES can be a right temperamental old bastard. It also has no idea about context at all.

Been sent two text messages? Sounds like harassment to me. CRAPPIES. Found a firework in your garden? Sounds like more harassment to me. CRAPPIES. Been gently pushed by your landlord? Ooh, nasty. Assault Occasioning Actual Bodily Harm. You poor thing. CRAPPIES. Been sworn at by a twelve-year-old boy with Tourettes? That's *intentional* alarm and distress. CRAPPIES. Can I just make something up to fit your set of circumstances? CRAPPIES. What crime haven't I used for three days? CRAPPIES. No, don't tell me what's happened, I need

---

22 It may have been PC Bean but I can't confirm this. Poor little mite.

to record it on CRAPPIES first. You're lying you say? You just want a crime reference number to claim on your insurance? No problem. CRAPPIES. Mental health problems? Burgled by a ghost called Vladivostock McSnot? CRAPPIES.

You're the victim – you decide. CRAPPIES. If you don't choose something, I will. Either way, you're going on CRAPPIES whether you like it or not. You *will* be a victim! I will find something to make you feel aggrieved, just you watch! CRAPPIES. It's all about CRAPPIES. Let's not actually bother going out to speak to people any more. Let's not even leave the station. Let's just sit in front of CRAPPIES all day and conduct theoretical and virtual 'investigations'. That way we can maintain some form of virtual justice. So long as CRAPPIES is all up-to-date and everything is neatly tucked away into some software-related compartment, it is really quite irrelevant what's going on outside. CRAPPIES is the way forward. The solution to it all. It has become a demi-god amongst software products. An *uber*-system.

CRAPPIES also gives us the chance to help *victims*. It even forces us to contact them! Goodness me, how novel. It makes us phone them and write to them and keep them aware of their case progress. Their trivial little problems. Their third party allegations of nuisance missed calls by a withheld phone number. Their mind bending shit. Their lies. Their apparent victimness (still not sure if that's a real word, but it fits …)

Of course, using CRAPPIES also allows us to be able to record and monitor our detections with a level of infatuation and obsession beyond all sense of sanity. Whole departments spend all day furtively searching through CRAPPIES for crimes that may possibly result in a detection. They spend all day reviewing and checking and auditing and updating. Sending emails to officers about why things haven't been 'actioned', or why things haven't been updated. People whose remit is to simply piss off the frontline guys and gals as much as possible.

It gets worse than this though. We even get emails about 'lost' detections. I'm sorry, I've lost my detection. Will you help me find it? I think I left it over there with the rest of my common sense and perspective, but now it's all but fucked off into the ether ... How in the name of all that is sacred, sure and sensible can you *lose* a detection? Fuck the bed! Trying to put this bizarre phrase into context is giving me a profound headache. It's an administrative cacophony of shit beyond all reasoning and reckoning. I think it all boils down to what we discussed earlier about facts, figures and targets. We've got targets and we've *got* to meet them. One of the many areas of performance management in the police concerns detections and, therefore, CRAPPIES is elevated to an almost god-like status, as it is our way of measuring this all-important aspect of policing.

Another major issue with CRAPPIES is that owing to its friendly companionship with the NCRS, it tends to like to record trivial bollocks. It treats as crime, situations that do not deserve that privilege. Not long ago, I was passed an incident report to deal with. It was already three days old by the time I got it. I read the initial log (remember the three principles of the NCRS) and noted that a fourteen-year-old boy had been chased by another teenager. Glory be. Sounds like a classic to me. Of course, the whole thing was already on CRAPPIES. Some bright spark had decided that it was a case of Section 4A of the Public Order Act 1986 – *Intentional Harassment, Alarm or Distress*. Apparently the victim was very upset by what had happened. Ah, poor little thing.

So I logged onto CRAPPIES. Here was the victim. Here was the offender. Here was the offence. Deal with it like this and don't bother about any context. A chance of a detection! Woohoo! Such a heinous breach of the Public Order Act is detectable and, therefore, an excellent chance of boosting the figures. Rock on! All I need to do is take a statement from the victim and arrest the offender. Hopefully he'll cough it in interview and then perhaps I can give him some kind of juvenile caution. Justice done! Detection gained! CRAPPIES updated. Chief's happy. Hallelujah! Well done PC Pinkstone, have a lolly.

So what had actually happened then? Do the Government and the senior management ever ask that question?[23] CRAPPIES certainly doesn't give a damn. Well it appeared that the victim had been playing cards with some younger boys. He'd then accidentally got some dirt onto some of the cards and one of the younger boys started to cry. So my victim put his hand over the wailing mouth to try to shut him up. Then a short while later, some other boys turned up and chased my victim into a garden.

That's it. Nothing more, nothing less. My goodness, I have a more stressful time cutting my toenails, but that doesn't end up on CRAPPIES. Of course, following the procedures given to us by the Government, we had no choice but to record this teenage squabble on CRAPPIES. We had to theorise as to which offence best suited the incident and allocate a crime reference number to it. After that, it was a case of following procedure in the rather desperate hope of getting a detection.

I really can't go on about this in too much detail, because it grates my cheese *so much* I feel I want to throw something very large and heavy out of the window. Every day I stare at CRAPPIES and the absolute *CRAP* that has been recorded as a crime, and think to myself, 'Why the fuck am I here?' If you recall the 'two text messages' story from the first chapter as well as the egg-man story, then it will please you to know that the egg-man didn't quite make it onto CRAPPIES (owing to some deft and fortuitous cuffing on my part), but the ex-partner-you're-a-slut-I-slept-with-your-friend-tit-for-tat-text-message argument ended up on CRAPPIES and was graded as full-scale domestic

---

23 The short answer to that question is 'No'. The longer answer is 'No, they don't.'

harassment. So let's get those offenders arrested! Let's get those victims supported! CRAPPIES is the daddy! CRAPPIES rules your world! I honestly think it would be far easier to club a stegosaurus to death with an inflatable banana than it would be to sort this dire bureaucratic farce out. But we really, really have to try. Gooboo and Bugflob eat your heart out.

If you were to read Chapter 1 again, you may be able to make even more connections between this administrative bollocks and the victim culture. We discussed how the police *have* to deal with pretty much everything that is reported and how we are not allowed to bat it off like the crap that it is. Hopefully, you are gaining a fuller understanding of just how fucking awful it has all become. This is a vicious circle of immense proportions. And CRAPPIES certainly helps to enhance this melee of dung.

You really wouldn't want to look on CRAPPIES at the moment, due to the amount of utter tripe that is clogging it all up. If you did, you'd feel pretty darn disappointed in the running of the police service. You'd feel betrayed by an incompetent Government and weak, political police management. You'd feel about as pissed off as most frontline police officers.

Here, let me pass you a CRAPPIES reference number for a 'domestic' to deal with. It might cheer you up. Some guy has called us saying that he's feeling emotional due to his divorce and it's his wife's fault. She called us three days before this, saying the exact same thing. It's *domestic violence*,[24] by the way, and it will take you at least two hours to deal with. CRAPPIES, itself, will also demand a great deal of your time to tick all the boxes and update all the irrelevant details. Now do another couple of those and forget about lunch. After that, I'll pass you another

---

24 What constitutes 'violence' these days has gone beyond the pale. If you breathe in a manner that upsets your partner, and they call us, it will be graded as domestic *violence*. If you don't do anything at all, but your lack of attention upsets your partner – and they call us – domestic *violence* it is.

CRAPPIES reference number. This relates to a *racist incident*, so it's pretty darn important and has queue jumped in front of all the real crime. Some person has reported that his neighbour was looking at him in a nasty way and he feels it to be racially aggravated. Go and spend ages with him, fill in loads of forms, and then come back to the station and spend quite a long time updating CRAPPIES.

Now let me pass you another incident. It's a tit-for-tat teenage text message debacle. Some thirteen-year-old girl has been receiving texts from a girl called Chantelle. She's slagging her off about some boy at school. It's harassment. It's on CRAPPIES. Go and deal with it in the way dictated to you by a computer system.

Had enough yet? I hope not, because that's pretty much what you'll be doing all day, every day. On some occasions, you may actually spend a few hours pretending you're doing something exciting, but for 98.3% of the time you are dealing with utter shite. Take a look at your list of outstanding 'investigations' on CRAPPIES and you begin to realise that this really is a festival of poo. This victim culture is seriously fucked up.

Never, ever assume that true policing in Britain is anything like *Road Wars* or *The Bill*. I watched *The Bill* for the first time in ages the other day, and after three minutes, I threw a heavy object at the TV and swore loudly. That programme is pretty naff. No sign of CRAPPIES anywhere! What would be exciting about watching an exhausted police officer talking to a moron for an hour about some negligible incident and then staring at CRAPPIES for another hour trying to make sure every drop-down menu is accounted for.

Road Wars is slightly more realistic in that it is actually 'real' policing, but believe me when I say that it constitutes that remaining 1.7% of 'exciting' police work. The rest is plain, bureaucratic nonsense. The rest is the plethora of dung that chokes up CRAPPIES. You don't see that on the telly.[25]

I have to say at this point, ironically enough, that there is nothing intrinsically wrong with CRAPPIES! As a system all by itself, it's rather benign. It's just the manner in which it is being used and the amount of time we have to spend staring at it that makes it all so horrendous. One could say that we are literally slaves to the system. We are bound by policy and procedure so much that we are strangled by it to the point of complete suffocation. I got so riled by the teenage-boy-chasing-teenage-boy incident that I mentioned earlier being on CRAPPIES, that not so long ago I stuck my neck out at work and perhaps said something I shouldn't have. As a result, I got blasted by somebody higher up the food chain than me and smacked over the head with the NCRS in hardback form. It didn't hurt though, because I truly believe I've got a point with this issue. Many of my colleagues agree. We think it's fucking unbelievable.

Not long ago, I read an incident Log at work that further summed up the current madness. It appeared that a member of the public had been driving past a field and noticed a poor horse that appeared to have been somewhat abused. The sight of this animal distressed the member of the public and they quite rightly called the police. Now, first things first. Name, address, date of birth and self-defined ethnicity. Phone number and location of incident. Get it all logged and recorded properly.

Then come the details of the incident itself. What's happened? Well, the member of the public had driven past a field and saw what looked to be a horse with a stick shoved halfway up its arse. Judging by the angle at which the stick was wedged it was ascertained by the person creating the incident Log that,

---

25 Rumour has it that a *Road Wars* cameraman went out and about with a police officer and got extremely cross with him because 'nothing was happening'. Actually, lots of stuff was happening – just nothing you'd want to watch on the TV at 9pm.

quote, '*the horse could not have backed onto the stick*'. Therefore, it must have been put there on purpose. Therefore, it was most likely a crime. Therefore, we must get it onto CRAPPIES as soon as possible! All of this farting around and no-one has actually been to see the poor horse yet. Poor bugger.

So some bright spark does the business and records it on CRAPPIES straight away (yes, animals can be victims too ...) and categorises it as some animal cruelty related crime. In effect, creating a crime report based on an allegation, irrespective of police attendance. The way it is nowadays.[26] Anyway, some police officers eventually found the time between updating CRAPPIES to go and locate the unfortunate creature. What they found wasn't quite what they were expecting. It wasn't a stick sticking out of the horse – it was a *leg*. The horse was giving birth ...

Thus, the crime report was submitted as a 'non-crime' and everyone could pat themselves on the back for a job well done. Procedure followed. It was all compliant with various standards and we got a gold star for doing it by the book. *Now* try to imagine the frustration of a police officer who has been tasked with going to someone's house following an allegation of something a little more difficult to establish than a horse with an unusual butt-plug. Something like an assault, or an harassment, or some other tricky human affair involving emotions and counter allegations and lies.

You see, by the time we get to an incident it has already been decided who is the victim and who is the offender, and what offence has taken place. Some civilian, albeit following procedure, has clicked on a screen and made all the decisions. CRAPPIES contains the relevant details and proposes the method by which the problem will be dealt. Yet there is something intrinsically wrong with this. It's almost as if CRAPPIES, and all the other

---

26 I believe that most crimes should *not* be recorded on CRAPPIES until frontline police officers have attended. I believe that most crimes should not be recorded on CRAPPIES until frontline *police officers* have attended. Yes, I just repeated myself. Hopefully the fuckers will take notice now...

awful procedural systems, *create* victims and offenders when they're' nothing of the sort. How on earth can a computer system decide who really needs supporting, or who really needs arresting? It's utter madness. Sorry mate, I have to arrest you – you've been recorded on CRAPPIES as an offender.

Let me just quote something I wrote earlier in Chapter 6:

> *'A detection occurs when a crime has been recorded and the offender has been either cautioned, charged or fined for the offence in question (please note that a crime only needs to have been recorded – it doesn't actually need to have occurred ...)'*

The part in brackets is completely true. Every day the police are dealing with and 'detecting' 'crime' that is not even worth dignifying with a police response, let alone granted a crime reference number and a criminal offence classification. We are also treating people as 'victims' and 'offenders' when they are *nothing* of the sort. It's all one big, huge, sticky mess. It's a carnival of CRAP ...

8. Discretion and Duty

If I were you, I wouldn't ever consider owning a garden pond. If you've already got one, get rid of it. Fill it in. Please be aware that it's a serious indictable offence and carries quite a substantial penalty upon conviction. Sound ludicrous to you? Of course it is. But not as ludicrous as this story.

Recently, a dear colleague of mine, PC Snipper, was trying to do some paperwork in the station whilst feeling guilty about not being outside. He'd already spent several hours updating CRAPPIES with what he described as 'non-updates', which were basically ticks in boxes and online notes reminding himself of all the work he hadn't done and why he hadn't had time to do it. After this he set himself some more targets of updating CRAPPIES at a later date, of backdating all the non-updates that he wouldn't have time to update in the first place. Then he post-dated several updates in the hope that he may have time to update them before they became outdated, in which case he'd need to add several more non-updates in an effort to counter-date the previous pre-dates. (You can imagine the conversations we have at work – they get much sillier than this.) Basically, he wasn't doing anything except pointing and clicking on a screen, which is what modern day policing in Britain is all about.

Anyway, in the middle of all of this hard work he was allocated a job. A *suspicious package.* The Royal Mail had discovered a parcel at their processing plant that looked a wee bit dodgy. So PC Snipper took a look at the incident Log on the computer. It had been reported about an hour or so previously and the basic details were that some workers at the Royal Mail had discovered a package that they believed contained cannabis. Excellent. That's what I like to hear. Get some drugs off the street. Disrupt those criminal bastards. Save some lives. So PC Snipper got his bits and pieces together and made his merry way to the Royal Mail to examine and most likely collect the package.

The incident was now about an hour-and-a-half old. While PC Snipper was driving to the Royal Mail, you can guess what happened. That's right. It was allocated a crime reference number and a crime classification. CRAPPIES eat your heart out. *Possession/Cultivation Cannabis with Intent to Supply.* After all, a crime had been reported. Best get recording it straight away. Doesn't really matter about anything else, so long as it's on the system and we've got all the boxes ticked. Ethnicity? Yes. Date of birth? Yes. Context? No. Common sense? Don't fucking joke.

PC Snipper duly arrived at the Royal Mail and took hold of the parcel. It was a bulging and slightly damp affair, which certainly had the pungent aroma of cannabis. More than a mere whiff of green. He placed it in the car beside him and drove back to the police station. Yet even now, seeds of doubt were beginning to germinate in his mind. Even now he knew that something wasn't quite right. Upon returning to the station he gave the package his full and fervent attention. There was something about this cannabis that didn't really tie in with his already extensive knowledge of the drug. This was perhaps due to the fact that it *wasn't* cannabis …

It was *pondweed.* Now this is where it gets even sillier. An honest mistake, yes. Worth police attendance? Definitely. Worth taking up half-an-hour of a police officer's time? Under the circumstances, yes. Did I say half-an-hour? It took ten minutes to drive to the Royal Mail and ten minutes to drive back, and perhaps ten or so minutes to discover what had happened and then rectify it by re-sealing the package and sending it to the criminal pond-owner. Job done.

Sorry, did I say *half-an-hour* of a police officer's time? Since when does anything take *half-an-hour* in the police service?[27] This, of course, was not the end of the matter. PC Snipper called up on the radio to say that the package did indeed contain pondweed. Ha ha ha, all have a giggle. End of the matter. Now he can get on with updating some more backdates, or whatever he was doing before the job came in.

Er, not quite. Nothing is ever that simple these days. If I was to tell you that it probably took a further *several* hours to sort out, would you be surprised? I don't think you would be surprised at all. Now please bear in mind that the package had been sent on its way; the Royal Mail wasn't visited again and the person to whom the package was addressed wasn't involved in any way. Neither was the person who sent the package involved in any way. The extra time spent dealing with the matter had nothing to do with any external influences.

Nay, it's all internal politics and bureaucracy gone mad. PC Snipper had to spend an age updating CRAPPIES as to the effect that what had happened was not in fact the *Possession/ Cultivation Cannabis with Intent to Supply,* but was rather the, er, *Delivery of Pondweed by Second Class Post.* Hardly a crime of notable proportions. Hardly worth too much time or effort. But he still had to sit there and justify why a crime *hadn't* happened. He had to sit there and type reams and reams justifying every action

---

27 A favourite quote used by some police radio controllers is: 'Can you take a quick job for me?' Always makes me smile. They know they're lying. We know they're lying. There really is no such thing as a 'quick job' in the police service.

he took and confirming that this evil crime was nothing of the sort. That it was a horticultural issue, not a narcotic one.

He then had to compile a written report saying pretty much the same thing as he'd written on CRAPPIES, but repeating everything just in case it wasn't repeated at least twice.[28] He then had to print off copies of the crime report, print off his request to have the crime report turned into a 'non-crime', and then submit it all to his Sergeant. His Sergeant then had to check the request for a 'non-crime' for any potential reasons as to why this incident still couldn't be classified as a crime; and once satisfied that this was the case, update CRAPPIES as to the effect that this was an agreeable decision. Once this was complete, the Sergeant could then send all the paperwork to a Scrutineer in another department who would check everything again and then update CRAPPIES *again* to say that the crime report was to be sent off to HQ to be considered for a 'non-crime'.

At some indeterminable time later, a Crime Registrar at HQ received the paperwork and decided, on the balance of probabilities, that the incident was perhaps not a crime after all and updated CRAPPIES *yet again,* to confirm that a parcel of pondweed was not, in fact, a criminal offence. The paperwork for this would then be forwarded to Archives where it would still be open to any form of scrutiny from the Home Office auditors to ensure that the police were actually doing their job properly and not playing silly beggars with the crime figures ... This story is completely true. Every single fucking bit of it.

Is it any wonder at all why many police officers are so completely and utterly fucked off? Is it any surprise? Does the Government have *any* conception of what it has done to the professionalism of our role? Does it have any clue *whatsoever* about the completely debilitating lack of discretion we now have? I think I sometimes want to sit down with a big box of Kleenex

28 Duplication. Duplication. Duplication. It would make a great TV programme.

and just cry forever. I use the example above because it is not only mind-boggling, but also rather sterile. After all, it's only a package with weeds in it. However, if a package containing oxygenating pond plants can cause so much grief through the most inordinate amount of bureaucracy, just imagine the paperwork trail and computer system attention needed for a situation concerning *people.*

Ah, my goodness me. *People.* They create a *lot* of paperwork. They almost crash the system. What about a job involving children, or some malicious counter allegations, or a homophobically aggravated harassment? How many sheets of paper and computer updates will they need? Blimey, one would think that police officers spend more time filling in forms and updating a crime report on a computer system than they would actually spend *dealing* with the incident itself ...

We spend so much time not actually *doing* anything, nowadays, that we have very little time to actually *do* things. We're not allowed to simply arrive at an incident and deal with it sensibly, appropriately and realistically. We now have to spend countless hours back at the station justifying our decision to make certain decisions; updating CRAPPIES with all the things we did or didn't do, as well as referring to things that weren't relevant but we considered anyway, such as checking CCTV, even though the incident concerned was an argument over a Brussels sprout in someone's kitchen.[29] Then there's the whole issue of treating everyone as a victim and everyone *else* as an offender, even though most of the time they should not be allocated such salubrious titles whatsoever. It's all gone completely mad. Common sense has buggered off into outer space.

---

29 There's a suggestion that the police should carry handheld PDA's to stop them having to return to the station to use computers etc. Oh what a great idea that is. Now we can sit in our vehicles on the streets and spend countless fucking hours updating the same information, but on a slightly smaller screen.

Last year, my colleague and I went to a 'domestic' incident wherein a female had argued with her husband because he came back from work late. Not a violent argument. Not a terrible one. Just a bloody argument. She'd then taken her cigarette and put it out on his roast beef dinner … That was it. The whole story. Nothing else to add. Unfortunately, one of them called the police. I can't remember which one it was, but for the sake of a domestic, we usually treat the female as the 'victim' and the male as the 'offender'. Anyway, what was simply a minor affair that needed some stern words of advice and, perhaps, even a giggle about putting a smoke out on some topside, turned into the usual bureaucratic debacle. One would have thought it was a fatal stubbing. The usual form filling and computer system updating. The ticky boxes and drop down menus. The reporting and the checking and the monitoring and the filing. The victim support and risk assessment. On and on like some never-ending paper trail. It's just madness.

Our ability to give advice, or deal with a situation there and then by means of our professional capacity or reasonable approach to life is almost entirely undermined by a rip tide of bureaucracy and senseless arse covering. The situation is so bad that no amount of political rhetoric can even begin to address the problem. The other day, I read in a police magazine that a particular party leader promised to 'give police their discretion back', if his party came to power. My goodness, that sounds fantastic! What are they going to do, distribute it in the internal mail? *'Dear PC Pinkstone, please find enclosed your discretion. We've been looking after it for several years and now you can have it back …'* The situation is far more complicated than simply suggesting something like that, even though we desperately *do* need it back! For discretion itself is almost completely incapacitated by the systems we employ to deal with things. The whole thing is so fucked up we might as well not even bother.

What we really need is discretion to be able to turn round and say, 'No. I'm not going to fill in that form, because it is a waste of fucking time'. Or, 'No, Government. We're not going to chase after those statistics or figures, because it's fucking pointless'. Can you imagine a police officer refusing to fill in a form, or not ticking a box? Bloody hell, the last time I refused to fill in a pointless form I was facing death by firing squad. The whole system comes crashing down if all the pointless bureaucratic crap isn't completed. In this environment, discretion is null and void anyway. Sadly, it hasn't always been this way.

* * *

Somewhere in the misty alleyways of my mind, I vaguely recall a time where discretion was allowed and encouraged, where it was appropriate to use it. A time when a greater focus on professionalism allowed for people to make informed decisions based on personal experience, life skills and common sense. That time has all but gone. No longer are the police a professional body. No longer do its trained officers have any confidence placed in them with regards to their ability to deal with life. No chance. Now we have to deal with things by procedure, by policy. By following a set of rules and regulations designed to make everything fit neatly into a box. Packaging everyday existence into conveniently labelled, monitored and audited chunks.

Unfortunately, you can't do that with life. It doesn't work. Life doesn't fit into a box or a pie chart. You can't deal with people by rote. You can't police society by ticking boxes and following neatly laid out and rigid procedures. It's destructive, dangerous and debilitating. Without flexibility you have disaster. This erosion of discretion and professionalism has affected pretty much everything in society, not least the police. Teaching, the Health Service and all manner of other organisations and job roles have been affected by the steady corrosion of trusting in people's ability to make decisions. There is a procedure for everything.

God forbid that anyone should make a decision! Arrgh! That does not toe the party line at all. We can't tell other people what to do! We might get sued, or something. We can't give advice – that's far too subjective. What if that advice isn't trustworthy? What we apparently need is a system designed to be all-inclusive, totally fair and not affected by anyone's experience or opinions, and certainly not impinged upon by common sense, or the lessons taught to us by history.

So this is what we are going to do. We are going to implement this policy and that policy. We are going to have rules and regulations for *everything*. We are going to measure everything and record everything. There's no room for latitude. No room for opinion. This is how it will be done. And from the statistics and figures that we collate, we will implement new policies. If those don't work, we'll implement newer ones. But we won't listen to reason or rationale. Common sense has no part to play in this. It must be done this way, or not at all. If you don't conform, we'll send in the heavies and *make* you conform. If you under perform, you get blasted. If you're results aren't up to scratch, you get blasted. If you somehow manage to do well, we'll cut your budget next year. But maybe we'll just cut your budget anyway.

We want anything and everything to be quantifiable, measurable, recordable and auditable. Don't forget – this applies to *everything*. Not just things that are inherently quantifiable, but *everything*. We want to sum you up. We want to assess you. We want to collate you. Strip you of your innate humanness and turn you into a set of ticky-box ticks and drop down menus. You will not be an organism. You will not live and breath and feel. There's nothing about your existence that cannot be compiled, monitored and summarised on a computer system. For the past several years, the Government has all but destroyed discretion and professionalism. With this decay has come an all pervasive lack of self-esteem, of morale, of sentiment. Life has become one big, sterile ticky box.

Now, all the police do on a day to day basis is record your lives on our computers. We measure you. Assess you. Define you. We deal with you by rote. You pass us by like identical items on a conveyor belt. You're all the same to us. If you report something, we deal with it by policy. If you're a 'named offender', you get arrested. If you're a 'victim', you get supported, whatever your case. No room for context. No room for reality. If you report something, we record it. No room for truth. No room for your own responsibility.

There's no backbone any more. No balls. No guts, no glory. No chivalry or common sense. No reasoning. No inspiration. No appreciation for the glorious irregularities of life. We take you, measure you, apply our procedures to you and send you on your way. Our quality of service depends on following rules and ticking boxes. Our duty is to abide by standards of measurement and calculation, not standards of common sense, reasonableness, or flexibility.

How on earth can the police display any sense of humanity, or a reasonable approach to life's foibles, if we are so bogged down by politics and procedure? On the one hand, the Government wants us to be victim focussed and approachable, but on the other hand, it destroys any sense of appropriate human interaction by applying choking policies and extreme administrative methods. By doing this it destroys morale, creates ill-feeling and internal strife, drives good people out of the job and makes us even worse than we were alleged to have been several years ago. Institutionally racist? Ha! Now we're institutionally fucked. Sorry folks, your police service is in decline. We have no frontline staff, no morale, no incentive, no feeling that we are making a difference, no flexibility and practically no money. If we smile, it's just wind. Thank you Government, you're *so* fantastic.

9. Taking the Blame

It's all our fault by the way. It's all the fault of the police. Forgive us for not making the world a better place. Forgive us for not sorting your lives out. Forgive us for not catching all the baddies and locking them all away and throwing away the keys. Forgive us for not turning up on your doorstep the minute after you call us. Forgive us for waking you up with our sirens or stopping you from driving down certain roads. Forgive us for everything. Forgive us for sounding negative and for moaning constantly, especially in a book like this – or any other book about the police service in Britain today. Forgive us for all of this and anything else I may have forgotten. It's all our fault.

I wonder what we do all day. We clearly don't do anything valuable, because we're obviously getting everything wrong. I wonder how on earth we manage to obtain some 'victim satisfaction' between updating CRAPPIES, getting sworn at, getting spat at, getting ignored and abused. Getting sent from allegation of crap to allegation of crap and not having any time to eat, drink or even take a wee before the next 'priority' incident comes in. How do we manage to deal with the important stuff when we're so completely overwhelmed? How do we fill in those forms, or send off those requests when we're not even in the station? How do we fill in those forms, or send off those requests when we're being told to go outside? Arrrgggghhh! How the hell do we do anything without screaming in utter frustration? Yes, dear victims, it's all our fault.

And apologies to all of you who had certain officers in charge of your investigations – the certain officers who are now dead and gone. The officers who died on duty, or off duty. The officers who just didn't make it. The ones who were shot, or who died in traffic accidents. The ones who left the station just after that morning briefing to find themselves stabbed and dead before tea break. A tea break they never would have had anyway. The ones who lived, loved and lost out. The ones who left behind only memories and a feeling of utter emptiness. A feeling of helplessness. A feeling of immense loss and sadness. A feeling that life is pretty fucking harsh. Pretty fucking unfair. Pretty fucking evil.

It's all our fault by the way. We should clearly know better. We're the ones who should have prevented all of this from occurring in the beginning. We should have foreseen it. We should have anticipated it. Negated it from taking place. Pre-empted it. We should never have had to leave the station in the first place. We could have had a policy in place to stop such things from happening. We could have stopped all of our officers from getting hurt or dead. We could have made them all desk-jockeys and mochaccinos sippers. We could have sat them all in front of a screen and ignored the outside world. It can all be policed from within. From the backline. From upstairs. From corridors and classrooms. Behind fences. Behind closed doors. From the safety and sanctity of a building – far, far away from the mean streets. While beneath the unyielding elements, a few remaining souls reap a harvest of political indifference, and pay the price with their own safety.

For we could reduce the level of real officers doing real work so much, that even when the shit hits the fan, there is no one else to help them. Everyone else is too busy staring at computer screens. They don't even have their radios switched on any more. There's five or six real police officers left and they are running completely ragged. Look at them – they are even *dying*. What a way to go. Killed on duty. Getting maimed *on duty*. My goodness, does that actually happen? Can you imagine being stabbed by a computer? Can you imagine being scalded by a coffee cup? Can you imagine those nasty biro rashes and paper cuts? The pain of being attacked by your latest well-groomed little policy? It's a cruel world in there. It's a cruel world indeed.

Yes, it's all our fault by the way. Well, someone has to take the blame. We're all pointing at each other here. Let's even blame the dead ones. They should never have got involved. They should have got themselves a desk job. Got themselves behind the scenes. Got themselves a 'support' role. Got themselves fat and useless. Got themselves so stressed they can't cope with the frontline any more. Yes, perhaps it's their fault. Perhaps they should have had a gun. Perhaps. Perhaps. Perhaps. And so it goes on. The cycle continues. The endless, monotonous rhythm of blaming, moaning and pointing the finger. It's been the fault of the police for years. The Government blames us. The public blame us. We blame us. Everyone blames us. It's all our fault. No matter what happens.

A few weeks ago, I turned up at work for a night shift. The usual story. Spent the first five or so hours blatting around town like an idiot. Far too much going on, and not enough people to deal with it all. Think we managed to reduce the level of outstanding live 'jobs' down from sixty-seven to about sixty-three. Great going team! Then suddenly, in the early hours, came the report of a burglary. Little old lady as a victim. She was quite literally little, and she was quite literally old. No stereotyping here. Some chap had forced his way into her house, pushed her over, *stamped* on her, and tried to steal her stuff.

We all made to the scene, desperate to actually do our job. My crewmate rode the speed bumps like a diva in a diesel, arriving in about three minutes flat. Area search. No trace. Bollocks. He'd got away. The usual story. So we took the statement and supported this little old lady. Covered in bruises and pretty shaken up. Gave crime prevention advice. Passed the reference numbers. Passed the phone numbers. Did all we could, bar moving her out into somewhere completely safe and secure. Did the necessaries to the best of our ability. Did it all properly. Stayed with her as long as we could. Held her hand and flew the flag.

The next night shift was the same story. The first few hours trying to deal with the drunk, the mentally unstable and the anti-social. The uninsured and dangerous. The dregs of Britain. The bottom of the barrel. The ones who rule the roost nowadays. The wife-beaters and love cheaters. The thieves and fraudsters. The usual suspects. The drugged up, fucked up wasters. Most normal people are asleep gone midnight, but that's often when the scum come out to play. Lurking on a street corner wearing a hoody at one in the morning? Yeah, sure – you're on your way to work. Yeah, sure – you've been at your mate's house playing Xbox. Yeah, sure – you're a worthy citizen of this country, you little skank. Why don't you pull your tracksuit trousers up, stop sucking your teeth and go home to bed? And don't call me 'bruv' – we're not even from the same fucking species, which negates the chance of us being genetically related.

So, the early hours arrive and a burglary is reported. Same house as last night! Same little old lady! You've got to be joking. We made to the area employing a classic pincer manoeuvre. This, of course, means that the six or seven of us who actually police the streets made to the area in a hodge podge of squealing tyres and flashing lights, blocking the road and waking the neighbours. Suddenly, a colleague can be heard on the radio. Male making off! My goodness, we've managed to find somebody! Fuck me, that's a stroke of luck. He could be the postman, but at least it's a suspect. My colleague calls up on the radio again. One in custody – he tried to stab me. Little fucker.

I drove to the scene in a transit van. Now there's more police vehicles than ever. There's at least five of them! Wow! I've never seen that many police vehicles. This local police station is certainly well endowed. Thank goodness for that. Er, actually that's *all* our police vehicles and they are *all* on this one street. There's no police vehicles and no police officers anywhere else in the rest of the area. All the other so-called coppers are asleep. They'll be back in the morning to moan about the frontline staff whilst sipping their nice hot cups of tea. Perhaps they'll even send an email as to why something wasn't done 'properly'.

Meanwhile, my colleague is dragging some human wretch out from an alleyway helped by another colleague. This piece of shit has a graze on his face and he's handcuffed to the rear. Police brutality! Evil nasty police! First of all, you can't call them wretches and secondly, you're beating them up! Independent Police Complaints Commission! Professional Standards! Get those officers fired! I want your number. I pay your wages, filth. I look at him with utter disdain. I want to bounce him off the floor like a human basketball until he apologises for all the pain and grief he has caused. Of course I do. I'm human. I joined this job to nail baddies, but they are always getting away. They are always getting let off. Prisons are full? Full of what? Sheep? Still, *this* baddy won't get away with it, surely.

So we get this scabby little wretch into the back of the van. He's clucking like a hen and talks with a peculiar, yet familiar, accent. He's the same guy who burgled the old lady yesterday. Fits the description to a T. In his pocket is a torch and a pair of gloves. He's already had his ten inch screwdriver confiscated from him because he tried to stab an officer with it (that would be PC Butch. I've changed his name by the way ...) Nearby is another male. He's also been arrested. This chap didn't decide to run though. He also has his torch and gloves confiscated. I wonder what they were doing out at that time in the morning all tooled up? I wonder why one of them ran away? Ah, perhaps he was just spooked.

Back at the station the males are booked into custody. One of them gives a false name. The other doesn't bother, because we all recognised him anyway. Local scumbag. Regular burglar. Typical drug addict. The usual scrote. The other is fidgeting and faffing and twisting his arms around in agitation. He's on a major come down. He's got more cold turkey than a Bernard Matthews industrial freezer. He's taken to his cell and searched by myself and PC Butch. Bugger me, drugs in his socks. Class A. Add that to the list. So we have a burglary from yesterday, an attempted burglary from today, and possession of a Class A drug. Anything else? Oh yes. We've discovered his real identity, and he's also got conditions not to come anywhere near this place – this town. Not to even enter its borders. He's not been long out of prison. He wasn't in prison long …

The following day, I come to work to find my colleague staring at an email. My colleague who was nearly stabbed with a screwdriver. The one who caught the little scumbag. PC Butch. He looks at me in bewilderment. *Bailed.* I say what? They fucking bailed him. They did *what?* They fucking bailed them both! I sit down and shake my head. Turn on my computer. Check my own emails. Ah, didn't fill in a form. Didn't send off a request for some tapes or something. That's right, I was too busy dealing with a burglary and some prisoners and seizing clothing, and all the other stuff that the few remaining frontline guys and girls do. Prior to that, I didn't even have time to have my dinner because I was being sent all over town like a twat.

So that's right. You tell me what I haven't done and you just bail the baddies. Undermined by my so-called 'support' crew and fucked off by the CPS. What a great way to start the new shift. Why did they bail them mate? Oh, something to do with some identification procedure or the other. Nothing we've done. Not our blunder. Just something to do with something else. Not even relevant. What does it matter? We did our bit. Now they've just let the fuckers go. Some drug taking skanks. Some burglars. Some real criminals and a real victim. A little old lady. But who cares eh? Still, it's all our fault I suppose.

I wondered what the CPS wanted. Was it a confession signed in blood? Was it CCTV evidence from the little old lady's house? Was it a DNA hit from her door handle? Stolen property concealed inside a jacket? What? What more did they want? Who were they blaming here? And whose fault was it that the baddies were let loose for a few more weeks so that they could continue their relentless reign of terror? So that they could fail to appear on the 16th. Perhaps it was my fault. Perhaps PC Butch. Perhaps we didn't do something right. Perhaps the raggedy bunch of exhausted officers left pissing against the wind on the streets of shame did something or the other wrong. Perhaps it *was* our fault. After all, we ended up blaming ourselves anyway. After all, we only nailed the fuckers. We must have done something amiss. The week was going very well so far.

The next day my colleague and I had to attend a 'sudden death'. I wasn't with PC Butch, thank goodness. He was still so mightily pissed off I think he may not have been the best person to comfort a grieving family. Nay, I was crewed with PC Oscar. En-route to the address, we were passed further details. Ambulance on scene. Eighty-seven-year-old male. Pronounced life extinct. Family at the house. You see, the police also have to deal with death and dead people. If someone dies in their home, we attend. If it's a suspicious death, we investigate it. This death wasn't suspicious, however. We arrived in due course to find the ambulance outside, which always helps in locating a house. My colleague and I turned off our phones and knocked on the door. I have found it good practice to do this with the mobiles in specific situations. Certain ring tones can be slightly unsuitable in certain circumstances. In fact, I once thought of starting a website entitled: www.inappropiateringtonesatsuddendeaths.co.uk but I felt this would be unprofessional. Either way, I turned off my 'Benny Hill' tone and entered the hallway along with my colleague.

We were greeted by a paramedic who informed us that the male was upstairs in bed. In the dining room was an elderly lady and a middle-aged gentleman. They were both smiling. Slightly odd, I thought, but not freaky. I looked at them again and realised that they had both smiled at my colleague and me, and now they were looking sombre again. I liked them already. I even liked the house. It was immaculate. It was a proper 'nana and grandad' house. It had little trinkets on a bureau and pictures of grandchildren on the wall. It had that pleasant, homely aura you associate with your grandparents.

My colleague and I went upstairs with the paramedics. Dead man in a bed. Still in his pyjamas. His frail, elderly body finally at rest. We all went downstairs again and back into the dining room. I noticed a plate on the wall commemorating the battle of El-Alamein. *War hero*, I thought. On the opposite side of the room was another memory of loss. A black and white photograph of a naval captain. I later learned he was the father of the widow sitting at the table before me. He'd gone down with his ship in World War II. The middle-aged man introduced himself. We all sat down at the table. I got out my form. It's called a *Sudden Death Reporting Form*. Seemed rather inappropriate in itself, but it had to be done.

After half-an-hour, I'd learned a fair bit about the man in the bedroom upstairs. He was indeed a war hero and a busy man. Spent his life working and contributing. Deaf in one ear due to wartime noise. He also enjoyed Guinness, just like me. One pint a day. Nothing in excess, unlike me. Loved his grandchildren. Some years ago he'd started to write down some of his memoirs. His stories. His tales of courage and decency in a bygone era. He never had a chance to finish them. At this point, and for the first time in my policing career, I felt that I would be overcome. I looked down at the form in front of me and swallowed it all in, fighting back that lump in the throat that makes your words sound all gluey. This wasn't the first time I'd seen death, and it wasn't the first time I'd filled in a form. I think it was more to do with the week I'd had. Yesterday a wretch stamping on an old lady and then set loose, and today an old champion dying. Didn't seem right. This stark comparison made me feel weak and emotional. I wanted to fucking scream.

Thank god for the undertakers is all I can say. They rescued me from the nicest house I have probably been in whilst on duty, and saved me from some of the most delightful and dignified people I have ever met. The other son had turned up halfway through the form-filling and hugged his mother – nothing over the top. Nothing hysterical. She brushed his arm and held back the tears. He then smiled and shook our hands and went upstairs to see his dad for the last time. His father. His own hero. And as this fallen champion was carried to the back of the private ambulance on a stretcher and covered with the cloth of death, the brothers came and stood outside together, side by side, under an eternal sky. They watched him leave their lives forever and shook our hands again. 'Thank you officers. Thank you'.

There was something intrinsically wrong with that week at work. Something not right at all. Why should I waste my time chasing after people who give this world nothing but pain and grief and sorrow, only for them to be given a short ride to freedom, and then have people thank me when their heroes fall? I wanted those lovely people to scream at me. I wanted emotion and despair and hate and anger and a general loss of dignity. I wanted them to tell me it was unfair. I wanted them to tell me that while goodness and decent old-fashioned values fade away, evil is allowed to flourish and take hold. I wanted them to tell me that this country has gone to the dogs and that it's all fucked up. I wanted to take the blame. I would have given anything to take the blame. I wanted to feel the full weight of what it meant to lose such a decent human being, in a town scarred with such undeserving scum. I wanted them to tell me it was all my fault. I wanted them to blame me for everything and I would have shouldered it just for them. I'd have worn it like a crown, because they deserved it. They all did. I wanted anything but a *thank you*. Anything but a smile.

I can't even begin to understand what has happened to this country, and to this police service within it. I can't understand why we take the blame for things that aren't our fault and why we don't take the blame for things that are. We can't stop people from dying, but we *can* try and preserve some sense of justice and decency, and punish those who truly deserve it. We can't stop bad people from being bad but we *can* stop them from taking over. We can surely do more than we are now. At the moment we have neither the support nor the manpower. Neither do we have the overwhelming desire to try. We've traded it all in for lies, wild promises and falsely promoted visions by beaming politicians. It's hopeless. It's fruitless. It's futile. We must begin to make more noise and stand up for what we all know to be the right thing. Not some spurious ideas of justice, but real, gritty and worthy conceptions of what it means to live with honour, valour and decency. What it means to be a hero. Else what is the point of even trying? What is the point? Do we stand by and watch our champions fall, only to be replaced by people who care not? Have we already done this? Are we doing it now? Maybe it is our fault after all …

10. Under-Classed or Over-Rated?

I wonder whether the largest percentage of little shits in our society live on council estates? I think it would be quite easy to believe this. After all, all you need to do is take a cruise around some of the less than salubrious estates in this country and you will be faced with the social, economic and mental disintegration we all associate with the less than classy. The chavs. The scrotes. The cerebrally challenged. The toothless and mass unemployed. The pot bellied mothers with scraped back hair, wearing pink tracksuits and lots of bling, pushing several prams around whilst simultaneously chewing, chatting, smoking and texting. There's nothing like a good stereotype to make us all feel better about ourselves. Council fodder is a very good benchmark for us to measure ourselves against. Makes us all seem like extremely worthy citizens of this life. Perhaps they should all be shot?

Unfortunately, stereotypes arise for a reason, and I have seen Miss Piggy and all of her ilk on so many occasions. In fact, I see her every day. She is a generic person. They are all the same, even though they don't all look like Miss Piggy, thank goodness. Their tragic little lives become monotonous after a while. Stepping over that abandoned sofa in the front garden to walk into a tropical lounge filled with half dressed and grubby children, only to listen with a kind of detached numbness to the trivia and folly and utter inanity of life from the shallower end of the gene pool, while in the background Jeremy Kyle witters on in the presence of more social misfits on a forty-eight inch plasma TV. The endless tales of woe, misery and hardship one associates with the muddied waters of everyday existence in these environments. The fickleness, frivolity and completely twisted concept of the word 'relationship'.

The blokes are just as bad, too. They often fulfil a stereotypical role. They can't seem to hold a relationship down very easily and tend to swap girlfriends like Top Trumps, often leaving behind a legacy of grubby little sprogs bearing various surnames. In fact, life *is* a game of Top Trumps to them. Height? Five foot seven. Children? Probably. Intelligence? Yeah bruv, I is got like no GCSEs, innit. Cars? Several. None of them insured. Convictions? Of course. Trousers? Halfway down my arse, what do you expect? Job? Don't be ridiculous. Benefits? Yes please – lots and lots. Language? A kind of stunted version of English, liberally scattered with chavved up words, accentuated by dismissive hand gestures, a slight limp, the sucking of teeth and the occasional pavement spit. Attitude? Fucking awful, bruv …

I really wish that all of this wasn't true and that it was a mere cruel stereotyping from someone who clearly had a good education and considers himself much worthier than the pond scum. Sadly, it is true. Sadly, there are collections of people who epitomise several pertinent aspects of this victim culture – the trivia; the corrupted mental state; the fucked up and contorted moral outlook; the mindless violence; the rather downgraded view of personal and social hygiene; the lack of employment and toothpaste. Everything you would expect to find living in the shadiest and seediest corners of the council estate. Yet it would be somewhat harsh to suggest that council estates in themselves breed such social ignorance. In fact, it would be more than harsh. It would be wrong. Completely wrong.

This victim culture isn't anything to do with council estates. It has everything to do with attitude and existence. Often the hallmarks of this culture scream out at you from the less than wholesome parts of town and suggest that all we need to do is raze those tenement blocks and scummy estates to the ground and round up all the scrotes and massacre them. It would be far easier for us to place all our emphasis on those we truly want to despise than take a stark look at ourselves and where we are going wrong. The social corruption and decay may be very well represented in that kind of social housing, and many of the shitty and inconsequential crime reports that end up on CRAPPIES most likely have a link with Miss Piggy and her offspring, but this is not the victim culture in its entirety. Not quite anyway.

For the classes of people who consider themselves above this melee of social mankyness are not without blame. Scumbags hail from all walks of life and from all corners of society. They may not provide the overwhelming trivia of the less than classy, but they provide more than their fair share of criminals, and a very large share of social aloofness resulting in a general lack of respect for anyone or anything. They are often morally inactive and just as demanding in other ways. No one is without fault in this world. Not even those up the higher end of the social scale. We must not for one moment think that the victim culture in Britain is simply all about less than classy people doing less than classy things to each other. It's about all of us. The victim culture affects everyone.

Unfortunately, the police *do* have to deal with the lower end of the market day in, day out. Sadly, it has become our all-consuming remit. Social responsibility is at its worst when it comes to dealing with the stereotypes. Petty criminal acts, anti-social behaviour and mindless violence are hallmarks of this corrupted mentality of the less than classy. They are hallmarks of a certain part of this victim culture and represent a huge majority of current police commitments. We really do deal with stereotypes every day of the year and, therefore, CRAPPIES is clogged up with the trivial machinations of a fucked up class of people. It is a very sad fact that a large aspect of the victim culture – namely the focussing on the victim – has simply made the police a kind of social overseer for stupid idiots acting like little shits in all areas of their lives and not being able to cope when it all goes wrong. And quite simply, the police cannot cope with trying to deal with it all. One of the tragic results of this state of affairs is that the country is falling into rack and ruin at the hands of scumbags, wherein the political morons seem unable to comprehend just how bad it all is. They wouldn't dare say anything anyway, due to this wishy-washy, pink and fluffy environment. Yet we must appreciate that far too many of this country's streets are ruled by asinine idiots, and the police seem powerless to combat the mindless, anti-social corruption of these less than classy pillocks.

Last Christmas was a very good example of this, as my team and I looked forward to a 4pm until 1am shift on Christmas Eve. It had to be said that those higher up the social ladder were most likely all in their beds by midnight and the ones on the top rungs were surrounded by so many electric gates and high brick walls it would have been impossible to tell anyway. Even the Skidpan Estate was quiet, believe it or not (name has been changed to protect its innocence) and the shift were looking forward to finishing on time and going home to bed, so at least we could enjoy the majority of Christmas Day without falling asleep halfway through cutting the turkey.

Sadly, it all went rather pear-shaped. The dregs of Skidpan existence came out to play. And by 'play' that means roving around in a large, yobbish and drunken gang across the estate, smashing up cars and causing as much wanton damage as possible. By the time the ninth person had reported their car being smashed up and nearly every police officer was running around the estate through darkened alleyways and empty garage blocks, it was getting a little bit tedious to say the least. I just love chasing hooded gangs through council estates at 1am on Christmas morning. I think it's a great idea. Managed to catch up with a few of them as well. Of course, trying to get a comprehensive description from a bleary-eyed victim looking out of their window at the rear end of a teenager wearing a tracksuit and a hoody is pretty difficult. As such, we really didn't have any evidence with which we could make any arrests. Believe me, I wanted to arrest them all. There must have been about fifteen of them in total, running around causing havoc. Arrest them and hose them all down with a blast of water so cold and so powerful it washes away every last bit of attitude and leaves the undeserving little fuckwits shivering in tears on the floor. And then hose them down some more. Little bastards.

Caught up with one of them outside his house. 'Hello James.' 'Hello officer.' He looked away and spat on the pavement. 'Up to much this morning, James?' Teeth suck. 'No, bruv.' Weary head shake. 'Do you know what day it is today, James?' Hand flick with teeth suck. 'Yeah bruv, just an ordinary day to me man. Just an ordinary day ...' At this my mind wandered. It entered into the realms of the impossible. The realms of illusory justice. I imagined being able to arrest James and take him down the police station. I imagined him spending the whole of Christmas Day and Boxing Day in the cells. He was then dragged before the court the day after that and shouted at by the Judge. He was not only handed down a hefty fine for criminal damage and anti-social behaviour, but forced to pay for it through closely monitored manual labour via an almost chain-gang like correctional department of the local council. After he had paid back in full for all the damage he had caused, he was warned that any further disgraceful behaviour would result in a six-month sentence behind bars where he would be forced to undergo re-education in what it meant to be a decent human being. Any lapses in attitude would result in a further month being added to his sentence. He came out of prison fully corrected and, while still a little rascal at heart, went on to learn a trade and contribute to society in some meaningful way. My mind wandered back to the real world. 'Good night, James.' 'Goodnight officer.'

I then went to several houses with smashed-up vehicles parked outside them and apologised profusely to all the victims that we were unable to identify any offenders. They gave me looks of desperation and I gave them a CRAPPIES reference number. After that, I got back in the police car and banged my head on the steering wheel several times. The car didn't start like it did in *Back to The Future* when Michael J. Fox did the same – it just hurt my head. But the night wasn't over yet. I nearly reached eighty-eight miles per hour driving to the next incident. By now, it was nearly 2am and the drunk and incapable were coming out to play.

I rounded the corner to see a sign of chaos. Well, perhaps 'chaos' is too strong a word. I think 'distress' is possibly better. Distress because it's Christmas Day, it's just gone 2am and we all want to go home. Unfortunately, there were five police cars parked all over the road and about six of my colleagues running around fighting with idiots. A drunk pregnant female is lying in the gutter, literally. She is being attended to by PC Oscar, bless her wholesome little heart. However, I wanted a more visceral challenge. So, I pile out of the car and charge at the nearest idiot who is struggling with a female colleague. Annoyingly, PC Hair gets there first because he's closer than me. Still, I'm the one who manages to get the little shit onto the floor. Not exactly a Home Office approved manoeuvre, nevertheless highly effective. I once did a World Wrestling Federation inspired body-to-back-suplex on a chap outside a nightclub. Winded the hell out of both of us, yet looked absolutely stunning to bystanders, including the duty Inspector who happened to be driving past at the *exact* moment. He simply nodded and said, 'Good move Pinkstone,' and then drove off. Typical.

Anyway, with this little scrote I think I employed the less than conventional Body Shake with Knee Knock and Swear Words, which is basically an adapted version of a straight arm bar takedown. You see, when someone is actually trying to hurt you or a colleague, it's very difficult to revert to those technically proficient moves you learn in training school. I think I grabbed him by both arms from behind, to stop him from landing any more blows, and shook him until his teeth rattled, while simultaneously kneeing him in the back of the leg and then throwing him sideways over the nearest garden wall and calling him a 'Fucking little shit'. Actually, I called him something far worse but if I say what it was then Professional Standards will come down on me like a tonne of bricks.

Sadly, this classic technique did not have the desired effect and he continued to struggle, fight and swear and do all the things you would associate with some less than classy pissed-up little council scumbag. He was eventually handcuffed to the rear by yours truly, after some more carefully considered control techniques, and leant against the nearest lamppost to be examined for cuts or breakages. Remarkably, he was fine. My body was knackered though. I had grazes everywhere and my left knee was aching like a bitch. Why is it that the scrotes always end up with hardly anything to show for their violence? Perhaps the fact that we are simply not allowed to point a gun at them and say, 'Stop,' may have something to do with it. I don't even like guns by the way. But there's something to be said for easing the physical element in a situation involving conflict by using a firearm.

So meanwhile, my colleagues are managing to get some control over the rest of the idiots who are kicking off. A van arrives and the more violent of them are dragged towards it. My little friend by the lamppost is then released. Yes, he is *released*. His handcuffs are removed and he's told in no uncertain terms to fuck off home. He's had his fight. He's been squashed and now he's been given the chance to slope off back to whatever hovel he calls his pad and enjoy the rest of Christmas Day. We'd love to take him to the cells but unfortunately the local cells are full and we really can't be arsed to go further afield. Plus, the time it would take to book him in, do the paperwork and prepare the write-up for the morning crew who would end up dealing with him anyway … what's the point. So, off he goes. I see him disappear around the corner. He actually left.

Three minutes later, he's back. And he's kicking off again. I'm assisting a colleague with another struggling moron and see PC Butch (bless him, he can't run) trying to chase him across the road. I recognise the stripey jumper and obnoxious little face. Fucking idiot! I charge like a rhino with a grudge across the road and into a garden where PC Butch has miraculously got him cornered. He's lying face down across an ornamental flower bed and struggling violently, shouting words that would frighten a T-Rex. PC Butch is employing the classic headlock technique and I think it might have been PC Hair again trying to gain some control over the legs. I leap over a wheelie bin and dive in with an elbow. It completely misses its mark. Of course, I didn't really do that. I simply try to gain control over the violently struggling body as best I can whilst using relatively legal force and adding to the general melee by swearing just as loudly. In fact, I believe I blended several well-known profanities together to create newer and more potent forms of verbal abuse. It was special. And I did end up accidentally knee striking a small decorative stone object which hurt like buggery, but I think at the end of it justice was done. The little toe-rag was dumped into the back of a van and spent Christmas morning nursing nothing more than a hangover and some bruised pride. Meanwhile, my colleagues and me finished around 5am and were all fucking exhausted, covered in bits of garden and nursing real wounds.

Perhaps I'm making it sound like I love all of this. Perhaps it all sounds fun and glitzy. Perhaps not. I think the point I am making here, is that the relatively few idiots who were out and about on Christmas morning causing chaos ended up causing grief for dozens of people. The knock-on effect was enormous. It was at least nine houses with smashed cars, which would be several people in each house feeling upset that their festive season was interrupted by such mindless behaviour. Then there were the dozens of residents on the street of distress who were woken by the sound of police officers swearing and their garden furniture being broken. On top of all of that there were several police officers with minor injuries and ruined Christmas plans (even though we should 'expect' such things) and on top of all that, nothing really happened as a result of it all. For all of our effort we didn't prosecute any of the vandals, and the drunken, violent and abusive idiots ended up with minor fines and stern words of advice.

It's a vicious circle. A never-ending cycle. The few affect the many who affect everyone else. It only takes one rotten apple to spoil the rest of the bunch. Yet those at the top of the ladder are not without blame. They are part of this cycle as well. And the police? Well, we're not really policing the nation. We're simply keeping a lid on anarchy. That's all it is. Meanwhile, the less than classy continue with their follies and the over-rated blame them without taking stock of their own condition. They would never, ever consider going out smashing car windows or fighting with the police in the middle of a quiet residential area, so they must be perfect! In which case all they do is point the finger and deflect the blame. So no-one ends up doing anything about it. It's all so bloody hopeless. The victim culture denotes far more than mindlessness. It also denotes indifference and inaction. Selfishness and greed. It doesn't just apply to those people who live in grubby blocks of flats and who drive battered old cars, as we all would prefer to think. Rather it applies to us all. It makes us demand more without even having to get off our arses. It makes us weak, pathetic and unable to take a stand against the things we seem to disagree with so vociferously. It's always someone else's remit to pick up the pieces. It's always someone else's remit to re-educate. It's always someone else's remit. It's pass the buck time. Whether we are under-classed or not, we are certainly over-rated. It's all about attitude. We're all pretty fucked.

11. A PC PC

I'm going to make another word up here ... *integritised.* You see, we're all supposed to have honesty and integrity as police officers, but you can't shorten the word 'integrity'. You can shorten the word 'honesty' down to 'honest' and say, 'I'm honest', but that leaves you with a bit of an issue with integrity. 'I'm honest and integrity'. Nope, that doesn't work. 'I'm honest and integral'. Hmm, different meaning altogether. How about, 'I'm honest and have integrity'. Nah, that's too cumbersome. 'I'm honest and *integritised*'. Ah, much better!

You see, there's nothing wrong with making words up. You can do it just like that, especially if you put those words into context. Now put *these* words into context: 'Political correctness is a fucking travesty beyond all comprehension and it's fucked up the police, the Forces, the country and just about everything else you can think of ...' There's no point beating around the bush ... I mean, let's be honest!

I'm not a big fan of political correctness as you can possibly guess. That's why I'm taking my time with this chapter. Political correctness is the mouse and I'm the cat. I'm going to toy with that little bastard until I decide to kill it. Spread its guts out all over the lounge carpet. However, I'm not going to kill it until the final chapter, but I'm certainly going to scare the living crap out of it now. Perhaps give it some sly digs in the head as well.

Political correctness. We've already seen examples of it in practice and linked it to this softly-softly organisational approach, but how bad is it really? How far has it affected our mentality? I think the best way to get a grip on this would be to share a day in the life of an average police officer and be as brutally and unabashedly honest as possible. No holds barred. It's a gladiatorial battle with a big thumbs down at the end. So what better way to address this issue than examine a day in the life of a PC PC …

* * *

Your name is Geoff, by the way. You are twenty-nine years old. You've been in the job for a little over three years and you're white. You have short, dark hair and a little mole on the left-hand side of your chin. Your previous job was an accounts manager. You have a two-year-old daughter called Louise. You live in a two-bedroom house in the suburbs, which cost you £175,000. Your mortgage is a smidgen over £748 a month. Your wife works part time and between you the bills are paid and life has some small measure of comfort, but not in any excess. You're a shift officer in a busy, diverse and crime-ridden town. You have thirteen other officers on your shift (on a good day) and so far your 'results' have been pretty good. Arrest rate: fine. Detection rate: fine. Everything else: fine. Supervisor reviews? Fine. Performance Development Review? Effective.

You're one of the team. One of the boys. Neither a lad nor a wimp. You are an ordinary guy. You get on well with your colleagues – male and female. No-one minds being crewed with you. Your decision-making is excellent. Your handling of difficult situations is superb. You get stuck in when necessary but don't use excessive force. You're not led by your emotions and you take time with your investigations. Like others, though, you're well and truly fucked off with the state of play. However, you don't moan too much because you're too busy! You get on with your job and go out occasionally and let off steam with a few mates and a few sherbets. You are an average PC in an average town in an average nick. PC Geoff Hopkins. PC Geoffrey Peter Hopkins.

You arrive at work at 3.40pm for the start of a late shift. Pissing down with rain and nowhere to park at the nick. Fucking typical. You eventually find a space in a 'marked police vehicles only' bay and trudge off to the locker room to get your kit together. Stab vest. Kit belt. CAPTOR spray. Kit bag containing paperwork folder, high visibility jacket, hat, jumper, gloves, notebooks and all manner of other crap you can't be bothered to sort out. Waterproof trousers somewhere at the bottom. Hidden, because they don't supply them any more. You have to hide them because kit goes missing in the station like kids from care homes. Always going fucking walkabouts …

So, you're ready for the shift. It's now 3.51pm and you make your way down to the office. The early turn are still hanging around – some of them are furiously typing away on CRAPPIES, or preparing handovers for prisoners, or lucky enough to not be doing anything at all.

'Hi Hopper, how the fuck?' You greet Doormat with a wink and say something equally as obtuse. 'I'm OK you filthy tart. Anything exciting?' Doormat says, 'It's all been rather Q. Not much happening. Just the usual shit.' You nod in acknowledgement and dump your bag somewhere near the photocopier. You know that every now and again one of the Chiefs sends an 'all-user' email about Health and Safety and demands that bags are left out of the way, but you don't really give a flying fuck. It's never enforced. It's all bollocks. Do you want me to do my job or what?

So you sit down at a PC (a PC PC looking at a PC …) and open your emails. Delete. Delete. Delete. The usual crap.

Something about an MG3 and a charging scheme? You skim through it and hit delete. Something about a delivery of a skip to the station car park next Thursday. Delete. Something about another place to leave your court files – that's about the fiftieth different change of plan this month already. Delete. Something about a burglar and a person wanted for breaching his ASBO. Delete. Something about paying passing attention to the Skidpan Estate – reports of criminal damage to vehicles and anti-social behaviour. Now *there's* a fucking surprise … Delete.

3.59pm. Time for briefing. You walk into the room with your colleagues. One of them is carrying a cup of tea and one of them looks mightily pissed off. Blimey, shift has only just started and there's already immense frustration in the air. You say nothing. Words of comfort are no longer any use. As self-appointed Shift Morale Officer, you have no remit but to agree that everything is fucked. In file the Sergeants. Tim, John and Naz. They sit there like the three stooges. Tim is forty-one and built like the rear end of a rhino; been a Sergeant for seven years; ex-traffic. John is thirty-eight; tall, skinny and slightly goofy but clever as hell. He's an Acting Sergeant and isn't particularly good at making decisions. Naz is twenty-nine; been a Sergeant for two years. He's … not really very good either.

You know pretty much everything about everybody in the police station, so there's no secrets. You know whose been shagging who and which officers have had their probation extended. You know which officers can't spell worth shit and which officers you can't trust. You know which Sergeants are wankers and which ones are good old boys, even if they are female. Being a good old boy has nothing to do with gender. It has everything to do with attitude.

You know which officers socialise a lot and which officers don't. You know which ones say things pretty close to the mark and which ones are corporate brown-nosers. You know which ones have passed their Sergeant's Part I Promotion Exam and which ones failed miserably. You know which ones always get a bollocking over their inability to update CRAPPIES and which ones are always 'poaching' arrests. You know which officers kick the arse out of the overtime and which ones love to leave on time.

You know which ones have joined which department and which ones *should* join a department because they are totally crap on shift. You know which officers should never have been employed, and which officers are excellent at their job. You know everything. You have an opinion. But it's all hidden away inside that little brain of yours. Maybe you share it, but not with everyone. You have a close circle of friends and colleagues who you can really trust. There's a core of you who socialise together and share things that could get you into trouble at work, but you all trust each other and that's fine. You even know which *Sergeants* you can really trust, but it doesn't really go any further up the ranks than that. Once your numbers are removed from your epaulettes, you tend to have a personality transplant and become a political moron. Not all of them though. There are some officers with pips and above who still appear somewhat realistic.

But back to more pressing matters. Back to your own shift. Back to your Sergeants … Tim is a good old boy and knows the score. John and Naz are fucking useless. John is useless because he's a goofy prick who dithers around and doesn't make any decisions. Naz is useless because … well, it's difficult. Briefing finishes and you trudge out to the office. You're crewed with Hoops which always makes for a good pairing. Hopper and Hoops: the dream team. A partnership of chaos. A duo of destruction. You'll go out and kick some scumbag arse. You'll go out and cause some damage. Not really. You'll go out and sit in some disgusting house, and listen to trivial tales of woe, whilst real crime is going on elsewhere undetected and undisturbed.

So, you go out in the car with Hoops. You've been allocated a criminal damage to a fridge for some reason. Domestic related. The usual story. Anyway, you pull out of the station and you start to chat. You and Hoops are quite close. You've not saved each other's life or anything of that ilk, but you're on the same wavelength. You start to gossip about people on shift. Sarah. Useless. Mick. OK. Sam. Steals arrests. Gemma. Good at her job ... on it goes until you've pretty much covered everyone. It's the same old gossip. Nothing too nasty. Nothing too unkind. Just realistic human behaviour. Your criminal damage to a fridge is over the other side of town so you have a fair bit of time to chat. Traffic is building up anyway so you have at least twenty minutes in the car. At least it will be a chance to drive past lots of cars that need pulling over and ignore lots of scrotes that need turning over. You have no time to do real policing of course – too busy clearing up crap.

You reach the main crossroads in the middle of town. Conversation eventually turns to Naz. You can trust Hoops, he's a good old boy. You don't start on Naz straight away though. It all needs putting in context, so you skirt around the issue first by confirming your opinions on the other Sergeants. Tim. Good old boy. John. Clever but weak. Naz ... it's a bit political ... he seemed to rise through the ranks rather quickly. Or so you believe. Suddenly the controller re-deploys you to a priority incident. The conversation halts and you speed off in the opposite direction. Theft from motor vehicle in progress. Skidpan Estate. Now *there's* a surprise. You arrive four minutes later and find the 'attacked' vehicle. Side window smashed. Registered to number twenty-two. You knock on the door. No one answers. You leave a card to say what has happened containing all the relevant details ... Log number, shoulder number and, nowadays, the crime reference number from CRAPPIES ...

You get back in the car and resume your conversation. Where were we? Oh yes, Naz. Long story. Bit political … fuck me, re-deployed again. Priority domestic. Female by the name of Nasreen reporting her husband is being drunk and abusive. Children in the house. You speed off in the opposite direction and arrive five minutes later. You knock on the door. It's opened by a tearful female wearing traditional 'Asian' clothes. This is how you define them, anyway. You walk inside. You can't help but noticing that it's a 'typical' Asian house. It's very clean and very well presented. You also notice it smells different. Not unpleasant. Just different. It's culturally distinct. The pictures on the walls are slightly gaudy and contain images of older men wearing turbans, smiling and waving. You ascertain, correctly, that you are in a Sikh household. The sofas are arranged in a square pattern with a table in the middle. No point of focus. What do they do? Sit and talk? Your mind wanders back to the issue. Tearful female. You take a seat on a green leather couch. It's hard as hell. The female sits down too. You look up on the walls and see little placards containing familiar but illegible writing. You've seen such things before, but have never asked what they are. Something religious you guess.

The female explains that her husband is always getting drunk and being abusive. Her language is faltering. Her English isn't so good. He's upstairs now, sleeping. A child walks into the room and stands by her mum. She's insecure. Afraid. You smile and wink and get your notebook out. Another child walks into the room. He's older, about ten. You speak to him and his English is much better, you notice. In fact, you couldn't tell he was Asian. Your mind wanders again. You're not even sure what you mean by that. Back to the issue.

The female explains that nothing has really happened, but that she was afraid of her husband. He's angry and aggressive. She's hiding something though. She's burying some dark secrets deep inside her trembling body, but you can get no more out of her. So you fill out the forms and do the necessaries. You do the same as you would with anyone. You ask which schools the children go to. You ask which doctor they visit. You ask the female if she works. She does, part time. You ask about her husband. He works too. A businessman.

You stay at least twenty minutes and ask the female if she wants you to speak to her husband. She says 'No.' You take the decision not to speak to him. Best not to wake him up. Best not to disturb him. You don't *have* to speak to him anyway. After all, there's no allegation of a crime. But you still support the female because she needs it and deserves it. You've already ascertained that she is genuine. A real victim. A lovely person in need of help. You must pass her details on. Multi-agency approach. There's people out there who can help. The usual story. You feel the paperwork is justified, even though it's all hopeless in the end.

You leave the house and get back in the car. Hoops says nothing for a while. He then explodes. 'What a fucker! What a complete and utter *fucker!* She was lovely! Those kids are gorgeous! They have a lovely home and both work hard! Why is he such a fuckwit? He obviously hits her … she just didn't want to tell us!' You sit in further silence. You contemplate the story. Is it a cultural issue? Is it because he is Asian? Is it because you've been led to believe that Asian men treat women differently? Your mind wanders all over the place and then back to the road ahead. 'Where are we going Hoops?' 'We need diesel …'

Back at the station, you fill in the paperwork. It's no different to any other domestic you've been to. The cultural aspect is not that important. It's not that relevant. It's not an 'Asian' thing. It's a 'life' thing. We're not that different after all… Someone looks over your shoulder and reads your report. Looks at the spelling of the names. Mumbles, 'Fucking typical' and walks off. You say nothing. You feel the same. You don't feel the same. You're not sure how you feel. You want to believe that the cultural thing is irrelevant, but a tiny part of you wishes that it *was* relevant. A small, unidentified part of your brain wants to scream out at the top of its voice, 'You bloody Asian twat!'

You also know deep inside that if this chap was white you would also feel the same. You'd want to scream out, 'You bloody twat!' So it's no different to any other domestic with a vulnerable female. But why the distinction? Why say he's Asian? Why not just call him a twat without making reference to his difference? You can't really explain that one. It's just the way it is. It's just the way things are. You can't understand the way you feel. You know you're not racist, that's the main thing. You walk into the Sergeants' office. Naz and John are sitting there. You give the paperwork to … John. You had to think about that one. You don't know why you thought about it but you did. Something in the back of your mind told you to give it to John. You shake your head and walk out, annoyed at how you feel.

Soon you're back in the car with Hoops. Getting dark now. Still busy. You drive to your next job. Conversation turns to the weekend. Going out on the piss. Team do. Off to the city for plenty of sherbets and a good laugh. Even John is going. You joke that he won't be able to drink more than half a pint of shandy. You're not being nasty. You actually like the goofball, even if he is a bit of a lettuce. Somehow both of you don't end up mentioning Naz again. Not in relation to going out anyway. Naz doesn't drink and he very rarely goes out with the shift. In fact, never. In that respect he's not alone. Loads of officers don't go out with the shift for various reasons, whether to do with family, money or whatever. It's just the way it is. Not a cultural issue, just the way it is. Yet somewhere in the back of your mind, that little voice is screaming out again. 'He doesn't drink and he doesn't socialise and he doesn't mix with the rest of us!' You feel shocked at yourself and continue talking about Saturday. But your mind continues its rant. 'It's because he's Asian. He's bloody Asian!' You shake your head to get rid of these thoughts, and carry on gassing about the weekend. Hoops has no idea you've just thought what you did. *You* have no idea that Hoops just thought the same. Neither of you say anything about it. The conversation turns back to other matters. Turns back to how crap things are. Turns back to the state of play.

Then you realise, quite suddenly, that you've never asked Naz *why* he doesn't go out and why he doesn't drink. You've simply looked at his outward ethnic status and made your mind up already. You realise you've *assumed* you know more about him than you actually do. You realise that you have rarely spoken to him at all. You realise that you have been reluctant to. You realise that he could be carrying the weight of some huge tragedy and you would never know. You realise that the current climate has made you *afraid*. It's made you afraid to even *talk* about issues. Afraid to address them. Afraid to go near them. Afraid to even mention the word 'Asian' out loud near Naz in case you might upset him. Afraid to share any emotion or feeling with him whatsoever about anything at all, except, maybe, a passing comment about the weather, or how shit the football was.

You realise that your mind is completely fucked up. You realise that Naz's mind is probably just the same. You realise that the environment in which you work actually encourages a lack of honest discourse and makes you less genuine than you would like to be. You realise that it's all one big shambles. You realise that you would love to talk to Naz about him not socialising and rib him for not drinking – and, believe it or not, Naz would love the same thing – but you just wouldn't dare. You've already made up your mind how he feels. You've already decided what's best for him. He is a victim of your own making. A *victim*. You realise that you have maintained this PC environment. You have perpetuated it. You are a part of it. Your weakness and *lack* of honesty and integrity have sustained the current nightmare. You end your shift and go home. You lie awake and wish it was all different. You wish it would change. You wish that someone would have the balls to say something about it. The balls to stand up for what is truly honest and integritised …

12. Ethnicity and Classification

I'm just going to pop across to the window to check what it's like outside. Meanwhile, could you please select from the following list what best defines your ethnicity:

A1 – Asian Indian
A2 – Asian Pakistani
A3 – Asian Bangladeshi
A9 – Any other Asian background

B1 – Black Caribbean
B2 – Black African
B9 – Any other black background

M1 – Mixed white and black Caribbean
M2 – Mixed white and black African
M3 – Mixed white and Asian
M9 – Any other mixed background

W1 – White British
W2 – White Irish
W9 – Any other white background

O1 – Chinese
O9 – Any other ethnic group
NS – Not Stated

This wonderful, useful and highly respected system of self-defined ethnic classification is what the police use on a daily basis with pretty much everyone we meet. It is known as the '16+1 Classification System'. It gives you a chance, dear Reader, to define yourself. Allows you to ask the all-important philosophical question, 'Who am I?'

The police have to ask pretty much everyone we deal with to define themselves. If we've spoken to you for three seconds, define yourself. If you've committed an offence, define yourself. If you've not committed an offence, define yourself. If you're a witness, define yourself. If you happened to be near someone who may, or may not have been a witness, define yourself. If you've been involved in a car accident, define yourself. If you're clearly a white Polish person, who speaks Polish, has a Polish name, a Polish passport, a Polish driving licence and says 'Hi, I'm from Poland,' define yourself.

We're not allowed to do it for you. It's your opportunity to tell us who you are. It is a self-defining moment. Now when I say that we're not allowed to define you, that is slightly misleading. We can slap some form of label on you:

IC1 – White
IC2 – Dark skinned European
IC3 – Black
IC4 – Asian
IC5 – Chinese
IC6 – Arabic
IC – Dead

(I made the last one up by the way.)

So, my Polish man from above would be an IC1, W9. Most documentation the police fill in has little ticky boxes for both classifications. One is *our* label and the other is your label. In theory, you can define yourself as whatever you want. If you're Black British, but define yourself as White Irish, that's entirely your prerogative. And we would have to note you down as such. In which case, if everyone took the piss out of the system, it would serve no useful purpose whatsoever. Not that it serves a useful purpose now, of course. And as a professional person I would never, ever advocate that anyone took the piss.

Furthermore, the issue of *self-defining* is somewhat blurred by the fact that when we record the details of babies and very young children on our paperwork and computer systems, for example, we have to fill in their 16+1 ethnicity as well. Not that I've ever been able to convince a baby to self-define, of course, but nevertheless, it's something we still have to do, which makes the whole thing rather amusing sometimes (after all, if you can't laugh you'll just cry).

Not long ago, one of my colleagues had something of an argument with an internal department. My colleague was quite rightfully trying to convince the person on the other end of the phone that a nine-month-old child couldn't self-define, but they weren't having any of it. In the end, it came down to the fact that the computer system (CRAPPIES – bless it) wouldn't allow for a blank space to be left in that particular drop down menu, so my colleague had to self-define the baby himself. There's also the fact that the crime report to which this debacle related couldn't be filed if any of the ethnic classifications were missing anyway, so either way someone, somewhere had to make something up.

Ethnic recording has long been a particular favourite of the Government and because of this wishy-washy victim culture, it perhaps makes it all the more deferential. I've no doubt that the statistics provided by such racial monitoring will allow somebody somewhere, or perhaps a group of people, to become a victim of something or the other. The wider issue of racial monitoring is also to ensure so-called equity when it comes to employment, for example, so that everyone is fairly treated and given an equal chance. That's the theory of course. Within the police service racial monitoring is also taken into consideration with boards and promotion (even though this is a very dubious and often despised form of discrimination, but it's OK because we slap the word 'positive' in front of it and suddenly it becomes acceptable.) It's known as 'positive action', and it's pretty typical of the current obsequious political obsessions. At the moment, there is also a recommendation by the Government that the police workforce should comprise (approximately) 7% of ethnic minority officers. This target will clearly take some years to meet and there are concerns it may lead to the employment of unsuitable individuals. As we have already seen, it's all very well appreciating (and for this chapter insert the word 'employing') people for their difference, but if they're unsuitable this should override everything else, including targets.

The Government also has many different agendas when it comes to racial monitoring, and at least it gives them the opportunity to examine the statistics and then come up with crap suggestions and ill-informed policies, if nothing else. For perhaps too many people of a particular racial group have been involved in car accidents. Perhaps there's not enough witnesses from another group. Perhaps there's too many victims of a certain race in a certain area. Perhaps too many police searches of a certain colour of skin. So we have to constantly chop and change if it appears that one group is more maligned than another group. Can't be seen to be racist after all! As we have already discussed, the police are allegedly institutionally racist to the core and, therefore, the Government will need negative racial statistics to continue to prove this.

Perhaps if the Government actually knew what was going on in the country and also that certain parts thereof comprise almost entirely of specific racial groups, it would understand that statistics in those areas will relate to the people who live there. There's going to be more black offenders in Brixton than there are in Plymouth. There's going to be more Asian offenders in Luton than there are in Brixton, and there's going to be more white offenders in Plymouth than there are Asian offenders. This, of course, is pretty general, but it's also a simple demographic fact. In which case your victims and witnesses will also relate to the percentage of racial groups living in an area.

To be as blunt as possible, the majority of your baddies in places like Brixton are going to be black. Therefore, your police stop-searches will reflect this too. This isn't some deliberate and concerted effort on the part of the police to malign a certain colour of skin. This isn't an issue of institutional racism. It's how it is. All you need to do is walk down the road in certain parts of the country and open your eyes. Take a wee trip into Southall for example and you'll realise that most of your offenders will be Asian. Goodness me, what a racist thing to say! No, it's an honest and realistic thing to say. Go to Truro and your offenders will be mostly white.

So what is the answer to this situation? Ah, I know. Let's try to ensure that our police service 'reflects' the communities they serve. Let's increase the percentage of ethnic minority officers in a weak and feeble attempt to somehow prove that we are in touch with our localities and obviously not racist. This will clearly enable the communities to see that the police are making every effort not to live up to their already shattered reputation, or something along those lines. Something about maintaining a false image.

Therefore, officers who are representative of the communities they serve will be able to much better understand and appreciate the needs of the locals. They will be able to speak the lingo and level with them in ways obviously foreign to non-ethnic minority officers. This in itself will stop the baddies in those communities from committing crime and make everything nice and perfect. It will ensure that the police do not deliberately target certain ethnic minorities and so maintain an image of unity and cohesion. With the exception of the odd idiot who manages to wear the uniform, however, police officers do not pick on certain racial groups for the sake of it. They pick on baddies. And if you're white, you're white; if you're black you're black. We don't create baddies out of thin air. We just want to lock them up, regardless of what colour they are.

The above points also demonstrate another very stark issue about ethnicity in this nation and that is the whole concept of 'integration'. Basically, Britain is like a very badly stirred cultural packet mix. It's a bit lumpy in places. It's not quite as dissolved as it could be. There are rather large areas of unmixed and badly integrated ethnic groups. Large pockets of either a certain colour of skin or a certain culture. Groups of people who can pretty much live exactly as they did in their 'own' countries and not even have to bother themselves mixing with the rest of society. They can shop in their own shops and socialise with their own kin. They can talk their own language and wear their own clothes. They can have their legal affairs sorted by people from their own race and have their documents written in their own tongue. In many respects they could be living anywhere. Britain just happens to provide the right environment to exercise the best or worst of their own culture.

Not long ago, I went to a delightful house in my police area and spoke to a lovely middle aged woman from Pakistan. Her home was a credit to cleanliness and order. Her husband was at work and her daughters were married and having families, except for one of her daughters who had died in a tragic car crash some years before. The woman spoke with tears in her eyes about this event, but the trouble was I could hardly understand a word she was saying. She kept on apologising about her bad English and then said that she had lived in the country for thirty-seven years.

There is an older generation of ethnic minorities in this country who, in all honesty, have not integrated very well at all, in the sense that their generation is slightly at odds with their children and grandchildren. They moved over in post War years and quietly and unassumingly got on with their lives, yet somehow managed to survive without really 'integrating'. Now, because communities are so well established in certain parts of the country, you have a situation where there are plenty of people from ethnic minorities born and bred in Britain who, quite rightly, call themselves British (even though they have to classify themselves as something else), yet you still have people being able to live in those communities and not really bother too much with anything particularly British, including the language.

I've asked some people from supposedly ethnic minorities who are older than me and speak better English than me to self-classify and they have basically been expected to say things like 'Asian Indian' or 'Asian Pakistani.' This is wrong. People should be able to classify themselves how they like. Unfortunately there isn't a classification for 'Asian British ' – or just 'British'. I have also asked other people from the same countries to define themselves and they don't have a clue what I'm saying because they simply don't speak English, and many of them have lived in the country for years. In other words, 'integration' can mean a few things. It can mean integration into Britishness, and it can mean integration into a community that skips around the edges of Britishness. It all depends on who you are, where you are and what you want. This is where 'classification' itself has no objective purpose.

Now we have an even more trying situation whereby peoples from other certain European countries are flooding into Britain and creating their own badly mixed pockets of existence, whereby their own shops and business spring up all over the place, and many of them also haven't got a clue what I'm talking about when I speak to them. Most of these people self-classify (with the help of an expensive interpreter) as 'W9' – any other white background. Unfortunately, this does not differentiate the country they come from and neither does it assist with anything else at all for that matter. Most people I ask to look at the 16+1 system simply frown in confusion at just how shit it really is. The most definitive answers I get are from white British or black British people (and you can always tell if the white British people lean towards the far right when they give their response – a definite emphasis on the word 'white.') Other people just stare at the list either trying to find a classification that actually suits their situation, or stare at the list because they can't read. The list proves nothing.

However, you could change the system but that wouldn't actually make much difference at all. The police need far more details about people than the system is able to produce, for it is unable to supply the most useful of information. We need to know where a person lives and where a person was born. We need to know their date of birth and how long they have been in the country. We sometimes need to know what that person does for a living and whether they are allowed to work. We need to know how long the person is permitted to stay in the country before they should leave.

Such information is usually available upon arresting someone, even though many people still lie to the police when in custody. However, it is not accessible through simply speaking to someone on the street unless we either make a million phone calls, or take the person home to 'prove' who they are by rifling through their documents. This is clearly not going to happen. Instead, we get them to look at our crappy little list, often in the most ridiculous of circumstances – like when they are lying half mangled in a hospital bed – and their response provides us with absolutely no substantial information whatsoever.

So all this paranoia and obsession with ethnic recording is just another example of the Government's clear lack of purpose and direction. What exactly are we doing it for? Not only is it divisive and unnecessary in the sense that it provides the Government with statistics that allows them to create stupid targets and make ridiculous proposals, but it is also a far cry from what we actually need. It is, perhaps, a rather limp attempt at establishing who is in the country and how they perceive themselves. I can see no useful purpose for it whatsoever except to supply a pathetic administration with bizarre statistics for them to propose even more bizarre targets. For if some statistician looks at the figures and thinks, 'Goodness me, look at all those Eastern European people being stop-searched by police in Slufftown,' he wouldn't be thinking along the lines of, 'Goodness me, there must be rather a lot of Eastern European people in Slufftown.' Rather, he'd suggest that the police are picking on the Eastern Europeans. He'd come up with something so stupid and frustrating that police officers across the country would be banging their heads against the wall in despair.

Surely a far better method than simply asking people to self-define would be to get in a car and drive around the country. To actually take a look at what is going on and who lives where. The police know what is going on. We see it with our own eyes and deal with the mess. We can tell you what communities are like. We can tell you just how fucked up some places are. We can tell you about the problems created by the ethnic mix (even though we're not allowed to) but the Government simply aren't interested and don't listen.

The crux of the matter beneath all of this nonsense is some wishy-washy and half-hearted attempt on the part of the administration at somehow appearing nice and fair and diverse. Bubbling away beneath the surface, though, is another matter, which civil libertarians and human rights groups would most likely malign. While the Government perhaps wants to keep some form of a lid on what is going on, it is unable to do so because it is weak and pathetic. It creates sycophantic policies that don't really address the issues. What it really wants to do – but has been faffing around for ages trying to sort out – is to implement things like 'identity cards' or other such methods of self-defining.

While the prospect of ID cards has been looming for a number of years – and is thus one of the few seemingly suitable decisions made by the Government in the past decade – the implementation is still a fairly long way off. They just need to get on with it. And if you recall something I wrote in the first part of my Introduction, namely that all political parties are a part of the current shambles, then perhaps you would not be surprised to hear that the leader of one political party suggested scrapping the whole ID card scheme in favour of something else. In other words, it's all a big pile of poo. Yet while the arguments rage back and forth, the fact remains that things are slowly crumbling around our ears. But we still have our little ethnicity classification charts to keep us going!

So, as police, we currently have the power to pull a crappy little list out of our pockets and ask people to tell us something useless about themselves, when what we really need to do is ask people to pull something out of *their* pockets and ask them to show *us* something useful. In this way, we wouldn't need to bother ourselves with getting someone to self-classify – all the information we need would be in one place. It places the onus on the person to demonstrate some form of responsibility (God forbid!) and prove that they are legitimate. But no. What a suggestion! What a breach of human rights! What a disgraceful thing for a police officer to say! Yet it's one of the few ways we can begin to get a grip again. One of the many methods that must be considered in order for this nation to find its feet and gain some form of stability once more. Self-classification my arse. What we need is a system for people to prove who they are, not a system for people to prove who they aren't. It should be called 'self-identification' and replace the current crap.

13. Frustration, Frustration, Frustration

A stable country needs a stable police service. A police service not constantly undermined by bureaucratic procedures. A police service with officers able to ascertain from people who they are and what they are doing without fear of being labelled 'Big Brother', or breaching some fucked up concept of 'human rights'. A police service equipped with proper legislation and proper equipment to have some impact for the greater good. As we saw in the last chapter, it would be useful to have a system where people have to prove who they are and that they are legitimate. I'd have no problem pulling an identification card from my pocket or answering specific questions put to me by a police officer. Got nothing to hide! It would also be useful to have the equipment and resources to deal with things properly in the first place.

Instead the police are farting around on the fringe of effectiveness and not really having much of an impact at all. Furthermore, we're facing budget cuts and varied threats of performance-related pay in some sick politically motivated effort to 'improve efficiency'. It appears that we have to justify our positions far more than criminals, for example, have to justify anything whatsoever. The whole emphasis is entirely skewed. If you're a police officer you get fucked about to the point of complete exasperation – and blamed for everything anyway – while undeserving little shits walk around with smiles on their faces. It's almost as if the police need to be kept in line more than the bad guys. Basically, the bottom line is that the Government doesn't trust the police and wants to keep them as squashed and subdued as possible. And cutting budgets is a prime example of making sure we're completely useless. Couple this to the fact that we are often woefully under-resourced, poorly equipped and treated like shit, and you might realise why many frontline staff have no morale left whatsoever.

Imagine turning up in a transit van to a darkened street to find four of your colleagues struggling with an eighteen stone woman who has slit her wrists down to the bone. She is screaming at the top of her voice and disturbing the whole neighbourhood. From a lounge window it looks pretty brutal. Several police officers manhandling a poor woman in such a rough manner? Disgraceful! Victim! I want your shoulder number, filth. What you don't necessarily realise from your lounge window, however, is that these police officers are trying to get this woman into the back of a van and get her to hospital to save her life. She's dying, but she doesn't want any help. Fortunately, she's outside so she's been detained under a certain section of the Mental Health Act so we can use a certain amount of reasonable force to get her to where we want her to go. And seeing as she's cut her wrists so deeply she's pissing blood everywhere, and generally being about as obnoxious as anyone could ever be. Also she's fucking strong. Not only is she completely crazy, she's tough. The combination of size, mass, blood loss and psychotic behaviour is a cocktail of total grief.

I arrive in the van, which I seem to do a lot. This is because I'm one of the lucky officers to have been trained to drive the darn thing. Others have been waiting for years. This isn't a joke by the way. We have to wait months, sometimes years, for basic training in various essential areas. For the most part, we are simply untrained. However, we have a fucking incredibly detailed idea of what diversity is all about. Very useful when you're on the streets and being flung about by a psycho. So I pull up and leap out with my customary grace, which in this case was an exclamation involving several profanities and a purposeful stride into the melee. The woman is nowhere near under control. She's fucking enormous. It's like trying to wrestle a rhino in a tank top. Not only that, but she's bleeding, screaming and kicking. She's biting, fighting and not in any way complying. Someone shouts out to me, 'Pinkstone, get the leg restraints!'

I run back to the transit van. Leg restraints? Hmm, let me think. That sounds like a piece of useful kit. In that case, no. We don't have useful kit. We have a short metal stick and a nasty spray. We have strange woollen-like trousers without any give in the waist area whatsoever. We have uncomfortable white shirts and clip-on ties. Would you like to fight a rhino while wearing a shirt and tie? Would you like to fight a rhino? I don't suppose it matters either way. We could all be dressed in Superman costumes and this woman would still give us one hell of a struggle. Still, it would be nice to actually be able to move in an unrestricted manner. So I enter the transit and start looking for leg restraints that I know aren't there anyway. In the background the screams are becoming worse. *Fuck*. Leg restraints? I start throwing things around in the back of the van swearing at the top of my voice. It must have been one hell of a spectacle, all told. Coke can? No, that's no good. Plastic shield? Not really. Brown paper bag for seizing shoes? Nah.

In the end I do the decent thing and grab a roll of police barrier tape and leap out of the van for the second time and plunge into the seething mob. Police barrier tape was not designed for restraining large, mad women. However, you have to make do and mend when there's only six of you actually policing a whole town and you're not even equipped to do it properly anyway. I suppose I could have got my Pocket Note Book out and asked her to self-define, but I fear this may have been somewhat useless. So here I am, wrapping a mad woman up in police barrier tape in the middle of the street. A moment I will never really forget. She's like an interactive scene-watch. A fucking dangerous scene-watch. 'Police Line – Do Not Cross' emblazoned across her shins as she continues to struggle with the ferocity of a hippo on crack.

In the end, the wrapping of the leg ceremony begins to have some effect and the screaming mass of blood, sweat and fury is lugged towards the open cage at the back of the van. When I say this woman was dumped in the cage, I mean that quite literally. We couldn't have placed her in there. We couldn't have popped her in the back with a kind word before the door shuts gently with a little click. This wasn't some china ornament being positioned on a shelf. This was about two hundred and fifty pounds of fuming carcass. She gets bundled into the back and two officers leap in and practically sit on her while the door is slammed behind them with a very loud, *'Thank fuck for that.'* Then a deft bit of driving on my part gets us to the hospital without an accident and she is further dumped on a stretcher to go into A & E. Fortunately, by this time, the blood loss and effort of struggling with five police officers has somewhat lessened her infuriation and she kind of resigns herself to being treated. The cuts on her wrist are examined by a doctor. I can see her bones. I lean against the cubicle curtain. This is only the first job of the night and I haven't even looked at CRAPPIES yet.

A few months after this we all received training on how to restrain legs properly. This had nothing to do with the police barrier tape adaptation – it was everything to do with the fact that we had now been kitted out with new gear. We had new leg restraints. Yes! Every police vehicle in the organisation now had them as standard, thank goodness. Better late than never I suppose. However, when we were experimenting with these wonderful pieces of equipment the trainer informed us that they were *roof-rack straps* because real leg restraints were way too expensive. I'm sure he was joking, of course. However, it wouldn't surprise me in the slightest if it was true. The fact of the matter is that when your policing budget is cut so much and you have so many political targets to meet then the officer on the street has to make do and mend with whatever is most cheap and cheerful. This inspires police organisations to come up with rather drastic measures in order to be cost-effective. Nevertheless, you can be sure that for every police officer on the street getting pissed on with blood and making do with police tape or a motoring accessory to control a highly dangerous person, there will be at least four of five officers behind the scenes happily sipping cups of coffee and tutting at how shit those frontline officers are.

Frustration? You bet your fucking arse there's frustration. But don't worry, every one of those police officers that exhausted themselves in dealing with that mad woman situation all got maligned in some way the next day for not ticking an unrelated box or updating CRAPPIES regarding all the stuff we didn't have time to do. Crazy female with slit wrists trying to kill herself and everyone else? Er, I'm sorry, that doesn't appear to be a CRAPPIES related issue. Therefore it's not relevant. Did it get you a detection? No? Well, in that case PC Pinkstone and colleagues, you are not really doing your job properly. Perhaps we'll link your Performance Development Review to your pay and *make* you get those results and hit those targets.[30] See down

---

30 This is the last time I'm going to mention the Performance Development Review system in this book. The Government wants to link it to police pay. They can fuck off.

to the bone you say? No, there isn't a ticky box for that. Got covered in blood? No, that isn't detectable. Oh, by the way PC Pinkstone, we need that woman's self-defined ethnicity after all ... Arrrrrrgggghhh! Who is the fucking victim here I wonder?!

* * *

Talking of frustration, a very short while ago my colleague and I were allocated an incident to deal with. One of the many miscellaneous things frontline officers are tasked with attending, unrelated to CRAPPIES or targets or political paranoia. In other words, it was a job that would take us pretty much all day to deal with and we wouldn't get anything out of it at the end. The number crunchers couldn't put the information in a pie chart. It was also nothing to do with supporting victims or creating a false image of effective police intervention in an area. Therefore it was crap. A meaningless and fruitless task that wouldn't earn any person any more than a dismissive pat on the back and the wrath of the Chief for not getting him his weekly drug detection or whatever the hell he's being forced to whine about now. Actually, I'm lying. We did get something out of it – a cleaning bill.

The radio controller called up to say that a female on the top floor of a block of flats hadn't seen her neighbour for several weeks. There was an extremely unpleasant smell emanating from the doorway and there was a large congregation of flies. Ah. Bollocks. Just what you want on a Friday morning at 10.30. Just what you want when you've been told your performance figures are crap and the Boss isn't happy. Just what you want when you know you'll be dealing with it all day and your workload, which is enormous anyway, won't even be touched yet again. In fact, it is *everything* you want to deal with as a police officer, but has become something you simply can't afford to deal with. In other words, we no longer like dealing with griefy stuff unrelated to

CRAPPIES, or anything else that is target related, as we're so performance driven that the paranoia is overwhelming.

Not quite as overwhelming as the stench of putrefying human flesh, but close. Hmm, let me just check CRAPPIES for the drop-down box that says I've dealt with a deceased male who has been lying face down on his sofa for six weeks in the summer. No, it's not there. Let me just check the performance graph that tells me we bashed in the door and got blasted backwards by a smell so horrific it took my legs from underneath me and made me retch. This was no egg-man smell. That was mild in comparison. Those spores were huge, granted, but this smell was more than just a smell. It was a life force all by itself. Let me just see if opening the lounge door with a scarf to my face and seeing a human carcass so bloated, blackened and gloupy you shudder involuntarily and nearly puke again, results in some form of tick in any box whatsoever. No? Well in that case, it doesn't count. It's not real policing then. It's just a miscellaneous thing you have to deal with quickly so you can get out there and support those poor victims by getting lots and lots of juicy detections.

Did I say juicy? Ever seen someone who is so rotten that when you move them the stomach splits and spills the rancid contents everywhere, creating an aroma so powerful it makes you stagger when you are fifty feet away? The layers of putrid fat. The indefinable goo. The decomposing sludge. The repulsive and repugnant matter that bears no resemblance whatsoever to the human life to which it relates. Hang on, let me check again whether or not this is a police matter. Yes, it appears to be the case. However, it's on the miscellaneous pile and you'll just have to update CRAPPIES when you get a chance, but we'll still tell you off for not doing it anyway. But, back to the flat. So my colleague – PC Latvia – and I have utilised the door bashing qualities of our armed crew (because we are not trained to do this apparently) and then spend the next four hours downwind of the stench whilst waiting for the inevitable arguments as to whose remit it was to actually clear up the mess.

Of course, owing to the fact that we have no resources and the resources we do have are committed anyway, then we have no one available to do anything about the situation. A body in such a state of decomposition requires a specialist unit in specialist clothing to remove. We're talking full on body suits with oxygen masks. We're talking the whole hog. We're talking about as little human contact as possible with what could be a serious health risk in rotting human form. It's the usual story. PC Latvia and I sit there, feeling queasy, while behind the scenes the arguments raged back and forth about who was or wasn't available and who should do the business.[31] Minutes passed. Those minutes turned into hours. Meanwhile, the rest of the shift – that would be about eight of them on this particular occasion – are running completely ragged. They are blatting all over town without any time for a break, being sent from job to job to job and still getting moaned at for not getting enough detections or updating fucking CRAPPIES. In fact, one of my colleagues is so busy he doesn't even have time to fill in a Domestic Risk Assessment Form on the same day he deals with a domestic. Panic buttons! Awoooga! Awoooga! How fucking *dare* you not complete that form PC Glasses! How fucking *dare* you! The following day, believe it or not, PC Glasses is so busy again, he doesn't find the time to fill in that form yet again. The last I saw of PC Glasses was his head on a spike somewhere, and yet another email about how shit we all are. Oh, and we're not getting enough detections.

Meanwhile, I'm sitting on the bottom step at the block of flats waiting for someone higher up the food chain than me to actually make a decision. Goodness, what a thought. That would be far too

---

31 Chief Inspector Raincoat tried his best for us but unfortunately he was undermined by morons further up the food chain than himself. The higher you go, the more detached from reality you become.

sensible. So instead, they persuade the usual undertakers to pop down and remove the body. We're talking men in suits here. Men wearing top hats and tails. Men who do a difficult enough job, anyway, without having to face what is lying on a sofa three floors up. Yet they got kitted up and did the business. That is to say they put on woefully inadequate paper suits and donned cardboard masks. PC Latvia showed them upstairs. They came downstairs again very quickly and put an extra pair of gloves on. Probably also phoned their families to say they weren't coming home, or at least to run them a nice hot bath.

At this point, it was entirely evident that they were not equipped to do the job properly. They should have refused there and then. However the true British spirit kicked in with a vengeance and those two undertakers went upstairs into that foulest of rooms dressed in paper, and heaved the putrefaction onto a plastic mat. The stomach split, as expected, and layers of rancid skin, fat and gloup remained stuck to the sofa to add to the general distress. I have never heard an undertaker vomit before. That is, I'd never heard an undertaker vomit before 2.35 on that Friday afternoon. He staggered from the room and retched his guts up, pulling off his mask and staggering down the stairs. Meanwhile, some Chief was sitting behind a desk somewhere feeling he'd made a great decision, and another Chief was sending out his weekly email regarding detections, crime figures and robberies being up by 3.2% – you useless shift officers.[32]

The poor undertaker leaned against the private ambulance, his face ashen. Then with a look I can only grade as fucking nails, he walked back up the stairs again and into the room of death. About five minutes later, the valiant pair had covered the deceased with enough layers of plastic to stop him from dripping

---

32 He never says that we're useless, because he's an extraordinarily decent chap. It's just that he gets his own arse kicked if his figures don't cut the mustard. The whole system is absolutely buggered from the top down.

on too many steps on the way down and put him in the back of the ambulance. Meanwhile, a small local crowd had gathered to pay their last respects, themselves retching and crying, and being generally noisy. PC Latvia and I had been speaking to them for most of the day. We'd been allaying their fears and comforting some of them who were clearly traumatised by the situation, not least the female who had called us. She'd spent the best part of three weeks buying air freshener for the landing in an effort to disguise the smell before she realised that perhaps something was amiss. So we both stood there for nearly five hours in the overwhelming stench, doing our job regarding the body and talking to people at the same time. Representing our police service with dignity and professionalism. Waving that banner. Flying that flag. What we both really wanted to do, of course, was be sick, or just cry. After all, it was a dead person. The rancid carcass was once a human life: someone who had lived alone and died alone. Yet we did our job, I believe, and did it well. We did what policing is all about these days. Getting our clothes infused with the aroma of decay, treading in rotten body fat and then going back to the police station to find some arsy email about a poor ticky box missing a particular tick. Frustration? You bet your fucking arse ...

* * *

Now, still on the theme of frustration, would you rather deal with a non-English speaking Asian Indian man with a UK visa stamped into a Russian passport, who is trying to cash £2,800 worth of cheques from his employer, using a fraudulent Italian passport as identification – bearing in mind that his UK visa does not permit him to work, but he's bought himself a new identity in this country, including said Italian passport, a false National Insurance Numbercard and a false Health and Safety certificate, and managed to gain employment under false pretences – or would you rather shove a cattle prod up your nose?

I propose that the latter would take far less time and result in far less pain. My colleague, PC Butter and I, had the pleasure of this little gentleman not long ago and I guess I could try and explain that the situation took just over thirteen hours to deal with, but ultimately, I would be lying. The truth is that we didn't really *deal* with it. We don't *deal* with things at all.

Despite the fact that we arrested him at a little after 4pm and left the police station at 5am feeling rather drained, there was little to show for our effort. Yes, the gentleman was in a police cell. Yes, he would most likely be facing a custodial sentence for his crime. Yes, some people might say this was a 'good result'.

No, it wasn't anything of the sort. It was a mere drop in the ocean and indicative of a much wider and more indelible problem. PC Butter and I had attempted to search the home address of where this gentleman 'lived' after we had arrested him, just to see if we could find any more documents relating to his false identity. What we did find was a grubby male with dyed ginger hair living in a shabby house who didn't speak any English, but was desperate to help us. He led us next door to the apparent 'landlord' of the house we wanted to search, who told us (in slightly better English) that our gentleman did not live there.

Ah, what a complete and utter surprise. We hadn't considered for one tiny little moment that false addresses exist as well. We hadn't even contemplated the fact that people use various addresses for their mail but don't really live there, probably because they are all part of some much larger network of people who are all living in Britain under false pretences.

The landlord, a middle-aged Asian gentleman, looked at myself and PC Butter with what I can only describe as incredulous pity. 'No good,' he said. 'You police are no good.' I stared for a moment. 'Pardon sir?' The gentleman smiled, but not unkindly.

'He use address, but no live there. This is big problem uh?' I nodded, still unsure why he had called us 'no good'. That stung a little. He continued. 'They know what to do. You police don't know. We speak different language. You don't understand. They want French driving licence? They get French driving licence. So many people. You police have no idea ...'

The penny was beginning to drop. He wasn't really calling us 'no good'. He was telling us that we were ineffective and practically chuckling in our faces, in a regretful kind of way. He was telling us that our house search was completely and utterly pointless and that what we had stumbled upon was the tiniest drop in the biggest ocean. I replied, 'It's not the fault of the police – I blame immigration!' The gentleman burst out laughing, again not unkindly, and patted me on the shoulder. I think he perhaps thought he was bursting my bubble; shattering my illusions. He wasn't. He was telling me what I already knew. He was confirming that the scale of the problem was quite simply enormous.

Must have been frustrating for him too, especially as he was living and working in the country legitimately and we'd disturbed him halfway through dinner. But we were trying to get a 'good result!' Well worth interrupting a meal for, don't you think? Hmm, I think the phrase, 'The Government hasn't got a fucking clue', springs readily to mind. Or, if they *have* got a clue, 'The police and the immigration service are completely powerless to do anything about anything at all'.

I spoke to an immigration officer back at the station about our detained gentleman, who we also believed had his mother and sister illegally stashed away somewhere else. His reply? 'Put them in the sausage maker along with all the rest.' I nodded, despite the savage brutality of his comments. We're not allowed to say such things are we? We're supposed to be *professional.* This suggestion, which flies in the face of being 'nice' and may get the civil libertarians and human rights groups tutting in disgust (and perhaps the creation of a racist incident non-recordable on CRAPPIES) – after all, everyone is a fucking victim – was merely borne out of the total frustration of being wholly unable to combat an endemic problem. Not an 'Asian' problem, although I have used this example. Simply a problem. A major fucking debacle. A categorical nightmare. I looked at PC Butter and said something about 'identity cards'. He looked at me and said, 'That's *so* last chapter …' He didn't say that really. He just nodded in weary agreement. I think he was as exhausted and dazed as me.

The bafflement is palpable. The annoyance obvious. I think I want to spend the rest of my life in Britain wrapping insane people up in plastic tape, or standing near rotting corpses for five hours while an under-resourced and over-political police organisation is helpless to do anything about it. I then want to spend a whole day 'dealing' with someone who represents many of the reasons why this nation is fucked up and have someone look at me and tell me I'm 'no good' when I'm trying my best to sort it all out.

The sad thing is that he was right. We *are* no good. We're fucking useless.

Frustration …?

14. The Police Family

Every police service is different by the way. We have different uniforms; different paperwork; different versions of CRAPPIES. We drive different makes of cars and respond to different call signs. We have a different emphasis on different types of crime relating to what area we cover and make different choices regarding the same things. Yet we're all the same really. Each police service is, at heart, the same as every other police service. We all face the same crap in the same way by the same kinds of people. We all have the same bureaucracy, which displays itself in different ways, but it's all the same shit. There's not one police service in the nation that has got the monopoly on getting things right and handling stuff properly. The Government fucks us all equally and without prejudice. So although I write the next couple of chapters from the perspective of the one police service I work for – each organisation will have the same kinds of problems, albeit manifest in a variety of ways. I also write from the perspective of a frontline shift officer. This role is completely different from that of a behind-the-scenes field intelligence officer, or a specialist search officer, for example. Therefore, my opinions will relate to my role. However, I am glad I write from the viewpoint of someone from the frontline because that's one of the areas being neglected by the Government to the extent that the wheels are coming off far too regularly. Frontline policing is in a state of disarray, as hopefully you will have gathered by now.

Not long ago, I asked a member of the public how many police officers she thought were 'on the streets' in her town. Her reply was 'eighty to one hundred'. I kind of just looked at her, stunned. Other people have also suggested similar amounts: 'fifty to sixty', 'one hundred or so', 'dozens'. It pained me somewhat to spill the beans to the member of the public I was dealing with, but sometimes you need to explain to people why it's taken nine hours to attend their burglary, or five days to attend a criminal damage they've reported. Irrespective of the fact that we're too often dealing with crap, we simply don't have enough frontline officers in many stations. And when it comes to responding to the majority of the calls and actually getting your pen out – this is the remit of the frontline *shift* officer.

I have a rather strong opinion on what it means to be a frontline shift officer, as well as what it means to be a frontline police officer, as the two are not quite the same. Basically, a shift officer means any police officer who turns up at work, gets kitted up, and goes out and deals with all the shit. That means *all* the shit. Their remit is anything and everything. They are the dogsbodies. The worker ants. The bread and butter. The core. The team. The 'plods'. They are what the public most associate with 'the police', unless they've been watching too many episodes of *Road Wars*, in which case they're confusing traffic cops with real police officers, which is entirely reprehensible if you ask me. Unfortunately I'm joking. *Road Wars* features more real police than any other programme, especially when the local units arrive in the picture and show everyone else how it's done.

The specialist departments fall under the broad category of frontline police, and they also arrive at work and get kitted up, but go and deal with remit-related shit. These are your traffic cops (bless them), dog handlers, specialist search, armed units and the like. Other frontline police include your beat officers, neighbourhood officers and PCSO's; and there's simply not enough of them either. For me, anyone who puts on their uniform, turns on a radio and leaves the station is a frontline officer.[33] A visible presence in the outside world – the kind of visible presence that the public recognise and generally appreciate, when they're not spitting at us or blaming us for not sorting their lives out. Obviously, there's loads of officers and civilians working in behind-the-scenes roles, but so long as they feel they can justify their positions, that's fine. So long as they are actually doing something of substance and not simply fulfilling a bureaucratic role, that's good. Then, of course, there's the essential CID and associated sub-departments dealing with priority crime and the like. I don't need to mention all the frontline departments, because there are far too many. The main point I am getting at here is that frontline policing is essential, and shift officers are a key element within this area. They are the ones who mostly represent that core of individuals who respond when you need them most in that first instance. Unfortunately the numbers are somewhat decreasing, along with morale and motivation. They are becoming slowly extinct. There are now less and less of them 'on the streets'. The Government appears not to give a flying fuck about them. Furthermore, other frontline departments face the same kind of dwindling numbers, and are still given ridiculous performance related targets.

Now the true figure for police numbers 'on the streets' varies on the police area and the size of the village, town or city. It also depends largely on what kind of incidents are happening in any one place. A serious GBH, for example, will tie up at least five to six shift officers at any one time, leaving practically no-one left

---

33 The only exception to this would be CID. They prefer to wear 'home clothes' but are most definitely frontline officers.

to deal with anything else. But whatever the relative number of visible frontline officers on the streets at any one time, it will be hugely smaller than anything suggested by the public. The word the police use to describe available officers is *resourcing* (e.g. 'Sorry sir, we can't attend your report of your car being smashed up by hooded thugs due to resourcing levels.') In reality, we do *not* have enough bodies on the front line.

This is not helped by the fact that we are living in a time of a change of focus. (e.g. from one blurred viewpoint to another …) The Government wants to roll out 'neighbourhood policing' across the country (see next chapter) and the practical application of this is to take officers from one department and put them into another. Nothing else changes – just the job title of the police officer. There are targets for the introduction of neighbourhood policing, and roles within the neighbourhood currently have to be filled, or some important police officers get told off. Therefore, the best way to fill these roles is to poach from shift. So shift numbers get depleted – and in some cases, completely decimated – while the workload remains the same. So to cut a long story short, you have less and less shift officers trying to cope with far too much work. Or, putting it another way, the same amount of officers, but with different job titles, trying to cope with far too much work.

The consequences of this are disastrous, because despite there being several frontline departments, it is shift that seems to be suffering the most at present, with significant impact to other departments also. Some stations call their shifts *team* and some stations use the word *party* to describe their individual shifts or teams. You may also hear the word 'response' or 'reactive'. Whatever the word and whatever the station, we are talking about the officers that most people see day in, day out. The uniformed guys with their protective vests, yellow jackets, top hats, metal sticks and nasty spray. The officers that deal with the endless calls. And at the moment, it's no bloody party. This may not be true for every police station in Britain, but the undeniable truth is extremely worrying – frontline police are losing grip, and losing it fast.

The reality is that not only are hundreds of officers retiring, but also hundreds are leaving the job early, anyway, due to the shit we're in. Hundreds are leaving the country, and hundreds are off work with stress or injury. Sickness is reaching new and unheard of levels. And new recruits are quite simply not filling the gaps. You may have guessed that I'm no number cruncher, and despite what the Government may spin on police resources, we simply do *not* have enough frontline staff. We do *not* have enough numbers to deal with incidents. And above all, we do *not* have enough officers to deal with the persistent and trivial problems of a society encouraged to be weak and pathetic. If the Government wants the police to be effective without society changing, then we need more officers. If, however, society is going to suddenly start behaving itself then we may be able to cope. Obviously the latter isn't going to happen, so we're pretty buggered. It's a vicious circle like no other, and it is simply getting worse and worse. So you can chop and change departments, call them different things and move officers from here to there, but without a *dramatic* shift in attitude, culture and expectation, nothing is going to change. In fact, it will only get worse. The population of Britain isn't exactly shrinking – but the police budgets to deal with Britain are getting smaller. Something is seriously fucked up. I think it may be Britain itself.

Therefore, we cannot be expected to deal effectively with *real* crime and *real* victims if this culture of fawning deference and political inaction persists. Day in, day out, across the country, frontline shift officers are turning up at work to be faced with a ludicrous amount of outstanding 'jobs'. We spend all day driving from allegation to allegation. And there is no real prioritising –

if you're a real victim you might as well just wait in line. That real crime you reported will not be considered priority over anything graded of the same urgency. You're on the list, and we'll get to you when we can. And the officers that will eventually come round and see you are already up to their eyeballs in crime reports, enquiries and a whole plethora of other unnecessary, time-consuming duties.

A few days ago in my police area, there were two serious assaults, in the space of about an hour, that happened in the very early hours of the morning. One was a pretty manky GBH at a local pub, and the other was some kind of revenge attack involving three males stabbing a female and then each getting stabbed by the female's boyfriend. The related arrests, scene management, victim duties and essential enquiries resulted in *every* shift officer being taken off the streets, as it were, for hours and hours. There was quite literally *no one* left to deal with anything else. I'm being deadly serious here. *No one.*[34]

While all this was going on, several other notable incidents happened, including a disorder where a male smashed the wing mirrors off seven cars and then pulled a replica gun on one of the victims who'd dared to challenge him. It was dark, the gun looked real, and it scared the living daylights out of the victim. Such an incident is quite rightfully graded as an 'immediate' response and would require the immediate attendance of a frontline officer, e.g. a shift officer. Using a firearm or imitation firearm to cause a fear of violence is an indictable offence with a lengthy prison sentence upon conviction, and the wanton criminal damage and related disorder prior to this cannot be discounted either. However, it was just over *nine hours* until police were eventually able to attend the scene and deal with the victim. This incident ended up in the local paper wherein the victim maligned the police for their

---

34 I am going to repeat myself *again* here. *No-one.* And this was not unusual. In fact, it will become the norm.

apparent lack of action and concern. I entirely sympathised with him. I sympathised because I was the officer who turned up nine hours later. The poor chap was very upset and despite my best efforts, I was unable to placate him. He went to the papers and rightly so, but he didn't mention me, thank goodness. It was more of a general moan, much like this chapter!

This is pretty much indicative of the state of play at the moment. The police service on the front line is running ragged. And what can make it all the more distasteful, for example, is that the only *real* victims from the above story were the people who'd had their wing mirrors smashed, and the chap who'd had the replica firearm pulled on him. The GBH in the pub involved two of the town's nastiest and most violent scumbags, and the injured party didn't want to make a complaint anyway. And the stabbing (which undoubtedly led to 'victims' of a sort) involved low-life criminals with nothing better to do than take drugs, drink heavily and arm themselves with weapons when they should all be asleep like most normal people. So not only do we have to deal with trivial crap, we also have to deal with serious stuff involving criminal scumbags who don't care either way, and maybe, eventually, we'll possibly deal with the decent folk who've really been the victims of a crime. Unfortunately, they figure way down the list.

The situation at the moment is leading to perhaps unprecedented levels of stress within the police service. Owing to this, many frontline officers moan constantly about critical manning levels, bureaucracy, paperwork and having to attend pathetic incidents that have been graded as urgent, treated as full-blown crimes and require hours of unwarranted attention. On top of this, it is not uncommon to also slag off what seem to be unnecessary departments within the police service. For criticisms can be made of the so-called *support* departments who, on the face of it, appear to do nothing more than push bits of paper around and then send nasty emails to shift officers telling them off for seemingly pointless and insignificant things. Most of the time though, they are fulfilling the bureaucratic demands of the Government, so cannot really be blamed.

However, there is nothing more dispiriting than buzzing around like a blue-arsed fly for fifteen hours with hardly any time to eat or even take a piss, and then receive some testy email about a ticky box that hasn't been ticked or a form that hasn't been correctly filled in. Ironically a lot of shift officers move from the front line to so-called support departments because life therein can be much less stressful. So the end result is very few officers on the streets, but a whole load of departments allegedly 'supporting' them.

There also seems to have been a gradual move away from reality and a definite shirking of common sense. As we have already seen from the first chapter, it is very easy to be a victim and even easier to get yourself recorded as one. All you need to do is contact the police. And the person you are most likely to speak to when you phone the police will be a civilian employee working in a call centre. Different police organisations refer to their call centres as different things – but that is basically what they are. The person you talk to will take your details and on the basis of your allegation will, more often than not, create a crime report.

This crime report is then passed to the shift officer to deal with. The shift officer turns up at the relevant location and discovers that it's either a complete and utter load of crap or worth investigating. However the decision has already been made either way, so there's almost no real point in a shift officer attending because the victim and the civilian employee have both decided what's happened anyway. If it's a false allegation and clear that things are certainly not as they seem and the shift officer tries to tell the civilian what has *really* occurred, the civilian simply ignores this and says that the original allegation stands as fact and the crime report is not to be changed.

You may or may not believe this, but every day myself and my colleagues spend far too much time trying to convince someone several miles away sitting behind a desk that the facts of an allegation are complete nonsense, to absolutely no avail whatsoever. It's completely mind boggling. We might as well not bother leaving the station, because whatever presence we have at an incident is constantly undermined by someone who hasn't been there, and that goes for pretty much every job we attend. I might as well sit at a desk all day myself and spend my time ticking boxes, filling in forms and updating a computer system with information as to the fact that I've updated it, because that's all I'm good for.

In many respects, you could imply this problem relates to the fairly recent introduction of large police call centres within the different police organisations – a centralisation process that undermines local knowledge, devalues the importance of station dynamics and de-skills the average police officer. We're being controlled by people sitting miles away facing computer screens, dealing with everything by policy. It has somehow strangled the raw reality out of policing and helped in the endless erosion of discretion and common sense. It is a terminal move towards policing by sitting in front of a terminal. We'll soon end up being a virtual police service. In twenty-five years time, I'll be discussing the good old days with my colleagues saying things like, 'Remember the days when police used to *leave* the station?'

This is not as bizarre as it sounds. Every day we come across more and more things that we're not actually allowed to do for various reasons. For example, at present there is a definite clamping down on vehicular pursuits. We get passed observations of vehicles that really need to be stopped but we are only allowed to look at them and then tell someone that we've seen them.

We're not allowed to approach anyone who may have a spud gun without at least an hour of consultation with those in the higher echelons. We're not allowed to be in any form of danger whatsoever. This, of course, is very nice and kind and I'm sure it's because we're valued and appreciated, but then again, perhaps it isn't. It's far safer to deal with things in a theoretical, policy-led manner than it is to deal with things in an actual manner. Life is clearly that uncomplicated. It clearly doesn't really need gritty, relevant, realistic or emotive involvement by trained and determined frontline staff.

Very soon, the police service will consist of a whole load of pen pushers and desk jockeys, with no one actually doing anything of substance at all. Shift offices will consist of a couple of computers, some odd bits of paper lying around and a lonesome bale of tumbleweed rolling across the carpet; while sitting at desks in faraway rooms, sipping coffee and munching biscuits, will be dozens of officers staring at computer screens. Don't bother calling the police as it will be no-one's remit to attend. Hi, I'm PC Pinkstone, I work on the backline …

* * *

But it's not all doom and gloom, because the neighbourhood officers will soon be out in larger numbers, on foot and riding bicycles. Top hats and tails. Beaming smiles and community minded. Clipping little thieves around the ear and walking between tea stops. A Home Office vision of a safe, cohesive and friendly society. A nice society. An all-inclusive, frilly-around-the-edges, happy and diverse nation. A Victorian parody. So the neighbourhood teams are rolling out in force to roll out this dream. Watch out, it's coming your way.

Well, that's perhaps an overstatement, as the neighbourhood officers consist of those who were already on shift, so it's the same motley crew with a different remit. And they were hardly out in force before they changed roles, so not a lot will be different, except neighbourhood officers don't seem to work regular night shifts at the moment, so that will have to be addressed. There seems to be quite a few rather pertinent and pressing concerns about the way things are going. But don't worry! It's all in hand ...

15. The Neighbourhood and Police Reform

I've decided to lump the neighbourhood and police reform together, as a natural progression from the last chapter, because I find it irritatingly jarring that the Government is pushing for 'neighbourhood policing' and a utopian ideal of a safe, just and tolerant society, without reducing the levels of bureaucracy and organisational paranoia within the police service. In other words, effectively nothing is changing.[35] Furthermore, the numerous underlying issues of social incontinence and lack of responsibility for one's own life enhance the need for more and more police time to be wasted. Couple this with the nanny state, fear of saying anything for fear of offending anyone and overwhelming lack of determination to preserve common sense and Britishness, and you have a rather naff situation.

While neighbourhood policing is, in theory, a rather splendid concept, the practical reality of it in many police stations is simply the removal of frontline shift officers to 'neighbourhoods', where

35 There are various plans to reduce bureaucracy ... perhaps by creating less – but more puissant – forms of legislation. It will be like drinking neat squash. My opinion is that they'll just replace the current bureaucracy with more shit.

they deal with the same old shit in the same old way. Frontline staff numbers aren't being increased. There won't be any more police 'on the streets'. All this sickly spin about safer neighbourhoods and a just and tolerant society is completely and utterly unrealistic considering the facts of what is happening. It's unquestionably short-sighted and uncompromisingly appalling. So while I am a big proponent of the theory behind neighbourhood policing, I am not entirely convinced that it isn't fucked up already – before it's even been completely rolled out.

In practice, the roll out of neighbourhood policing is having an extremely negative impact – mainly on shift numbers, morale and general police attitudes. I'm also of the opinion, as I have mentioned before, that the real problem is more of a social one as opposed to an administrative one. Nevertheless, police administration perpetuates social incontinence. So we can chop and change all we like, but until there is a visible and concerted effort to change the way we think and the way we are expected to deal with things, as well as much deeper changes in social behaviour, there will be very little positive effect in our neighbourhoods. It will be the same deck of cards dealt in a slightly different way. Same crap hand though.

If significant changes aren't going to be made at the deepest levels of police organisational behaviour – e.g. let us begin to *police* the nation as opposed to nanny the nation, then there is little point in promoting the neighbourhood vision. I fear that my views are perhaps a touch hard line and old fashioned, compared to this pink and fluffy victim based mollycoddling, but we surely cannot believe that this current level of grovelling will promote a healthy, self-sufficient and law abiding culture. Furthermore, the criminal justice system needs one heck of an overhaul too. In fact, it pains me somewhat to use the words 'justice' and 'system', because there is no justice and there is no system. My own confidence in 'the system' - on a scale of 0 to 10, stands at a teeny-weeny bit over 0.0044, and that's being generous.

There's also a lot of talk about public confidence in the police. There's very little talk about police confidence in the public. We are confident, however, that we can do nothing right and it's always our fault. If you're going to blame anyone, blame the police. I can't speak for every one of my police colleagues, but there's a huge percentage that have very little faith or confidence in the criminal justice system, too. The public, by and large, feel the same way. In which case it appears that the public and the police have very little confidence in each other, and very little confidence in the system. What a healthy environment that is.

So I don't really expect any tangibly positive changes to be brought about by simply promoting the neighbourhood vision. Ironically, nobody seems to know what it is specifically anyway! However, I believe it to be along the lines of creating safe, tolerant and cohesive communities; where people value and respect each other and where differences are resolved on a mutual basis. The police, therefore, become social overseers and moral guardians (no change there then) and our visible presence on the streets creates this aura of safety and security, so citizens feel safe in their homes and protected when they leave them. Disputes over land, property and all manner of civil issues continue to be the remit of the neighbourhood officer, as well as ASBOs, crack houses, anti-social behaviour, curfews and dispersal orders, and plenty else besides. The public call and officers respond. Reports are taken and meetings organised. Other social and economic agencies are informed. It's all sorted out reasonably, fairly and dispassionately, to the mutual benefit of all parties concerned.

Initially, the neighbourhood officer will not respond to those 'priority' incidents. This will still be the job of the 'response' shift officers – those that are left anyway. The neighbourhood officer will deal with the slow-time enquiries. The jobs that take ages;

the ongoing problems of an ever needy and highly dependent society. The jobs that aren't critical but, nevertheless, require a significant amount of time, effort and input. Jobs relating to social incompetence and moral ignorance. A festival of shit. And the neighbourhood officers, with the PCSOs in tow, will be the champions of this victim focussed mollycoddling. They will park their bicycles and sit in people's lounges, sipping tea and listening to the never ending life stories. They will build bridges. Make friends. Give advice. Help old ladies across the road and clip little rascals around the ear for scrumping apples. They will be the true English bobbies again, parading with dignity in this Victorian utopian fantasy. This playground of dreams.

Soon, though, it will become apparent that the dwindled shifts simply can't cope with the incidents coming in, because they are barely coping as it is. For the system of reporting and recording won't change – they will still be expected to deal with the same amount of stuff, fill in the same amount of forms and get the same amount of arrests and detections. Meanwhile, the neighbourhood officers will be submerged beneath a plethora of trivial social problems and struggling to maintain any form of effective presence, because the system of recording, reporting and ticky-box ticking won't change for them either. Then the wheels start to come off and the neighbourhood officers are required to attend critical incidents due to severe under manning of shifts. Everyone runs ragged. Nothing changes. Crime levels stay the same (even though crime can never be effectively monitored). The shifts blame the neighbourhood teams and the neighbourhood teams blame the shifts. The support departments blame everybody. The senior management blame anybody and no-one takes responsibility for anything. The Home Office blame the senior management and new policies are implemented. And regardless of what your job title has become, everyone ends up doing exactly the same things in exactly the same way as they did before.

In the end, everyone realises that nothing has changed. It's all the same and it's all shit. There's still not enough frontline staff. The country has still gone to the dogs. The safe, just and tolerant society promoted by the spin doctors and Government fools is an ill-conceived and imbecilic dream. There's still no faith and still no confidence. Everyone remains a victim, and those who want to be victims can still lean on their ever present crutch of a softy-softly police service. And the well paid dolts inside their ivory towers turn a blind eye to the truth of what is really going on outside.

This may sound a bit general and more than a touch depressing, so there are some that might disagree and say that the new neighbourhood teams will do this and do that and be proactive and get results and blah blah blah, but I've heard it all before. They know as well as anyone else that nothing is really going to change. The current problems are much deeper and cannot be resolved by a relatively minor alteration of job roles. It's like painting over the cracks without filling them in first – it will look shiny and new for a few weeks but will soon reveal the faults that are there; faults that desperately need sorting out. But the Government would rather get the tin of paint out than the filler.

Police reform has focussed far too much on the superficial – a layer of paint here, a touch up there. A new policy, a new power. A new Act and a whole load of new paperwork. Now we can seize vehicles used in an anti-social manner. Whoopy do. Now we can demand the name and address of youths acting in an anti-social manner. Wow, how cool is that? We can close crack houses. Fantastic! We can give out ASBOs. Yeehaa, they're *so* effective. And under SOCAP, we can arrest people for *anything,* providing it's justified. My goodness, society must be reeling at the police state we live in. The effect has been awesome, the results tangible. Not at all. The problems are at the foundation level and require something far more incisive to make a dent.[36] We're just scratching at the surface at the moment and reeling at the carnival of crap flooding in every day. It's all very well politicians advocating some good ideas to sort the mess out, but most of their ideas do not work in practice! This is the way of the world, and especially the way of Britain.

For while any Government minister or senior police officer sounds, quite rightly, justified in promoting neighbourhood policing, or any other aspect of police reform – and even believes wholeheartedly in the ideologies contained therein – by the time the concept has filtered down through the ranks, flitted its way through corridors, and faffed its way through rooms where policies are dreamed and implemented, there is very little left that is tangible and effective. By the time it reaches the police it is ragged, breathless and almost without shape or form. All we're doing now is filling roles and babbling on, vaguely, about concepts and ideals that really don't have any substance whatsoever. We're filling positions for the sole purpose of filling positions. We're creating roles for the sole purpose of meeting requirements. Any glitzy or inspirational concepts put forward in meetings and conferences that get people clapping and nodding are simply ineffective and inappropriate in practice. By the time it's all rolled out and re-jigged, neighbourhood policing will probably have come full circle and we'll be right back where we started. Which is to say, completely fucked.

---

36 Problems are never really solved. They are either moved elsewhere or deferred until later.

16. Domestics

Try to imagine, if you will, the average police officer turning up at work. If you already are, or were, a copper, then you shouldn't have any problem with this. If you aren't a copper, try to take on board all that I've written so far and place yourself in front of CRAPPIES at a desk in the station. Also place yourself in front of the other software system that displays the 'initial Logs' – those incident reports. The primary means by which the police record something when someone calls us.

There are basically two main systems – the 'live' reporting system and CRAPPIES. If a crime is reported it gets logged and then the details are transferred onto CRAPPIES for the investigative process. The initial Logs are then 'closed' and the details are later archived. As you can imagine, there are *lots and lots* of Logs. People call the police *a lot*. Not everything ends up on CRAPPIES though. Not everything gets passed to officers to deal with. Sometimes the Logs are closed almost straight away. I can't give you an exact percentage, but let's say for the sake of argument that about 40% of reported incidents are not necessarily concerning criminal offences or things that need officer attendance or investigation. However, the remaining 60% constitutes a sumptuous array of crap to be addressing.

So imagine, if you will, staring at the screen. You look first of all at the list of 'live' jobs. We call them 'jobs' by the way.[37] Whether you've been burgled, assaulted, or have discovered a skeleton in your back garden, it's a 'job'. We don't mean to sound dismissive when we say it. Each 'job' is graded according to some priority or the other. Anything racist tends to queue jump and land itself beaming at the top of the important pile, while miscellaneous stuff tends to be bumped down to the bottom. Because the system is 'live', then the grading is updated accordingly. If you call us reporting something pretty nasty happening right *now*, it is graded as 'priority' or 'immediate' and, therefore, takes precedence over anything else graded lower. Different police areas use different words but we all mean the same thing. When you see the police vehicle speed past you on the road it is most likely responding to one of these priority incidents. There are other gradings as well depending on the nature of what has happened – usually about four or five gradings in all, with the lowest form of police intervention being information passed over the telephone.

The jobs are also further classified according to the nature of the incident itself, such as criminal damage, theft, harassment, drugs, fraud, assault, burglary, robbery – basically any criminal offence you can think of that may warrant police attention. Then there's all the miscellaneous stuff that police deal with – including domestic incidents that do not involve criminal offences – as well as traffic stuff, breaches of the peace, missing persons, dead persons, mad persons, suspicious incidents and the like. Rural areas may have jobs concerning abandoned sheep or combine harvesters making off, but inner city strife tends to be a little different. Anything really serious has been passed to CID to deal with and they spend their time with long and complex investigations, as well as loads of other matters pertaining to quite weighty affairs

---

37 Jobs, Logs, CADs, URNs – all the same thing.

in the locality.[38] However, for the average shift officer it's not quite as momentous. For you, it's a festival of poo.

Unfortunately, you don't see too many open jobs concerning skeletons in gardens. That would be far too interesting and exciting. What you *do* see when you come to work are pages and pages of outstanding drivel. Some of them are real jobs that need real attention, but for the most part – especially nowadays – they are pure and utter crap. Your heart sinks. The victim culture has created out of thin air more 'jobs' than you can shake a stick at. The police incident logging systems are being pushed to the limit, even when we do manage to bat a load of shit off. The focus on ensuring everyone gets a 'quality of service' and allowing everyone be a victim whatever their trivial tale of woe, has inspired a lot more 'logging' and ultimately, CRAPPYING, than ever before.

So, at 7.15am on any given morning, you can see the rest of your colleagues reading these many Logs and feeling the same emotions. You've just come out of the briefing meeting and already the controller is reminding the Sergeant that there are at least fifty outstanding jobs. You know this. You can see them in front of you. Not only is it an endless and relentless carousel, it's also a carousel of nonsense. Half the stuff that's on there is mind-numbing trivia. You read through some of the Logs. You select one for closer inspection. There's a report of a domestic harassment where the best friend of a friend has called the police to say that her best friend's ex-boyfriend is sending them both nasty text messages. Your heart sinks even more. Yes, that's *two* victims. Sure enough, a crime report has been generated for both of them. There's a CRAPPIES reference number for each poor, poor victim in the Log and the system is just waiting for an Officer in Case (OIC) – e.g. *you,* to start investigating the matter.

38 Other really serious stuff gets passed to other departments too, such as child protection or anti terrorism. There are, of course, lots of behind-the-scenes police officers who deal with pretty grim or sensitive incidents that are not known to the average shift PC.

You wonder which unlucky bastard is going to get *that* one. You wish you had a CPS appointment, or a person coming in to make a statement. You wish for anything but Log number 735 of today (based on a true Log, of course).

The controller pipes up on the radio. You hear your call sign. She's asking you to view a Log. She passes you the reference number. Your heart reaches knee level as you realise it's the double whammy domestic harassment. You think you might be able to get away with only *one* of the crime reports being domestic related, until you realise that the best friend of the friend also used to shag the now ex-boyfriend of both of them, so you're completely stuffed. You even faintly recognise the names and addresses of all the parties concerned. You think you've met these people before. You most likely have.

You look on CRAPPIES by typing in the crime reference numbers with a slow and heavy finger. You start with the number relating to the best friend of the friend. Yes, *domestic harassment*. Full-scale, full-blown domestic harassment. You then type in the second number. This one concerns the most recent of the ex-girlfriends. Your heart reaches sock level. Assault? Common assault? Domestic common assault? Are your eyes deceiving you? You read through the notes. 'Third party report from caller from related crime report (other harassment) that her best friend was pushed by her now ex-boyfriend following verbal argument. Ex-boyfriend now harassing both parties by sending abusive text messages.'

Your heart hits the floor and starts seeping into the carpet. You feel the weight of helplessness crushing you and suffocating you like a thirty tonne duvet. All around the office there are gentle whimpers and sighs of anguish as your colleagues are allocated equally awful jobs. Occasionally a burst of anger emanates from one corner of the room. 'Oh for fucks sake! For fucks *fucking* sake!' You hear a desk slam and the sound of stomping feet to the printer – which is nearly always dysfunctional – as someone collects their printed-off Log. Their job. Their report of a theft involving a teenage brother and sister. Apparently, one of them has 'stolen' the other one's watch and pawned it. Full-scale domestic theft on CRAPPIES.

You glance back at your trivia. You shake your head in despair. Forget breakfast. Forget your other investigations – including the real ones with real victims. Forget the fact you've got so much to do you might as well just leap out of the window and put an end to it all. Forget everything. Drop everything and go to this domestic. It's *urgent.* It needs to be dealt with *now* (or at the very least within forty-five minutes[39]).

Do I need to go into the nature of this so-called domestic harassment with added common assault? Do I need to tell you what those two females were like? Do I need to burden you with such depressing information? I don't think I do. Suffice to say, that after about three hours of form filling, statement taking and CRAPPIES updating, you're pretty exhausted. Mentally, physically and emotionally drained. But don't have a rest – there are still fifty outstanding jobs, because new ones are coming in all the time. They're stacking up like bodies after a one-sided battle. They are spilling over the edges and dripping down the sides.

The Sergeant reads your Domestic Risk Assessment Form. He signs it. He puts it in the box to go 'upstairs' to the Domestic Violence Unit, or the Public Protection Unit. The Fucked Up Relationships in Britain Unit. You then update CRAPPIES with another non-update to say that you intend, at some point when you have time, to 'speak' to the offender in this domestic-harassing-text-message-tit-for-tat-push-and-shove-debacle. This complete lack of ability to get a life and grow the fuck up. You lean back in

---

39 The latest local policy on attending domestics in my police service is that we *have* to get to it within forty-five minutes, even if it is utter CRAP. It's called an *'Escalation Policy,'* otherwise known as an *'Arse-Covering Risk-Aversion Policy'.* If relationships go wrong, it's the fault of the police.

your chair and let out a sigh. The controller pipes up again. A job has just come in. It's graded as priority. It's another domestic! It's only half past ten but apparently the caller is reporting that her ex-boyfriend is outside the house drunk. He's banging on the door! Female at risk! Previous domestic violence between the couple! All units, go *go* GO!

You race to the car, leaping over obstacles like a gazelle. Your crewmate hurries along behind you eating a yoghurt. Strawberry. You pile into the driver's seat and start the engine. The controller updates you. Apparently the line has gone dead. They no longer have contact with the caller! Arrgh! She's dead! She's been brutally murdered! It's all over! The diesel engine roars into life. Actually, it kind of coughs slightly and whimpers. You strap yourself in and press all the buttons.

You speed out of the station car park with squealing tyres and flashing lights. Well, *speed* is somewhat ambitious. It's a diesel and the turbo is fucked. It's been fucked since its second week on shift. Still, you're making a lot of noise and you're visible from space. Sirens blaring and adrenaline pumping; only if you're new, of course. If you've been in the job a while, you have no adrenaline left. You have no emotions left whatsoever. Driving at top speed through heavy traffic in a bright and noisy car doesn't really float your boat that much. Driving to a 'priority' domestic such as this is not exciting at all. Not in the least little bit.

Of course, in the back of your mind, you are fully conscious of the fact that something serious may actually have happened! Of all the hundreds of domestic incidents that are reported, there are many that truly deserve police intervention. You *know* that domestic abuse is horrible. You know it's particularly nasty. You really do feel compassion for those victims, but you can't help the cynicism. You can't help the feeling of hopelessness and frustration. You can't help feeling that, despite all of your best efforts, you're not even making a dent.

You screech around the corner into the relevant street. There's no further updates. You park your car outside the house and get out. There's no sign of anyone or anything untoward. You knock on the door. It is opened by a female in her thirties. She welcomes you inside. The house is clean and tidy, and there's no sign of disturbance. You say, 'Are you OK madam?' She says, 'Yes ... he's gone now ...'

You sit down and talk about what happened. She split up with him six months ago. He wants to get back together with her. She doesn't want this. She's moved on. He's got a drink problem. The usual story. You've heard it before so many times. Although you feel sorry for this female, you know that there's nothing you can do. All he's done today is turn up and knock on the door, while a wee bit pissed. He hasn't made a habit of it. He doesn't harass her. It's just that every now and then, usually after a few sherbets, he gets a bit emotional. Men are weak, especially nowadays.

So, you do the necessaries: you have to – there's no choice in the matter. You fill in the forms and assess the risk. You drive back to the station and complete everything. You update CRAPPIES. You hand over the paperwork. Your Sergeant signs the Domestic Risk Assessment Form and puts it in the box to go upstairs. This isn't a domestic with added complications of a criminal offence. It's a 'non-recordable', but you record it anyway. By now it's way past lunchtime and you still haven't had any breakfast.

Fortunately, you manage to grab a bite to eat. Not from the canteen, of course – it's closed down. Government cutting budgets and your police organisation scrimping and saving wherever it can. You call up to say you're available for more jobs. The controller passes you a six-day-old domestic. Haven't been able to get hold of the caller since last Thursday. Circumstances are that a female had called the police requesting help – with the sound of a disturbance in the background – and then hung up. Called on a mobile number that is now switched off. Nothing more than that. However, the number comes back to a female who'd called us eight months ago regarding criminal damage to a fence. However, this incident is graded as domestic, just to be on the safe side. Other officers had been round to the address in the past few days, but no-one answered the door.

Is she dead? Has she been kidnapped? You know that this is highly unlikely, but not ultimately impossible. You can't rule out anything in this life. Because of this, you know that the matter will not rest until you have somehow located this female and checked on her welfare. By some fortuitous coincidence, the female is at home. She's absolutely fine. Her mobile phone had been broken and she works nights. Why had she called us? Well, her husband who is working at the moment, had got quite aggressive and threatened to smack her face in. He's not usually like that. He started throwing things around the house and shouting angrily. So she called the police. He then grabbed the phone off her and smashed it. In the morning everything was fine.

He was mortified. Absolutely horrified at his behaviour. Bought her a new phone and made it all up to her. Stresses at work, he said. The pressures of life. He didn't hit her. Didn't hurt her. Didn't do anything too awful except smash her phone. Even he couldn't believe it. A glitch. A momentary loss of control. So you do the necessaries. How does she feel about the broken phone? You know how *you* feel about the broken phone. You want her to say that it doesn't matter! You wait with baited breath for her response. Does she want to pursue the matter? Does she want to make a report of criminal damage? Does she want her husband arrested?

Scenario One: She does. Scenario Two: She doesn't. The answer hangs in the balance. It sits on the fence. There are two options here. What will she choose? She looks at you, almost frowning. She asks you what you mean by how she feels about the broken phone. She's already told you that things are OK now and she's got a new phone. She didn't even feel the need to call the police again.

You wince inside. You try to explain that she could have her husband arrested, or not support such an outcome. She certainly doesn't want him arrested! Why would she want him arrested? She's quite shocked you even suggest such a thing. However, you know better. You know the system. You know it's all fucked up beyond repair. You know that *you* have to justify every course of action you take. *You* are responsible for everyone you ever meet and even people you haven't. *You* are responsible. And when it comes to domestics, it's your arse on the line. So you whip out your statement paper and pocket notebook and write down everything that's happened. You mention the breaking of the phone and explain in laborious detail that the female doesn't want to make a specific complaint regarding this. You get her to sign things. You cover your arse. You cover your arse completely. Does my bum look big in this? Don't know – can't even see it. Too much butt-concealing paperwork in the way.

You leave her house and inform her that she shouldn't feel afraid of calling the police whenever she feels the need. You do the whole victim thing. You fly the flag and pass advice. You give support. You treat her like the police are the only people she can trust in times of domestic need. So you go back to the station and complete the paperwork. But this has a twist to it. Here, you have an *offence* with the added intricacy of no support from the victim. You have a criminal damage! What's more, you have a *domestic* criminal damage. How the hell can you bat this one off without arresting someone? How can you justify *not* thinking about getting a detection?

You phone the CRAPPIES hotline and pass all the information. Sure enough – domestic-related criminal damage. Sure enough, there's the 'victim' details and there's the 'offender' details. Their lives on our screen. Their complexities and complications; their emotional and intricate human affairs in virtual form, boiled down to scrutinised simplicity. Report. Arrest. *Detect.* Done and dusted. No room to involve common sense or reason. No room for emotion. Their lives are sterilised, sanitised and compartmentalised. Conveyor belt justice.

So you wonder what to do. In the back of your mind you recall some previous emails from important people. You recall your Domestic Violence training. You recall every bit of advice or admonition about familial affairs. You know that if he was to ever end up killing her, then your actions today will be called into account. You know that if he was to beat her or hit her in the future, you would be asked to explain why you didn't do more today. You will have to explain why you didn't save the day. Why you didn't intervene *positively.* Yes my friend, it will be *your fault* if something happens to her. She cried for help, and you just cuffed her off with indifference!

You decide, in the end, to follow your instincts and not pursue the matter. You decide *not* to arrest this chap. You decide to file the crime report after suitable advice and leave it at that. Yet others may not have done the same. Your colleagues are all different. They are all affected in different ways by the paranoia. They are affected in different ways by the performance-related nagging. There's a chance of an *arrest* here. There's a change of a *detection!* They know they can justify it because it's domestic related. So they end up nicking the chap anyway. They end up doing this despite the wishes of the female. They interview him and he admits doing it. He admits breaking the phone. What else can he say? He's a decent bloke and tells the truth. He's a normal guy. Average Joe. Not a criminal or a saint. He's like you. He's like me.

He's also got no previous convictions whatsoever. He's never been arrested before today. So guess what? That's right, he's eligible for a caution. Done and dusted. Detection gained. Victim supported. Justice done. Pat on the back. The police can then say they've got a super clear-up rate with domestic violence! Look at all those detections and neatly disposed of crimes! Look at all those victims who have been indemnified and their relationship made all the better for police involvement!

Look at all of those normal people who now have criminal records just for being alive and in a relationship. Look at all of those men, and sometimes women, who've never been arrested, never been in trouble with the police and who would never hurt their partner intentionally, or unintentionally. They've now been nicked, interviewed and kicked out of the door with a fly in their ear and a criminal stamp on their chart. Bad, bad people. We will not suffer domestic violence!

* * *

It is a minefield. It is truly an immensely complex situation. It is one of those issues that is never going to go away. Domestic violence is a major problem and consumes a major part of police time and effort. Unfortunately, we live in a time of paranoia and procedure. The combination of both creates huge and convoluted problems when it comes to policing the domestic aspect of life. Of course, we tend to err on the side of caution and therefore we *do* end up criminalising people when they don't need to be. But we also send out a message that domestic violence is not acceptable. Which of these is winning the day? Which of these has had the most effect? Has the policing of domestic situations in the past several years been positive or negative?

I would say that owing to the plethora of paperwork and completely unnecessary form filling, as well as the mind-numbing arse covering, the overriding feeling will be one of negativity. Frontline police have so little discretion and are blamed for pretty much everything that has gone wrong, or might possibly go wrong, that we really don't like domestics any more! It's a rather sad fact that while we want to do our job and protect vulnerable people from domestic abuse, we feel bogged down to the extent of complete annoyance and indifference.

That 'Escalation Policy' I mentioned in my last footnote is a classic example of the procedural paranoia we face. It may very well be that not every police organisation has the same policy but, as mentioned before, we all face the same crap, albeit manifest in a variety of ways. The only way I can demonstrate the absurdity of this policy in action is by doing this:

The time is 1.15am on a Monday morning. Tango Zulu is the controller and Mike Bravo Nine-One are two officers driving round trying to catch real criminals. Unfortunately, this is based almost entirely on a recent true story:

(Faint hiss of static ... then a female voice ...)

Mike-Bravo Nine-One, Tango-Zulu.

Nine-One, go ahead.

Nine-One, can you take an outstanding domestic for me please?

Yes, yes, pass details.

Nine-One, thank you. The address you're going to is number 34 Wilkinson Path. We've had a call from a Mrs Duhane at that address reporting domestic violence from her husband. There are several previous domestics at that address. Could you go and see if you can raise our caller and do the necessaries?[40]

Nine-One copied. When did the call come in please?

Call came in Friday night at 11.29pm. We weren't able to go at the time, so the caller stated she would be going to stay with her sister. Caller hasn't been able to be seen since then. However, she contacted us again at 9.34pm yesterday evening stating she was available to be seen.

---

40 The 'necessaries', in most cases like this, means about an hour of pointless paperwork.. So, Mrs Duhane, how safe do you feel on a daily basis? Well, I feel safe generally, but not when he's been drinking ... (If I had a pound.)

Nine-One received. Is her husband also there?

Nine-One, that's not known, er, there's nothing in the Log that mentions him. Received?

Nine-One copied. Did the caller state what the nature of the domestic was?

Nine-One, that's a negative. She simply stated she was having domestic issues with her husband. The Log doesn't state any more than this.[41] Previous incidents have all been non-recordable. Arguments, mostly related to drinking.

Nine-One received. We'll go to the house to see if anyone's around.

(Four minutes later ...)

Tango-Zulu, Mike-Bravo Nine-One.

Nine-One, go ahead.

Nine-One, we're at the address and the house is all in darkness. No answer at the front door. Top window is open. We're going to leave a card for the caller to contact us.

Nine-One, that's all received. As stated, she did contact us yesterday evening waiting to be seen, but owing to the time of night, er, card drop it is. I'll add that to the Log.

Nine-One, card has been dropped, can you show us resuming please?

Nine-One, that's all received.

(Three minutes later ...)

Mike-Bravo Nine-One, Tango-Zulu.

Nine-One, go ahead.

Nine-One, apologies for this. From the Control Room Sergeant, owing to the Escalation Policy can you please make more attempts to raise our caller, er, as there is a fear for her welfare. Received?

---

41 Nowadays, all people have to do is mention the word 'domestic' and a Log is created with practically no details. Circumstances are irrelevant. The police then simply have to attend.

(Pause)[42]

Nine-One, all received. Have we tried a phone call?

Nine-One, yes, yes. Phone is switched off, received?

Nine-One copied.

(Six minutes later ...)

Tango-Zulu, Mike-Bravo Nine-One.

Nine-One, go ahead.

Nine-One, we're back at the address. There's no answer at the door again. No lights are on. We've tried knocking several times, quite loudly. Received?

Nine-One, er, that's all copied. I'll attach that to the Log. Er, you may as well resume Nine-One.

Nine-One copied. Nine-One further.

Nine-One, go ahead.

Nine-One, did you state that the female called us yesterday evening?

Nine-One, yes, yes. She called us at 9.34pm requesting officer attendance.

Nine-One copied. Did she sound distressed?

Nine-One, that's a negative. She stated she was home now and available to be seen.

Nine-One all copied. In that case it sounds like this job can be deferred until the morning. No real welfare issues, received?

Nine-One, er, that's all copied. I'll show you resumed.

(Two minutes later ...)

Well, you're going to have to wait for a short while for the rest of the radio transcript. I need a quick break, or I'll throw something really heavy in my room and break something I'll regret. That's because I know what's coming. I hope that you can see, so far, that a significant effort has been made to contact this 'victim' after her initial report. However, the fact that she's called us is enough to

---

42 Mike-Bravo Nine-One will be swearing profusely during this little break in radio communication ...

create a Log and get the bare details onto CRAPPIES, and initiate policies so unrealistic, unnecessary and unbelievable you can but swear and swipe papers off a desk in rage.

Let me just quote something from Chapter 3:

> *I don't think that whoever had taken the call from the 'victim' had asked too many questions. As soon as the word racist was mentioned, it set off all the alarms. People started panicking ...*

In this case, all you need to do is replace the word 'racist' with the word 'domestic'. It's all the same paranoia. For as I will mention time and time again until I'm blue in the face, there is quite literally no appreciation of context any more – with anything. This lack of context itself has fucked up discretion like a rebounded killing curse.

With our domestic scenario here, we simply have a female reporting 'domestic issues'. However, owing to the grading system, it is automatically referred to as 'domestic *violence*'. That's the first fucking annoyance.

The second fucking annoyance is that whoever took the call really didn't ask too many questions. Unfortunately, though, such questions are probably irrelevant, because if someone reports *anything* domestic related, a 'domestic violence' Log and associated CRAPPIES number are generated for officers to 'investigate'. Why, it was only yesterday when myself and PC Crash had to deal with Log number 1186: 'domestic violence'. The circumstances? Well, as a direct quote from the Log: '*Caller reporting his ex-wife is buzzing on his buzzer.*'

Believe me when I say that this was it. The full shebang. It meant a police Log, a CRAPPIES reference number, a Domestic Risk Assessment Form and associated CRAPPIES updating until self-harming seemed like an appropriate means of escape. Any wonder why many officers are simply leaving this fucked up debacle of a profession?

The third fucking annoyance is the Escalation Policy. By the time you read this paragraph, it may very well be that such a policy has been changed or altered. Either way, you can be fully assured that something else just as risk averse and arse covering will have sprung up in its place.

Er, Mike Bravo Nine-One, Tango-Zulu.

Nine-One, go ahead.

Er, Nine-One, apologies for this. From the Control Room Sergeant, could you please try knocking on the door again once more. If there is no answer could you please try knocking on the neighbour's door to see if they have seen our caller. If no luck there, please try another neighbour. Please make every effort to speak to someone who lives next to, or near, the caller, so that we can establish where she is and if she is all in order.

(Quite a long pause.)[43]

Nine-One, copied. Er, wait one please. Just going to contact the shift Sergeant.

Nine-One, er, that's all received.

(One minute later.)

Tango-Zulu, Sierra Five-One.

Sierra Five-One go ahead.

Five-One, I've spoken to Nine-One and agree with them that there is no real welfare concern for this female. She's called us only a few hours ago and my officers are not prepared to wake up the neighbours at half past one on a Monday morning. I've updated the Log to that effect.

Er, Sierra Five-One all received. Er, however, er, wait one ...

(Six minutes and several angry phone calls later.)

---

43 It's 1.30am and Mike Bravo Nine-One have reached new heights of profanity in their vehicle. By this time everyone else has tuned in to their frustration. All they want to do is some real police work, but instead they are caught up in this complete melee of political paranoia.

Mike Bravo Nine-One, Tango Zulu

Nine-One, go ahead.

Nine-One, er, from the Control Room Sergeant, we have a real welfare concern for this female. We haven't been able to contact her for nearly four hours and she specifically stated she wanted to be seen. There's lots of previous domestic violence between the couple and the Escalation Policy also states that we must make every effort to attend, so could you at least try to raise one neighbour to try to establish the welfare of our caller by asking them if they think she is OK. The Log has been updated to that effect.

Sierra Five-One, can I come in?

Please do Sierra Five-One.

Five-One, as stated I am not prepared to wake up the neighbours. It's 1.30am and people will be getting up for work in a few hours. We don't have a welfare concern for this female – *I've* updated the Log to this effect – and I think I could justify that in a bloody PSD interview …

(Eight minutes, more phone calls and several updates later, the Log is eventually deferred until Monday morning at the earliest opportunity.)

Meanwhile, Mrs Duhane is happily sleeping off her two bottles of wine, whilst her husband snores peacefully next to her, completely oblivious to the past half-an-hour police pantomime. And inevitably, at about 9.34pm on Monday evening, some officers go round to see Mrs Duhane who is perfectly safe and happy (and pissed) and all she wanted was to report to us that her husband kept 'getting aggressive' at her when they were both wankered. How long has this been going on for Mrs Duhane? Oh, since we both met about eighteen years ago …

I truly believe that those in their ivory towers have absolutely *no* comprehension whatsoever about what it is like to be a frontline police officer in Britain nowadays. They haven't got a fucking clue. Do they have any conception about our *total* lack of discretion? And this obsession with domestic incidents has gone beyond all forms of mental coherence. If the police service was a person it would be sectioned immediately and strapped to a bed.

* * *

We *desperately* need some discretion back in order to do our job properly and effectively. It should be for the frontline officers, their colleagues and their Sergeants to decide whether or not a domestic incident is worthy of following up, or batting off without the need for so much unnecessary time, attention or paperwork. It should not be up to the political morons – or arse covering supervisors sitting at Control Room desks – to make decisions about people's lives according to policies that jar so gratingly with common sense it makes you weep. *We* are the frontline guys and gals – the Government put us here, now let us do our fucking job. At the moment, it is all out of our hands. We're just robots in uniform. This also applies to any situation, not just domestics. Any situation where two minutes of advice could replace two hours of bureaucracy.

The current state of play has determined who is a victim and who is an offender before we even knock on the door. It's been decided by policy before any attempt is made to even establish the facts. Mrs Duhane became a domestic victim on a police computer system about eight seconds into her phone call, irrespective of what had taken place. The emphasis on supporting those poor little domestic victims seems even more frustrating when they are nothing of the sort. While we enjoy nicking bad guys and gals, we don't enjoy what is happening at the moment. We don't enjoy dealing with such mind-numbing trivia it makes us throw up our hands in utter despair. And we don't enjoy nicking normal people for doing nothing. For in recent times there has been a general blurring of who is bad and who is not. The words 'victim' and 'offender' have taken on new meanings. How on earth can we bring back some sense of perspective and proportion? I think a good place to start would be to look at the *real* criminals and the *real* victims. Perhaps if we can somehow define who they are, we might be able to clear our minds a little.

17. The Real Criminals

Criminals can be called many things. I can think of a few choice words to call some of them. However, they may also be called 'offenders', 'suspects' or 'baddies'. There's lots of words we use. But who, if anyone, is a *real* criminal? From a police point of view I think it is fair to say that a criminal is a person who persistently commits crime. There's always going to be rascals and one-off offenders who do something stupid and get into trouble, but such people are not necessarily criminals. The other week I arrested an extremely drunk and abusive chap who, when he had sobered up and seen the CCTV evidence of his misconduct on the street, was completely mortified at his behaviour. Obviously, we had to get a detection, so he got a caution for his sins, but I would certainly not call him a 'criminal'. He clearly deserved no more than a slap on the wrist and a stern warning that any further behaviour of a similar kind would result in him going to court.

A real criminal is one who ruins the lives of others on a regular basis. One who routinely abuses the welfare of other people. There's obviously so many different offences that it would be practically impossible to cover every kind of criminal, so I am only going to focus on the types of crime and criminal I deal with every day. Persistent burglars and street robbers, for

211

example, are not pleasant characters. Being on drugs is not an excuse. It's a reason. Such people ruin the lives of others and do not get punished properly. Neither do they repay their victims enough. The sentences they receive are completely poxy and are nowhere near sufficient. They need to be locked up for longer. I feel, like many others, that the criminal justice system is far too soft and that the criminals themselves are running the show. Surely if someone routinely commits crime, they should face much stiffer penalties. For example, by the time someone has committed their 4th or 5th burglary, they should be looking at a jail term of at least five years, not a couple of months. I have heard rumours of various plans in place to solidify criminal justice, and you may hear the odd ruse or speculation about extending certain sentences, or whatever, but it is simply not enough. It sounds a bit basic and simple, but criminals should spend longer in prison and be forced to contribute to society. They take enough away from it – now they should start to give something back.

Whilst in the joint, criminals should be put to work in some way by contributing to the welfare of the nation and earning money to pay back their victim in full. If they refuse to comply with any conditions of work, licence or whatever – their jail term should be extended. The same goes for drug dealers. People convicted of dealing, or being concerned in the production and supply of drugs, should be given very lengthy prison sentences. Whilst inside, they should be put to work and a percentage of the money they earn should be given to charities and organisations that help people get off drugs.

I could go on like this all day, but I hope that this gives you an indication of how the average police officer feels. We don't like criminals. We don't like crime. We also don't like the fact that when we are fortunate enough to catch a bad guy, the system lets them go almost straight away. Days and days of work and case file preparation and thousands of man-hours later – all so some bastard can do three weeks in jail. Wow, what a result. When it comes to faith in the justice system, the average police officer has almost none at all. It's rare that I express what other people think, but in this respect I know I am well and truly correct, and justified in saying so. Most police officers and, I dare say most citizens, would like to see real criminals locked up for longer and pay back towards the economic and emotional damage they have caused. This isn't some kind of 'lock em up and throw away the key' mentality, rather it is a heartfelt cry to get those bastards off the streets for longer and instil some much needed fear back into the criminal justice system.

Not long ago, I arrived at work to be informed of a case that had just been through court. The case of a man arrested for burglary. In this case, *distraction* burglary. A distraction burglary is one that results, in most cases, with frail and elderly victims. Those almost completely unable to defend themselves. Burgled in their own homes by vicious predators who demonstrate the sort of iniquitous indifference to life common to certain evil individuals. So this chap got himself charged and convicted at court of such a burglary. Now please bear in mind that the maximum penalty for this kind of offence is pretty hefty – fourteen years if convicted in the Crown court. However, this chap didn't get fourteen years – he got four-and-a-half years.

Well that's not too bad a result. To be quite honest, that's not a bad sentence at all. Four-and-a-half years.[44] But I haven't told you the whole story yet. You see, when we catch a burglar it's a damned good result to get a conviction. Any conviction. We like convictions for burglars. Unfortunately, though, they tend to be able to get away with several burglaries sometimes before we can catch them. There's usually a veritable trail of victims and heartache before they end up getting nabbed. I can't ply you with

---

44 Four-and-a-half years usually means about two years in real terms.

statistics, but it's fair to say that we respond to dozens and dozens and *dozens* of burglaries, but don't catch dozens of burglars.

Once these scumbags are caught, though, they have the option of *taking into consideration* any other crimes they may have committed. This allows them some latitude and leniency in the court. If they admit to these other crimes, which have been reported and recorded, then the police clear-up those crimes (and get detections, yippee) and everyone is happy. Or, not so happy ... For some reason I simply can't get my head around the whole issue of taking something into consideration. If someone admitted to me that they'd done some other burglaries, then the way I'd take that into consideration would be to send the fucker down for longer. But what do I know? I'm obviously not privy to the political importance behind this administrative and legal issue.

So this dear burglar was asked if he wanted to take into consideration any other crimes. Bless him, he did. He took into consideration over one-hundred-and-seventy burglaries, many of them distractions. That's over one-hundred-and-seventy poor victims, most of whom were completely shattered by the crime. *One-hundred-and-seventy* burglaries. But well done to the police. We got lots and lots of detections! We rang the victims and told them that we found the baddy who burgled them!

What we didn't tell them, however, was that irrespective of the administrative and legal issues of taking crimes into consideration – and the frankly bewildering complexities of the criminal justice system – the baddy burglar, if he was to serve the full four-and-a-half years, would actually serve a maximum of about *nine days* per burglary. Ain't that a daisy! Hello Mrs Smith, I know you're an eighty-seven year old pensioner and this chap pushed roughly past you in your own home, ransacked your drawers and stole your handbag, but I am pleased to inform you that he served a week-and-a-half for doing that. Good result don't you think madam?

In other words, there's something a wee bit wrong with the system. It would appear that criminals are somewhat ruling the roost and taking the piss. It's a right royal pain in the arse to come to work for a police service that is having its budget cut left right and centre; where overtime is almost impossible to get due to shortage of cash and where Government incompetence creates a choking and burdensome organisational environment anyway, for all of this to be compounded by the fact that when we arrest a criminal – that swine gets free transport, free meals, free legal advice, free accommodation and then pretty much a free ride to freedom, where they start committing crime all over again.

They leave a trail of destruction and a general feeling of helplessness. What's the bloody point of arresting them in the first place? We might as well not bother. It's a never ending carousel that appears to be having little or no effect in curbing criminal conduct. Criminals *should* begin to pay for their crimes in ways that instil a true fear of re-offending. They need to know that this country will not suffer their behaviour. We really have got to toughen up.

Such statements, though, are obviously far too harsh and hard line for this weak and quivering country. We can't punish people! Gosh no! How right wing! Unfortunately, there is no fear left. There is no apprehension of consequence. The system is so pathetic that criminals are having a ball. The police and the baddies know this, and it's all one big game. I also believe that it has very little to do with police powers. For in many respects, the police currently have quite adequate powers under the various Acts. However, we are *constantly* undermined by a prosecution service that routinely safeguards criminals, and court sentencing that is not in any way commensurate with the crime. If sentencing reflected what was stipulated by law and reflected the economic and emotional damage caused by the crime in the first place, we might see some of our more regular criminals going down for much more appropriate lengths of time. And once they are safely installed behind bars, they can then make themselves useful and actually contribute in some way – first and foremost to any victim, and then to the rest of the country.

Justice has nothing to do with detections as we have already seen – it *should* have everything to do with the system as a whole. Beginning to end. And the end result should be baddies sufficiently punished and victims sufficiently compensated. Unfortunately, real criminals are getting away with crime day in, day out. The police know who they are, where they live and what they are doing. For all our powers though, we do not have the power of justice. There is quite literally nothing we can do about it.

18. The Real Victims

Real criminals leave behind real victims. It's actually quite obvious to a police officer if you are a real victim or not. Unfortunately, lots of people lie to the police on a regular basis and often people who appear to be real victims are nothing of the sort. Clearly the police are not allowed to suggest to people that they are liars though. Oh my goodness, how unprofessional. How unkind. *Every* victim must be given a true quality of service, regardless of whether their case is so inane as to be mind boggling, or a lie, or a counter allegation, or aggravated by some negative element that would result in the alleged victim actually being the criminal, if common sense was allowed to be applied.

But, no. That would be far too sensible. We have already seen how the police are working within a victim driven culture, perpetuated and encouraged by numerous factors, not least the Government.

I'll give you an example. Not long ago, I received a report of a robbery to deal with. It was already a couple of days old by the time I was given it and upon reading the Log, I recognised the name of the 'victim'. A couple of checks proved my suspicions that the victim was indeed a well known criminal (burglar in fact) and police eyes were on him regarding several criminal acts in the area. I also checked CRAPPIES to note that, of course, the report had received a crime reference number on the basis of the allegation according to NCRS and other stupid administrative procedures, and I duly set about attempting to deal with it.

I visited the 'victim' at his home and he told me a completely bewildering and arse-about-face story of how he was robbed by a guy he knew, who also happened to be a very well known scumbag, and that he wanted him arrested. My 'victim' also had two witnesses who, it transpired, didn't really see anything and couldn't really add anything of substance to the allegation. It really was a load of old bollocks. Not only was the story itself completely inconsistent, but there was no evidence to back up the claim. I didn't doubt that he was involved in some kind of incident with the people involved, just not in the way he was alleging. My victim really wasn't what he claimed to be. He was, in fact, a streetwise young crook with a string of criminal convictions and a propensity for being a little stinker.

You can guess that under no circumstances would all of this be allowed to undermine the investigation. Under no circumstances would I be able to convince the number crunchers and administrators that it was all bollocks. It would *have* to be dealt with as a robbery, and the named offender would have to be arrested. This would be after wasting several hours trying to obtain a statement and doing other procedural things. I then decided to do some more checks on my 'victim', and it turned out that he was on court bail for a burglary and that he had bail conditions attached.

One of his conditions was not to contact another very well known local scumbag and burglar, and the other was a home curfew between 9pm and 7am. In other words, he was not allowed out of his home between those hours. Such conditions are imposed for a reason (e.g. public protection) and never without good cause. Breaching those conditions is a criminal offence.

Yes, you may have already guessed that my 'victim' was breaching his bail conditions at the time of the alleged robbery. He was driving around the area at 10pm on the night of the incident, several miles from his home. He was treating his conditions with contempt, breaking the law, and making a mockery of the system.

Now what *should* have happened as a result of this? Well, I think that he should have been arrested immediately and dealt with extremely firmly: remanded and put before the court to attempt to explain himself. No latitude. No excuse. Given short shrift for his inability to comply with serious legal conditions and preferably handed a suitably cumbersome community order for his behaviour.

No. That would reek of justice and common sense. That would be far too hard line and in no way pink and fluffy enough. Too nasty. Not wishy washy and pathetic enough. Not deferential enough. Too many vertebrae in that decision. The end result was that I went on leave, giving instructions for the 'victim' to be arrested as soon as possible, which was ratified by my Sergeants and other people at the station. I came back from leave, three weeks later, to discover that the 'victim' had been arrested and let off scot-free for no particularly significant reason. He'd then subsequently made a complaint as to why his robbery allegation hadn't been dealt with properly. Unfortunately, the Inspector who took the complaint pretty much grovelled in agreement and displayed exactly the fawning sense of spinelessness I have come to expect from some senior officers. My opinions were overruled, and yet again, the victim culture won the day. Common sense and justice were rejected in favour of obsequious mollycoddling.

Now imagine this kind of thing happening day in, day out across the country. Imagine the amount of people who actually call the police purporting to be 'victims' – the sheer volume of souls who, mainly by their own incompetence and irresponsibility, have got themselves into a variety of trivial scrapes, then call the police because they cannot live their lives any other way. The Bugflobs of this world. Mixed in with these thousands and thousands of so-called victims – who not only create inconsequential crime reports, but false ones too – will be hundreds of people who truly need police assistance. Yet owing to the methods employed by the police to deal with crime, for example the rigidity of CRAPPIES and the NCRS, coupled with our lack of discretion and professionalism, we are unable to prioritise appropriately, or permitted to distinguish between what is worthless and what is worthwhile. There is no separating of the wheat from the chaff, as it were. Of course, while most police officers are fully aware of what is crap and what is not, we are not *allowed* to differentiate.

This goes to show that it doesn't really matter about context any more. There's no room for such a thing. I know I've mentioned this lots of times, but it's a pretty fucking serious point. If you are a real victim, just join the queue. And it's a bloody long queue. Real victims are those people who, first and foremost, have been the victims of a real crime. That crime could be a one-off like a burglary, or criminal damage, or they could be the victims of ongoing crimes like harassment, domestic abuse, or persistent anti-social behaviour. They may have been assaulted without reason, or had something truly horrific happen to them. Real victims of real crimes. The police really do want to deal with you, by the way – it's just that we don't have very much time or resources. Too busy mopping up social incontinence and compiling data for the Government.

So believe it or not, the police really are interested in helping real victims. We do want to arrive on your doorstep as soon as possible and help you. We want to stay and chat with you and give you reassurance. It's our job, and by and large, we enjoy it. I certainly do. It's one of the main reasons people join the police. There is a great deal of job satisfaction in helping a victim. There is very little satisfaction in the way things are at the moment, however. As you can hopefully see by now, we are in a world of shit.

In recent years, the distinction between those who are real victims and those who need to be given a bollocking for wasting police time has become extremely blurred. The almost total eradication of discretion and professionalism, as we briefly examined in Chapter 8, perpetuates the whole situation. Police officers are now no longer able to make reasonable and informed decisions. We are no longer able to say to someone that they need to grow up and take responsibility for themselves. We are not allowed to differentiate. Not permitted to look at the context. I vaguely recall reading *The Handmaid's Tale* by Margaret Atwood whilst at college. One sentence in that book is particularly succinct. It reads: 'Context is all'. Ironically, I can't remember the context of the sentence itself, but I guess that's OK. The gist is enough. *Context is all.* I like that.

Nicely put Margaret, I entirely agree with you. It would appear that the Government doesn't. There is no context allowed anymore. It's all but disappeared. And it's all rather depressing. If you were to put together every negative thing I have mentioned so far in this book – and there has been a fair bit – you will, hopefully, appreciate that the police truly are running ragged, and true quality of service at present is but an unattainable dream. Therefore, if you are the real victim of a real crime, I'm really, really sorry.

* * *

So that's victims of crime. Lots of crime, and lots of real victims. Sometimes victims can be companies or organisations. Sometimes the offence is committed against *Regina*; but there's lots of other victims as well, wherein the mere definition of the word can become so broad as to be limitless. Yet crime itself is not the only remit of the police, or other professionals dealing with society.

Not long ago, I was sitting in the station, most likely pointing and clicking, when the radio controller called up so say that a person on a train had seen what he believed to be a female body lying on the track. The chap on the train had only caught a glimpse of what he believed to be a partly naked person and that he thought he saw them somewhere between two particular stations.

Bodies on railway tracks are, unfortunately, a rather common occurrence and so this information was of no particular surprise. Two of my colleagues left the station and drove to one of the several local bridges passing over the railway line in an effort to look for this person.

About ten minutes after leaving the station, my colleague called up on the radio to say that he could see a decapitated body on the tracks just below a bridge. He and my other colleague stayed at the scene and a supervisor and CID were informed.

Owing to the potential need to preserve the scene and keep human traffic away from a possibly distressing sight, I also attended the location. I recall parking the van with the blue lights flashing about fifty metres shy of the bridge and walking up the path towards my colleague. There he stood with his high visibility jacket on and a rather sombre look on his face.

I looked over the edge of the bridge and several metres below I could see bits of body. Unidentifiable. Mushy. Spread out across the tracks. Maybe a finger here. Looks like a stomach there. A pulpy mass. I say this not to sound gory or gratuitous. It's how it was. A life ripped apart and scattered across the metal and the stones. Discarded like rubbish. My colleague then indicated a bit further up the tracks, just underneath the bridge. I had to peer through the railings to see it properly.

A man's head. Severed at the neck. Lying on its side between the railway tracks. Brown hair and open mouth. Tattered and bloody. Surreal. Distant. Somehow fake. I looked at my colleague and neither of us said a word. After about two minutes of rather awkward and cumbersome silence, I think I mumbled something about getting some police tape and putting a cordon around one side of the bridge, so pedestrians wouldn't have to look at the ragged human flesh dispersed with an almost disdainful casualness across the grimy tracks. So they wouldn't have to witness this waste. This mess. So they wouldn't have to see ... him.

Whoever he was. His life a sad story to end like that. A suicide note and a fare-thee-well. That was my life, goodbye. I leave you to put what remains of me in a bag and take me away. Here's my driving licence. My watch. My bits and bobs. My receipts. I paid the price, and this is *my* receipt. It all ends now. I give up. Can't take any more of this shit.

No human deserves to be so completely destroyed, emotionally or physically. We weren't born to bow down in such desperation, or stand in the path of momentum and mass and energy so powerful it rips us and splits us and cuts us. To lay down our lives in such despair with no hope of help: no chance of redemption.

The real victims are those who, by circumstances beyond their control, fall foul to the terrors and tragedies of life; either by man, machine or nature's power.[45] They cannot help it. They cannot foresee it. They cannot resist it. They are truly aggrieved and truly hurt. Life is no playground. It never has been. No matter what they say.

Life is raw, restless and relentless. It cannot be quantified, measured or summed up. It refuses to comply with most requests

---

45 For all of those people swept mercilessly away by floods, landslides and earthquakes. This world can be a dangerous and destructive home. Yet we content ourselves with trivial crap, while millions of souls on distant shores have a truly woeful existence. We really do need some fucking context.

for it to behave and will never abandon its follies. It declines to yield. It will never stop doing what it does. It is a powerful and predominant thing.

Yet we must never forget what we're made of. We are but flesh and blood and bone. We've seen it crushed and broken. We've picked it off the floor. We've washed it from walls and cleaned it from roads. Removed it from wreckages. Bagged it from breakages. Scraped it from fields and dragged it from rivers. We've pulled it and pushed it and pummelled it. Picked it and poked it, and prised it and peeled it. We've all loved it, lost it and buried it. We all started the same, and we all end up the same.

No matter who we think we are, or why we think we're here, we cannot ever escape the fact that we all have this one thing in common: we are but mortal, fragile little humans all trying to make our way in this world, whether by force or by favour. We are like wild flowers that bloom, wither and fade away in unseen fields. We are terrible and we are tender. We are a paradox beyond all understanding. We scale the highest heights of benevolence, yet descend into the uttermost depths of depravity. We are makers and breakers. Menders and shakers. Lovers and haters. We are everything and we are nothing.

The police deal with this. All of this. It's our job. We deal with *life*, and its terrors and triumphs. And we swore an oath to protect and preserve it – to *prevent all offences against people.* We walk amongst the living and the dead, and all of those in between. We have no special powers or privileges that make us different to others. We're not superhuman, we just have to try our best. Sometimes we just have to pick up the pieces. Sometimes it really isn't our fault. We can't stop everyone from being hurt, no matter how hard we try.

Thus, into this arena of the unpredictable, the untameable, the unruly and unmanageable, we must try to decide what, if anything, is our best option. Our best choice of direction. Where do the police go from here? What is our place in this arena? This society. This nation of ours. This life. How do we police such raw and emotional existence?

Yet the Government has tried to sterilise us. Neuter us. Display us on a screen. Control us with plans and procedures whitewashed with spin and bribery. It's turned life into a sick comedic sketch. A parody. An illusion of betterment. A vision of social cohesion and cultural coherency, nourished by falsely promoted aspirations and specious dreams. Broken promises and tainted truths. We are all victims of this. *All* of us.

The police are running ragged. Life is getting the better of us. We are losing grip. Losing touch. Losing sense and direction. Floundering and flapping around, treating life like it's something tangible and certain. Like it follows rules and fits into neat compartments. A ticky box trinket. Twee, gaudy and sickly sweet. We've lost the grit. Lost the nerve. Lost the will to stand and fight with honour, decency and courage. We've sold ourselves cheap. We've sold ourselves out to the victim culture and turned our backs on those who truly need our help. It is time to put everything back into the context it so desperately deserves and face the momentous task of clearing our minds of this fogginess; this political correctness. Clearing our heads of this sickening, grovelling, scrabbling around to please and perform. It's time to leave this playground. It's time to grow up and get real.

19. Full Moon Shift

In this penultimate chapter, I hope to sum up a great deal of what I have written so far about policing within this victim culture. The final chapter will focus more on the victim culture itself and further examine political correctness, race and diversity issues and other pertinent topics. But for now, we will content ourselves with looking at one single day at work that truly represents pretty much everything about what it means being a frontline police officer in Britain at the moment.

As explained before, every police service is different. Therefore, various bits in my account will relate to localised policies and procedures. While these may differ to other police organisations, the bureaucracy and frustration is all the same. Everything about the following account is true. It is the story of one particular shift at work that sums up a great deal, as we will see.

I have decided to call it the 'Full Moon Shift' because it happened on a full moon. Clever that. You may have recently read articles about the full moon and how this could potentially affect the behaviour of certain people. I would perhaps agree with this if it were not for the fact that people don't generally need a celestial reason to behave like little shits, and what happened on the night was in no way extraordinary.

My shift was due to start at 4pm. It was a late shift on a Saturday. Finishing time was 3am the morning after. At 10pm the covering shift would start in parallel with ours, and officers from that shift would be out in the town centre dealing with the bars and clubs. My shift, however, would be dealing with the rest of the town, along with the other frontline staff who were also on duty, which included a few traffic cops, a couple of beat officers and the odd armed officer here and there. Add all the numbers together and you're talking about fifteen officers 'available' in vehicles in the town at any one time. Ten of those officers would be from shift, including myself. And it would be those shift officers who would deal with most of the calls and get blasted with the most bureaucracy and paperwork.

So I duly arrived at work at 3.27pm and walked into the office. Various colleagues from the morning shift were sitting at computers updating CRAPPIES or typing information into different systems. I could hear the background noise of the radio because a couple of my colleagues didn't have their earpieces in.

I made my way to a spare terminal and logged on. First things first: check the emails. Seeing as it was a Saturday I wasn't expecting too much grief because all the people who send you annoying messages don't generally work weekends. Therefore, Saturdays and Sundays are blissfully inbox-free and a chance to pretend that you're actually doing something right.

My feelings of comfort were short lived, however. There was one email from a 'crime reviewer' from another department. I'd love to be a crime reviewer. All you have to do all day is look at CRAPPIES and then send police officers emails about why they haven't done something trivial. I'm sure they do more than this, but I don't actually care. The point is, that there seems to be far more people sitting and staring at a computer screen than there are doing real policing, but that's obvious by now anyway. Sad thing is, that naff all is ever done about it, and it's getting worse.

Anyway, I opened the email with my usual sigh of annoyance and read through it. After shaking my head and shouting 'Fuck off!' at pretty much the top of my voice (remember: *Shift Morale Officer*) I stomped off to get my kit together. The email had been sent by a civilian who had checked through my list of outstanding investigations (I had twelve on the go at that point) requesting that I update CRAPPIES with certain information regarding a criminal damage to a car that I was dealing with. The email had been sent at the behest of a Detective Inspector, who himself had appeared to authorise it at the behest of a Chief Inspector. So it had pretty much come from the top. Must be important then.

The crime in question involved the discovery of a damaged car in a nearby estate. I'd awaited its recovery about a week previously after someone reported its presence near their garage. The car turned out to be registered to a chap in a neighbouring police service, but had not yet been reported as stolen. Obviously by the time I'd arranged to have the car removed, and before I'd even driven back to the police station, the whole thing was on CRAPPIES and the crime reviewers and investigation managers were already updating, ticking, checking and suggesting lines of enquiry.

Obviously as a trained police officer with a few years' service, it would be difficult for me to think of my own lines of enquiry and, therefore, I was very grateful to my colleagues for suggesting things such *as 'Obtain Witness Statement'* or *'Check CCTV'* in the relevant drop-down menu boxes. There was even one for *'Identify and Record Witnesses'* and, my favourite one of all time: *'Update CRAPPIES'*. Yes, we have to update a computer system as to the effect that we've updated it. We even have to update it as to the fact that we *haven't* updated it.[46] Remember PC Snipper *'backdating all the non-updates that he wouldn't have time to update in the first place'* from an earlier chapter? Well, we

---

46 You may be laughing at the ludicrousness of this. I'm currently crying!

jest about it, but it's all true. One day, in about thirty years time, I hope to be able to look back at this chapter and shake my head with a little wry smile; perhaps thinking just how insane it all really was. For at the moment, our sanity has but fucked off into planes of untold existence and no amount of rhetoric appears able to beckon it back.

Anyway, all of these lines of enquiry, and more, were entered onto CRAPPIES by other people and given a time limit for completion. Clearly, this case now took priority over my other eleven investigations that, in themselves, had dozens of other stupid lines of enquiry suggested by other people. Basically, these lines of enquiry are added to the investigation to make us look like we've done something. The Home Office would be cross if we weren't superficially thorough. So if we're dealing with a racist incident, for example, you can be sure that the lines of enquiry will be about as bizarre as a two-headed goat. It's a drop down menu frenzy. Recently PC Snipper, bless him, dealt with a racist incident where a female had been called a nasty name in a park by four hooded people who immediately ran away. She didn't see them properly; she didn't know them; she wasn't particularly upset, and she simply wanted to report it to the police to 'make us aware'. This was all clearly written into the investigation notes by PC Snipper, who was ready to 'file' this incident owing to its non-existent 'real' lines of enquiry.

However, regardless of these circumstances, PC Snipper found on CRAPPIES several unnecessary lines of enquiry suggested by people munching biscuits and ticking boxes in their quest to appear busy; and because of their desire to at least *look* like the 'crime' has been investigated properly. After all, we work for a virtual police service and it's all about public perception. So their proposals included *House to House* (in a park?); *Identify Suspects* (how?); *Obtain Witness Statement* (there were no witnesses); *Obtain Witness Statement From*

Victim (what is the evidential value of doing that?). *Obtain CCTV* (none anywhere near, of course); *Liaise With Other Department* (this would be the Race Crime Unit, who were already aware of the incident because they were the ones suggesting the lines of enquiry in the first place, but they still suggested that PC Snipper liaise with them anyway, just so that box could be ticked …). *Make Local Beat Officer Aware* (like he gives a fuck and has time to do anything about it anyway); and, of course, *Update CRAPPIES* (the least said the better). There were a few more as well, but it's just too painful to write. Now multiply all of those lines of enquiry by about a dozen, and you have an indication of what your average police officer faces when he sits down at a computer. We spend more time staring and swearing at CRAPPIES than we do out on the streets actually *doing* stuff. You may think that these lines of enquiry actually equated to action, but they didn't. They just meant that PC Snipper had to justify *inaction* because they were all pointless. If he was given a tiny bit of responsibility and discretion, it would save a whole load of time.

You see, we're not actually in charge of our own investigations anymore. It's up to people sitting in comfortable chairs to stare at CRAPPIES and tell us what to do. Anyway, I digress somewhat. So I'm sitting at a desk looking at my own damaged car crime report on the system. *'Obtain Witness Statement?'* Nah, that sounds silly. I would never have thought of that. What difference would it make even if I did get a bloody statement, anyway? *'Check CCTV?'* The fact that there is no local CCTV in the estate at all is irrelevant. Obviously, without someone telling me to check it, I would be incapable of considering such an investigative device. My local knowledge and skills are irrelevant, but I still have to pretend I've checked, just to make it all look nice and precious. It's all got to be done by the book. Tick those fucking boxes.

Anyway, with this particular damaged car incident, the person who had reported it to us remained anonymous. He refused to be involved in any way. Therefore, he went down on CRAPPIES as 'anonymous'. Thank goodness, this negated the requirement to obtain his ethnic details and date of birth. However, there was another name on CRAPPIES. This person had phoned us stating that he was looking after the car for a friend who was on holiday. However, he refused to give us a contact number and then refused to give us the name of his friend, who we assumed had to be the person mentioned on the DVLA system, and then hung up on us. I then looked at further updates and noticed that a random female had also called us, but wasn't able to make a report. She turned out to be someone's cousin, but her details were not entered into the system and nothing appeared to be matching up with anything else.

After sitting and staring at CRAPPIES for ages, trying to make head or tail of what had happened, where it had happened and who was actually involved, I was called to attend other jobs happening outside and, therefore, didn't have much time to do anything else. The fact is, that by the time the darn car was towed away and I'd found the time to actually log on to CRAPPIES, the whole thing was completely fucked up and I had several rather bizarre lines of enquiry to complete and only a few days to do them. The fact I had three days off coming up was also entirely by the by.

Yet here I am, looking at this email a week or so after last finding the time to think about this fucking damaged car, and the crime reviewer is asking on behalf of the Detective Inspector, who is asking on behalf of the Chief Inspector, for me to update CRAPPIES *as soon as possible* with the victim details. Ah, the victim. The poor fucking victim. The victim who either wasn't in the country or didn't exist, or simply didn't care. Trying to trace the owner of a car who hasn't updated their details with the DVLA is nigh on impossible. If someone has had their car stolen and it is properly registered, then it is fairly easy to obtain victim details. If, however, you have a witness who refuses to be identified, a friend of a friend who doesn't want to be contacted and a random female who happens to be someone's cousin – and who is far too busy to make a report – then you have some trouble with your investigation. I noticed that someone had utilised their brain cell and sent a letter to the address supplied by the DVLA, so it was clear that pretty much all lines of enquiry to trace this bloody car owner were covered. If I'd have been able to speak to the people involved myself, it may have been a different story in the first place, but I'm not allowed to conduct my own investigations half the time, but certainly get blamed when others bugger it up for me.

As you can see, it's taken me several paragraphs to explain what was entirely obvious to me concerning *my* 'investigation'.[47] In fact, it was so obvious it didn't really need explaining to anyone, especially some 'reviewer' who sits behind a desk all day. Unfortunately when you have a virtual police service, people tend to look at drop down menus and ticky boxes and then panic because certain parts aren't updated within a certain acceptable time scale. Certain parameters on CRAPPIES start to send warning messages and 'flash up' with reminders if those parameters are breached. Context and circumstances, however, as we have already seen, are completely meaningless and irrelevant. Of course, I'm not really moaning at the 'reviewers' here. Well, I am and I'm not. It's just a wee bit frustrating.

The time was now about 3.41pm, and even though I'd only had this one email, I was already rather riled. You may think that it's a bit pathetic to get annoyed by a single email,

---

47 I thought I'd go on about it for ages to give you a small indication of the quagmire we are in. All of that updating; all of those stupid lines of enquiry; all of those emails from important people and now, several paragraphs in a book. The context? A crappy damaged car. Now *that's* quality of service...

but please bear in mind that this sort of thing is *relentless.* It is never-ending. And it was a Saturday. My day off for fuck's sake! Come Monday and you can multiply that kind of email by ten. Sometimes more. You can also add another twenty emails about changed policies and altered procedures as well as information about how badly we're all performing, or some prisoner being released after serving seven weeks for a serious offence, and you begin to get the picture. It is utterly relentless, and for the most part, it is frustrating beyond compare. In this climate it is perfectly possible to get extremely ratty over one single request. That's because you have dozens of people making the requests and by 3.50pm, the few of you who actually police a busy town of nigh on 200,000 people, are sitting at the computers all reading similar emails and awaiting 4pm for the shift briefing. That briefing in itself will deal out several jobs and tasks, and if you're lucky, you won't be harassed by the controller to deal with other jobs and tasks until at least 4.12pm, but you will most likely be sent out to a priority incident at 3.55pm, anyway. You have your dozens of jobs on CRAPPIES, the jobs given to you in the briefing, the several dozens of jobs outstanding on the 'live' terminal, various emails requesting immediate action and a room filled with only ten officers. Some of whom are on the verge of breakdown. This isn't a joke. Of all the things I have written so far in this book, this is one of the most pressing issues. We have but a few cops on the streets but literally *dozens* of other officers and civilians sitting at desks telling them what to do in a 'virtual', policy-driven kind of way. It is an absolute fucking disgrace of the highest order and needs to be sorted out *now.*

Anyway, several of my colleagues already have a variety of appointments they have managed to arrange – a statement here, some CCTV seizing there. Then there's the others who desperately need to arrest an outstanding suspect or complete an urgent case file. In which case, there's really a maximum of about four or five officers who are truly 'available', but even those officers are putting aside loads of enquiries just to respond to the never ending flow of incidents. I don't really need to go into it all again. It's way too depressing.[48]

So that was just the start of the shift. Only eleven hours to go! After the briefing, myself and PC Fresh – my lucky crewmate for the night – spent about ten minutes each frantically updating / backdating / pre-dating / post-dating CRAPPIES and writing emails and other such admin, and then had to pop to B & Q to obtain some CCTV. On the way, we passed several cars that really looked like they needed to be stopped, or crushed, but we were far too busy to do anything proactive. Halfway to B & Q we were allocated a theft to deal with. An eighty-four year old lady had been conned out of £385 by someone purporting to work for a double glazing company. It was graded as 'Urgent' (and quite rightfully so) but we requested we quickly seized our CCTV and then make our way there.

4.48pm and the CCTV wasn't going to be ready until Wednesday. We weren't working Wednesday. The CCTV was regarding two persistent juvenile offenders caught shoplifting. That's another long story, but it was being dealt with by PC Fresh so thank goodness I don't have to go into that one. 4.58pm and we arrived at the old lady's house.

Bless her little cotton socks she was a *real* victim. A slightly senile victim, but nevertheless a real one. She didn't stop talking for an hour-and-a-half. PC Fresh was trying valiantly to steer her away from her extremely confusing stories about life in the 40s, and did his best to elicit information about the scumbag who knocked on her door and said he'd mend her porch. After conning her out of the best part of £400 he drove off, never to be seen

---

48 Oh, and don't forget the cell watches, scene watches, bed watches and 'let's just watch something for the fucking sake of it' watches, which eat up a lot of time, resources and morale.

again. After ninety minutes I had something resembling a witness statement and asked that the little old lady sign it in about nine places in case one signature wasn't quite enough and then we got cornered by another long, rambling tale about some Inspector somewhere on the Isle of Wight and other details about life in early part of last century which would have been far more interesting if the female wasn't a wee bit crazy. It was like listening to the verbal equivalent of a Jackson Pollock painting.

You can't tell an old lady to be quiet though. She was lonely and wanted someone to talk to, but as we listened with one ear to her tales, our other ears could hear the controller reminding the Sergeant of the several outstanding jobs and various important Logs among them that needed extra special attention. PC Fresh and I managed to back out of the door with our paperwork and say goodbye to the little old lady who would never see her money again and would never have the satisfaction of knowing that the person who conned her paid the price for his sins. No, she went on CRAPPIES as standard, and I knew that as soon as I had the time I would be filing the job.

PC Fresh and I then knocked on a few doors to see if anyone had seen or heard anything suspicious, but unfortunately not. Our last line of enquiry was therefore pretty much completed, except for the suggestion of checking CCTV by someone sitting at a desk several miles away. Thanks for that you git. Do you not think I would have checked it if there were cameras around the place?

It was now about 6.35pm and the evening was hotting up. Actually, it was pissing down with rain and we made our way back to the station very briefly to have a 'comfort break'. That means a wee (yes, we managed to have a wee!) and a quick ten minutes on CRAPPIES, because withdrawal symptoms are quite acute after two hours. Ah, that's better.

As it neared 7pm (please allow for the time it takes to actually drive between places in a sprawling town) PC Fresh and I popped down to one of our other local stations to collect some paperwork before being sent to a miscellaneous incident fairly nearby. It appeared that a little old lady had called us stating that some youths were kicking a ball against her window. She'd then asked them to stop but they had all laughed at her. It looked like we were going to be the Blue Rinse car for the evening, so PC Fresh and I drove through the sodden streets to where the incident was occurring.

Two elderly sisters with exactly one hundred and seventy years on earth between them were sitting in their lounge. Across the way was a small recreational area where a group of five to six youths were playing cricket and football. Unfortunately, these youths often kicked their football deliberately against people's houses and laughed inconsiderately when asked not to. The old ladies were very sweet but were concerned that the police 'don't do anything about it'. Nothing is ever done about it. No one ever takes any notice. I could only but agree with these poor little old ladies. Policing this victim culture in all of its glory is pretty darn impossible so I told her that we'd do our best and have a word and inform the council and blah blah blah. What else could we do? I guess I could have gone outside and extended my metal stick and beaten the shit out of the little fuckers but that may have got me into trouble. Could have given them a quick squirt in the eyes with my nasty spray but that also might land me in a world of shit.

Instead PC Fresh and I trudged over to the smirking group and told them off. That is to say we gave them advice not to kick a ball near other people's windows. Some of them nodded and solemnly agreed. Others smiled. I thought of my own little old nan and decided that if PC Fresh and I teamed up we could probably massacre all of them without one single scrote getting away and calling for help. So you terrorise a little old lady and then smile at a police officer who is trying his best to tell you that this isn't acceptable? I think people, especially certain youths, are just *great.* They are the *future.*

7.48pm and we were wet. A trudge back to the car and a short drive in a random direction until we decided we may want to eat something before we didn't have time later. After a quick drive to the nearest suitable establishment we saw that the queue was backing out the door so we cancelled our intention to have some form of sustenance for the next four hours and were allocated a job to deal with just around the corner.

This is where the night really began to get fruity. By this time, myself and PC Fresh were about the only available car driving around the town. Other colleagues were tied up with statements, arrests, or trying to find an interpreter to deal with someone. Arrest a person for a domestic common assault who doesn't speak English and who wants a solicitor and you are talking an absolute minimum of about five hours from time of arrest to time of release, if released at all. One of my colleagues had that lucky, lucky job so you can count her and her crewmate out for most of the night. So that's eight of us left. I mean, that's two of us left. Everyone else is doing something else. No one to respond to any priority incidents once PC Fresh and I were allocated our next task.

Female reporting her partner had smashed up her house and punched her. She's at a nearby kebab place making the phone call as her mobile is broken. Amazingly, we were only just around the corner and managed to locate said female in less than a minute. What incredible service. I recognised her almost straight away. What a surprise. For the past few weeks her relationship with her boyfriend had been getting steadily worse. Apparently he was beating her up more and more and today he'd lost the plot again. It was only last week when he was kicking her on the floor in some random street in town at about 7.30am. He was eventually arrested for it, but she didn't support police action.

This time, however, she was determined to *press charges.* Determined to go all the way and go to court. That was it. Finished. Done. Caput. End of the relationship. She was settled in a new house and had a decent job. Didn't need him in her life anymore. Didn't need the aggro. He was an alcoholic, drug taking little shit. She was far better than that and a poor, poor victim.

8.22pm and we go back to her house with her. Kitchen door off its hinges. Big hole in the bedroom door. Wardrobe broken. She's got a big bruise on her left cheekbone. She is a domestic victim. The fact she is also a suicidal, self-harming emotionally fucked up female with psychotic tendencies is irrelevant. She is a victim. I genuinely believed her when she said she wanted to get it all sorted out and I was determined to assist. This isn't sarcasm by the way. I really did want to help her. For the next three hours, myself and PC Fresh built up a good rapport with her. We took her back to the station and filled out all the necessary paperwork. Well, PC Fresh took the seven page statement and completed the Risk Assessment Form and I did all the background stuff including creating a CRAPPIES report, writing my own statement, printing off the Log and creating a special warning marker on her address in case her 'boyfriend' was to turn up again and cause more hassle. It was a lot of work and it was all done very expeditiously, but it still took a long time. On Monday I planned to inform our Domestic Violence Unit that a panic alarm would be appropriate for her house too, and that we really could get this girl back on track.

Apart from the obvious emotional difficulties, our victim was quite normal and chatty and seemed extremely genuine. Irrespective of this fact, we would have treated her exactly the same anyway, but every now and again you feel that you can actually make a difference. Truth and lies aside, there is something satisfying about helping a real victim, or assisting a not quite so innocent person get themselves sorted. Our victim was definitely a not quite so innocent person but was real enough to warrant the best the police can give. We knew that she'd been in trouble with the police on a number of occasions and probably gave as good as she got, but that's not the point. Apparently.

So after doing all the necessaries, we dropped her back home at about 10.55pm. This was her decision, by the way. It was also ratified by the Sergeant. The house was considered 'safe' and we all felt it was appropriate for her to go back home. However, it was what she wanted anyway and she couldn't be persuaded otherwise. Her boyfriend was nowhere to be seen, of course. He'd left the scene very shortly after hitting her and kicking the doors in. Other officers had already checked his home address and the car he was believed to have been driving was passed over the airwaves for general observation.

PC Fresh and I installed our victim back at home and checked the whole house. It was a shared house with one other person living there, but he was at a wedding. We'll get to him later. Other than that she was alone, but safe and happy, and locked herself inside. The front door was double locked and her bedroom overlooked the main road with a large porch roof beneath it. Owing to this, we advised that she keep her windows closed in case the delightful boyfriend should try some roof climbing antics.

Back at the station, we quickly completed the final instalment of our master plan, which was a typed page of circumstances and a lengthy updated Log in order to pass the paperwork to the night shift to try and arrest Mr Boyfriend during the night or in the morning. No stone was left unturned. We literally did all we could bar taking the female back to our own houses, or finding her some skanky anonymous hostel to stay in. More often than not, these hostels provide little refuge for victims especially when they want to be found, but that's another story.

It's now about 11.30pm – and nearly four hours since we started dealing with this particular domestic – so myself and

PC Fresh manage to grab a quick bite to eat and then drive to our victim's address to make sure she was all in order. We wolf down our food and after five minutes a car pulled up outside. A chap in a suit staggers to the front door. He's the other tenant and manages to get himself into the house with the assistance of our victim who is still up and about. We drive past and wave and ask if everything is OK. She says 'Yes.'

Excellent, time to drive on. We've had a five minute break in seven-and-a-half hours of work, so that isn't too bad so far. It's often much worse than that. Meanwhile, the town centre is beginning to liven up slightly. CCTV spots a variety of males fighting and they are soon squashed by the officers on foot. Some arrests are made and things are kept on an even keel. The night is young though.

PC Fresh and I quickly popped back to the station for a comfort break. That is to say we didn't really have a break. We don't take breaks at the station. What we do is have a quick piss and then sit at the computer working, even if we're eating. There are no real breaks if you are a shift officer. I see PC Latvia in a corner. He's looking harangued and holding a printed Log. He says something like, 'This job is just fucking grief. You would not believe the fucking, fucking grief of this job, for fucks sake.' Ah, a man after my own heart. Having fun PC Latvia? No, PC Pinkstone, this job is fucking grief. I think I may have gathered that. He then tried to explain the circumstances to me, but I confess I hardly listened. PC Latvia looks like a hobbit, and apart from being an absolute top bloke, he sounds quite negative far too often and as Shift Morale Officer, I can't be doing with stuff that brings the team down. Good gracious me. So I counter his negativity by shaking my head and saying something like, 'It's all just fucking stupid, for fucks sake ... I don't know why we fucking bother.' PC Fresh laughs. I feel sorry for him because he's new and he's crewed with me.

It's now gone midnight and PC Fresh and I regain our motivation after being so depressed by PC Latvia, and subsequently make our way to Mr Boyfriend's house to see if he is there. He's not. We then stop a dodgy looking car, which is the first car I'd pulled over in three months. The driver is fine. I do the naughty thing and don't give him any paperwork. That's because he hasn't done anything wrong and hasn't really got anything to account for, even though we ask him the kinds of questions that mean we're requiring him to account for something or the other. He really should have got a 'Stop and Account Form'. However, at the time we were between forms. The old forms were being replaced by new ones, obviously, but we had not yet received training on how to fill the new ones in. Now you would have thought that it would be fairly easy for a police officer to fill in a form, but then again you haven't seen the new ones. I'd glanced at them in the station a few days earlier because the transition between old and new didn't coincide with training, or any other form of sense, and there were some forms available for inspection on the shelf.

I had never seen anything more fucking stupid in my life. Not only is 'Stop and Account' a completely pointless and bureaucratic pile of shit, but the forms were quite simply mind-boggling. PC Latvia, bless him, had actually tried to fill one out a few days before whilst on the street (and *before* his training session) and actually gave up after twenty minutes. This wasn't because he's a hobbit and was preoccupied with destroying an item of jewellery, but because the forms are unbelievable. Owing to the Government's infatuation with recording and ticky box ticking, the new forms are beyond a joke. There's nothing quite like ensuring people don't become victims of mistreatment by the police on the streets. Know your rights!

After chatting to the chap for a minute or two, PC Fresh and I then decided to do a drive-by of our victim's house. The bedroom light is on and the windows are open. We see our victim wandering around. She's fully dressed. She's been back for well over an hour and assured us she was going straight to bed, but this clearly wasn't the case. Still, at least she's safe and well and at home.

Meanwhile, the rest of the team are truly dealing with grief. For some inordinate reason, PC Fresh and I have managed to keep ourselves out of too much trouble. Yes, we've been busy. Yes, we've had about ten minutes of actual break time in nearly nine hours of work, but that's OK. You see, by the time it reaches midnight, all the outstanding live jobs often get deferred until the morning (unless they are domestics). That's because most of them either really don't need police attention, or aren't quite as urgent as made out. Yet they all have to be attended. Most of them have their relevant CRAPPIES numbers grinning away from the Logs to greet those weary officers commencing their tour of duty at 7am. Early shifts really are crap.

Anyway, it's now getting towards 1.15am and the night is truly beginning to hot up. The town centre is starting to bubble and there's a few fights and scraps and not a small amount of blood to clear up. A male bleeding from the head; three males running to a car park after a fight. Other updates from an earlier job involving a domestic where a sixteen-year-old had gone mad at home and smashed the place up. There's no respite. Some minutes before this, PC Glasses and PC Oscar had gone to a violent domestic a few miles away at the far end of town.

Even so, by now PC Fresh and I are considering the possibility of leaving on time.[49] We've still got a fair bit to do at the station with regards to updates and things like that, but should manage to fit it all in. Obviously we haven't even attempted to deal with our outstanding investigations – they don't take

---

49 After all, hope can keep a man alive. I've seen The Shawshank Redemption. My own tunnel leads to a country without political correctness and a police service dominated by common sense and gritty reality. I guess I'll be digging for a while …

precedence over the live jobs coming in every minute, so they'll have to wait.

As we contemplate things like sleep and rest, PC Oscar can be heard on the radio asking for a transit van. They've arrested a chap who's kicking off. Believe me when I say that the next *five* minutes of radio traffic is not what you want to hear about. What you want to hear is that this well resourced police service dispatched a van immediately for the assistance of its staff. For the assistance of its three or four officers bravely dealing with everything that is going on outside, while the rest of the team are incarcerated inside and submerged beneath procedures so cumbersome they make you snarl.

Suffice it to say, that we didn't have a van available. Well, we had a van, but it wasn't available. The other one was broken because it's shit. The other van was also defected because it's shit, and the other van was parked elsewhere with its keys hidden because some departments get very precious with their kit, which is not surprising because there's so little kit to go round it certainly is bloody precious.

I was already driving to the assistance of my colleagues when PC Fresh called up on the radio to say that we would assist. He couldn't get in on the radio for a while due to the frustrating transit van discussion. We were in a car, but my feelings were that, between the four of us, we could perhaps subdue this chap into behaving. After all, we would have two cars, four metal sticks, four nasty sprays and four pairs of handcuffs between us. Who needs a nice, safe van? That would be far too easy. Perhaps the Home Office would like to cut our budget even more?

PC Fresh and I arrived to find PC Glasses and PC Oscar in charge of a very pissed six foot moron who'd beaten his wife up and then decided to sit calmly on the front doorstep cradling an eight inch carving knife, while his partner sat cowering in the house begging for police assistance. She got police assistance and he got arrested. Bless him, he couldn't understand why he'd been detained. Fucking no-hoper.

We managed to get him to the station without too much trouble and eventually PC Fresh and I leave PC Glasses with his prisoner and set off towards our victim's house for a final check. On the way to the car, I walk past PC Peas. She's the one dealing with the non-English speaking domestic common assault with interpreter and solicitor. We exchange an unspoken glance. Words were irrelevant. I knew what she was going through, and I knew she wouldn't finish on time.

It's now about 2am and PC Fresh and I pass by the victim's house again. The lights are still on and we can see her standing in the bedroom. She appears to be alone and not in any way distressed. She looks like she's making her bed, or something. Do some people never sleep? We drive on and check the house of Mr Boyfriend. His car isn't there so we assume that he isn't there either. On the way back to the station we drive past the victim's house yet again. It's 2.15am and I see the silhouette of a male standing in the bedroom. It's not her housemate. It's *him*. I'd never met *him* before, but you don't need a degree in intelligence to guess that it was Mr Boyfriend and he had somehow managed to wheedle his way back into the house. (In truth, she had let him in and had intended to do so from the start ...)

Anyway, this was irrelevant at the time. So I parked the car outside and called up for assistance. Mr Boyfriend could be quite nasty by all accounts, and may very well need subduing. Perhaps he was beating his girlfriend up even as we pulled up outside – not a moment to lose! So PC Fresh and I get out of the car and walk towards the front door. Raised voices can be heard. Our victim is shouting, 'Get out! Just get out!' It all sounds a bit tense, so I request on the radio that officers get here sooner rather than later.

I knocked on the door loudly and shouted something I can't remember. Something like 'Police!' It's quite a good thing to shout when you don't really know what to say. I took a step back and heard PC Fresh say, 'He's coming down!' If only he did. I looked up above the large porch to the bedroom window. Framed behind the glass is our victim and Mr Boyfriend. She's crying and he's looking drunk and incapable. So he does the normal thing and climbs out of the window and stands eight feet above me on the porch with his arms out wide as if to say, 'What?' That kind of innocent stance that suggests nothing is amiss. That's right, nothing is amiss. He said something along the lines of, 'What, you going to arrest me again? You fucking cops take the piss.' In the background our victim is hysterical and banging on the window as hard as she can. I shout up at her to come downstairs and open the front door. It's double locked. She ignores me and continues screaming and banging the window. Mr Boyfriend, meanwhile, continues pacing around on the roof and ranting about how it's always his fault and he always gets arrested because of her and can't understand why he deserves to be so badly mistreated.

I know, let's walk around on a porch roof at 2.17am, having smashed up a bedroom and punched a woman – and having driven a car to get there in the first place when completely wankered and on crack – and then tell the police they are taking the piss. Do these people ever hear what they sound like? PC Fresh is shouting just as loudly as me to our victim, as well as yelling commands for Mr Boyfriend to keep away from the edge of the porch and just to be quiet. But it all goes even more pear-shaped when our victim shatters the five foot by four foot window with her bare hands and leans out through the broken glass screaming at her bloke. He walks towards her and she punches him twice around the face, smashing her hand through the remaining glass to do this. Blood spurts over his face and glass goes everywhere. He steps back and pleads with her not to do anything silly. At this point I'm shouting at pretty much the top of my voice for the victim to just come downstairs. She can hear me, but she doesn't care. She's thrusting her head out of a window with big bits of broken glass hanging from the frame above her neck. Has she never seen the film *Ghost?* Glass *kills.* She really was in danger.

PC Cheer arrived on the scene at this precise moment and then Mr Boyfriend did what any normal person would do under the circumstances. He ran across the porch at top speed and launched himself through the air like one of those tree jumping rodents you see on nature programs, ten feet above the ground, to land on the neighbour's porch. The gap must have been at least two metres, with a brick wall dividing the two porches. He would have hurt himself if he'd have fallen down. This would have been the fault of the police, by the way.

PC Fresh and PC Cheer run next door, but Mr Boyfriend is just japing around. He's having fun. After all, he's *innocent.* He stops mid track and says, 'It's OK boys, I'm only joking.' In the meantime, the victim isn't coming downstairs to open the front door – she's still screaming hysterically and leaning through the shattered window. Mr Boyfriend leaps back onto the porch and approaches her again, whereupon she turns even more apoplectic, if that were possible, and starts climbing through the frame. Not good.

Two pissed, crazy people on a roof having an argument is not a recipe for joy. It's not something you want to consider when you are responsible for the whole town, and anything that they do, or don't do, is your fault. At this point, things were getting quite serious. In that case, there was nothing else but to try and boot the front door in.

I run towards it and extend my right foot like they do in films. My heel connects with the frame with my fifteen stone weight behind it. I bounce off like a rubber ball. A quick glance up told me that it was getting even more serious on the porch, so I kicked the door again, while yelling, 'Open the fucking door!' I think I was yelling to myself. I kicked it twice more, but a double locked wooden front door is pretty solid, even when you are *really* trying to get through it by force. Fortunately, there were two glass panels in it and my hand was reaching for my metal stick to smash those in (more broken glass, why not?) when I decided on one more kick. I backed up about ten feet, steadied my nerves and concentrated all my energy into the bottom of my heel. With a roar of untamed passion I charged the door like an angry bull, my will bent on getting through it. Mid charge, I saw a human shape materialise behind the glass panels. It was a skinny bloke wearing a T-shirt and boxer shorts. He was clutching a mobile phone in one trembling hand and keys in the other. I lowered my foot and crashed into the door with all the gracefulness of a spider on roller-skates having a seizure – my shoulder impacting on the frame and my face squashing sideways against a glass panel, legs and arms akimbo. I almost expected to slide slowly down the door with a squeaking noise like they do in cartoons. With a muffled groan of pain, I whimpered, 'Door,' and prized myself away, shouting, 'Door!' again, but this time with a lot more authority.

The poor chap in the porch fortunately understood the need for brevity in the situation and started fumbling with some keys while I assisted by hammering on the glass and shouting, 'Door!' again. I'm sure it helped, because he managed to open the door in at least seventeen seconds and PC Fresh and I charged into the house and upstairs. By this time, the victim and Mr Boyfriend were both on the porch roof shrieking and I thought that it was time to join them. Why not create as much fucking noise and commotion as possible?

I arrived at the bedroom window to find my victim laying into her boyfriend with a bloodied hand and yelling in his face. I joined in with the yelling and leaned through the frame to try and grab her. My fingertips narrowly missed her arm and she continued her assault. I was just about to climb onto the roof myself when they both turned and faced me. Amazingly, and for reasons I cannot ever really fathom, Mr Boyfriend got a cigarette out of his pocket and tried to light it. He stumbled towards me and then tried to explain to me that the police don't understand and that it was all his fault, even though it wasn't. Miss Victim, meanwhile, is whacking the shit out of him and pissing blood everywhere from a deep cut to her hand. By now my temper was beginning to fray around the edges.

'Will you two shut the fuck up and get the fuck inside this fucking house before I fucking spray you both for fucks sake!' I had no intention of spraying either of them, of course. Can you imagine squirting a noxious gas into someone's eyes while they are standing on the edge of a porch and then watching them fall off? Try batting that one off in court.

So instead of getting my nasty spray out, I leaned through the window again and grabbed the victim. PC Fresh leaned through as well and took hold of her arm. She struggled violently but we kept hold, bits of glass from the frame digging into my leg. We managed to manhandle her inside the bedroom, but she is beside herself with rage and emotion. Blood squirts up my clothes and up my face from her hand as she swings wildly around and screams for us to get off her. In the midst of her shrieking, she says that we should leave her alone or she'll 'switch'.

I can't tell you how much I fucking *hate* that word. Ever heard someone boasting that they *switch?* Teenagers with ADHD like to 'switch'. It's their excuse to be little fuckers and be cool about it. It's their chance to ruin other people's lives because they can't help their behaviour. My fucking arse. I shout in the victim's face to calm down. She doesn't of course. She's *switching.* She continues struggling in the trashed room, next to a mattress covered in broken glass and pissing blood everywhere. 2.20am. We're not going home for a while …

* * *

3.15am, back at the 'office'. Both Mr Boyfriend and Miss Victim have been arrested. One of them is sitting in a cell moaning about it always being the fault of the bloke (and the police), while the other is screaming and banging on the cell door. She had to be carried in there. And when I say carried, I mean carried. Myself and PC Grin took the arms and PC Yellow took the legs. We dumped her on the blue wipe-clean mattress and removed several items from her that she could use to harm herself, such as her belt and earrings. She didn't stop screaming the whole time. She also didn't stop bleeding, but she'd refused to be seen by ambulance staff and refused to do pretty much anything else (probably due to her 'switching') so there was nothing for it but to lock her in the relative safety of a cell and leave her to calm down.

So there I am sitting in the office, covered in someone else's blood, sweating like a Derby winning horse and feeling pretty fucked. PC Peas is nearby with her head in her hands. Her predicament is somewhat worse, believe it or not. Elsewhere, PC Glasses and PC Oscar are typing and writing furiously. Not bad going since they've been working for nearly twelve hours straight. In the meantime, I've just started writing my statement which I know is going to take at least an hour and then I have to get all the paperwork together to hand over to the night shift who in turn will hand it all over to the early shift to deal with.

4.55am. Still typing. 5.12am. Yes, still typing. I left home fifteen hours ago and it's getting light outside. Very soon the early shift will be getting up and getting ready for work. 5.25am. Time to request overtime.

Local procedures differ on trying to claim overtime. I wouldn't say that my police service has the monopoly on an efficient and stress-free method, but I can't speak for every other police organisation. Perhaps others are just as fucking awful.

Current procedure dictated that you had to request overtime from the duty Inspector *before* incurring any. First you had to locate the Inspector and then you had to ask them. You could do it by phone, but that's rather difficult when you're rolling around in custody with a screeching female who's bleeding all over you.

So you know you're going to be late and you have to make contact with said Inspector and ask them, humbly, for about two hours in which to do three hours work. They allow you an hour-and-a-half for which you only get paid an hour anyway.

Fantastic. So I'm requesting overtime I have already incurred when I haven't even finished what I'm doing. I'm fucking exhausted, drenched in perspiration and plasma and need to send an email. You see, there's the *requesting* and the *confirming*. I've already fucked up on the requesting side of things, so I need to ensure that the confirming procedure is somewhat comprehensive. I just want to go home.

Instead, I minimise every computer system I'm working from and load up my emails. There's an Overtime Request Template on there somewhere. It's a table that you have to fill in and email off to the Inspector *before* you go off duty. It has several columns to fill in, most of which are meaningless overtime codes relating to what you've been doing. What have I been doing? I guess it comes under the broad category of 'Dealing with Prisoners', so I choose that one. What else? Ah, yes. The *circumstances* through which I incurred overtime. Well I'm still fucking here aren't I, you bunch of fuckwits, what more reason do you need? Do you think I'm claiming this for fun?

I only think this for a very brief moment, of course. I'd never get really angry with my employers. 5.32am. It's taken me seven minutes to load up my emails and get all the right codes in the right columns. Someone else interrupts me while I'm doing this and I lose my thread. 5.35am. Right, time to grovel.

'Dear Ma'am, apologies for not requesting this overtime

before I incurred it, but I was leaning through a broken window frame trying to stop a crazy female from falling off a porch and couldn't really get on the phone to you. After that, I was kneeling on her legs in a police cell trying to stop her from kicking PC Yellow in the bollocks and getting drenched in blood. Does this in any way mean I can get paid for my efforts even though I've not followed procedure? P.S. I didn't ask her to self-define, but I can do that now if you want?'

My email wasn't really quite as sarcastic as that, but it might as well have been. 5.39am. Think it's actually time to go home soon. I collate all the paperwork together (thanks to a large portion of rainforest) and hand it over to the night shift Sergeant. It's now someone else's problem, thank goodness. All the while I've been listening to the radio and the night shift had had plenty more fun with fighting males, big trouble kicking off in a nearby town, and a chap who'd decided to run through the streets with a large Samurai sword down his trousers. The sort of chap who would be surprised to find himself arrested.

Meanwhile, the other jobs were stacking up for the early shift to deal with. People ringing the police at 1am stating that they were receiving nuisance text messages from their ex-partner's cousin who lives in Australia. I wish I was joking. Why do they even bother creating Logs for this sort of thing? And why the hell do they have to involve CRAPPIES? Ah yes, something about a *standard*. I have a quick look at my particular Log before I leave. It's nineteen pages long by now, and the equivalent of about twenty hours work. By the time the lucky officer dealing with it in the morning finally boots Miss Victim and Mr Boyfriend both out of the door, it will have taken up at least thirty hours of police time. It also involved a smashed window, two smashed doors, a badly cut hand, a fat lip, a bloodied nose, a broken clock, a ruined mattress, a significant domestic cleaning bill for the poor landlord, a cleaning bill for the transit van that the female bled all over, a cleaning bill for the cell she bled all over and the hassle of several police officers having to clean most of their uniform.

Of course, after all of this the end result was super. Both Miss Victim and Mr Boyfriend suddenly decided to be normal human beings and they both lived happily ever after. Police time wasn't really wasted after all. We had some impact for the greater good and made a positive step in improving the corrupted mental state of the nation.

The sad thing about that shift was that it was completely normal. This was not the most exciting shift I could think of, and it was by no means extraordinary. Just a typical fucking day. I could have chosen a slightly busier one, believe it or not. I could have chosen Easter Sunday from two years ago when my shift dealt, amongst other things, with a murder, some serious public disorder, several extremely violent domestics and a whole host of incidents that warranted immediate police attention – let's just say that the wheels came off good and proper. The public disorder was significant enough to be classified as violent disorder bordering on riot, and the murder was only regarding a chap who'd had a screwdriver plunged so deep into the side of his head it penetrated his spinal column. I ended up nicking the chap who did it. He was extremely calm and was far less hassle to cope with than Miss Victim. This job is really quite bizarre sometimes.

This job is also more frustrating than anything else in the world. We're not really doing anything except keeping a lid on chaos. My sixteen hours on that one particular shift did not have any impact whatsoever. Now multiply that shift by tens of thousands, and you have an indication of daily policing in Britain nowadays. We're not even making a dent. Nothing is changing.

All we do is react when something happens and then spend hours and hours picking up the pieces. We also spend hours dealing with people when *nothing* has happened, because we're following procedure. I sometimes wonder what would happen if we did have a virtual police service with all officers just sitting behind desks. Perhaps that's the way forward, because at the moment we might as well not fucking bother going outside. In fact, we might as well not bother at all. And all the while the Government is banging on about 'quality of service'. 'Building bridges'. 'Strengthening community ties'. Promoting 'public reassurance'. It's just an illusion. Apparently the public would be dismayed if they knew the truth, so we all have to pretend.

The truth is, that when we're in the station we're not really doing anything substantial, and when we leave the station we're not really making any difference, and when we do actually manage to catch a bad person from doing something bad – they are just released. Maybe not straight away, but soon enough. It truly is fucking hopeless.

Quality of service my arse. All we do is fly a flag and try to maintain a fantasy. This cannot be stressed enough. We're not really *police.* We're like Standard Bearers. The Roman armies used to have Standard Bearers – soldiers whose remit was to enter the field of battle with the rest of the troops and simply hold the standard. They'd pick their way through the screaming, clashing, bleeding horror and wave a flag. If it was me, I'd at least want something else to protect me, or to fight with – something better than a pole with a rag on the end.

But that's the police in Britain. We walk, poorly equipped in every sense, through the melee that is this nation – picking our way among grim social disorder and cultural chaos, waving our little banners; our emblems of safety and security; somehow managing to have a visible yet indistinct presence. A role of nothingness. Here, look at me, I'm waving a flag while people are dying right next to me. Sorry Bob, I'll let your misses know you loved her. What the fuck *are* we doing?

The victim culture in its entirety is a nightmare of such immense proportions it cannot truly be summed up. We are living on the fringe of complete social meltdown and not even coming close to addressing the major issues. For the organisations that are trying to address the problems are beginning to disintegrate anyway, which leaves society to implode without any hope of redemption whatsoever. If we don't address the problems *now* it will be too late. If we don't start from the bottom up and repair the foundations, the whole thing will collapse around our ears.

It's all one big show. It's a façade. A fantasy. An imaginary sanctuary. A game. It's a Victorian playground. It's a victim culture. And this victim culture *is* Britain. And Britain, at present, is completely fucked.

20. The Victim Culture Part II

So, here we are at the final chapter. As you will see, it's pretty long. I feel I must also say at this point, that this book is clearly full of my opinions, and this chapter is no exception! Nevertheless, I hope I do some justice to how many of my friends and colleagues feel about things. How *you* feel about things.

We'll be summing up a lot of what I have written so far, and further examining the consequences and potential conclusions of the current behaviours, and the possible impact on the police and society in general. It's always good to try to round things off, so let's get going without any further ado.

***

In the first chapter, we looked at how Britain could have been described as a 'rage culture' in the early 90s, and how such a negative social climate needed some form of intervention. The Government certainly softened things up, including the police. Everything became very distilled and insipid and the nation began to revel in its new comfort zone. The minute things get a bit testy; the minute things don't go your way – ouch! Call the police. Call someone. Make a complaint. Know your rights!

Everyone seemed to become much more demanding and socially objectionable. We demanded more choice, more options. Sit back and relax and let everyone else come to you. They are there at your disposal. A kind of coffee shop mentality. No more hard chairs at plain tables. We want couches and mochaccinos; bagels and fancy flapjacks. Chrome plated wine bars: bright, glitzy and full of twenty-something clones in suits. It's fresh. It's trendy. It's modern. A new Millennium and a new direction. Moving on up. Reaching for the stars. We're not angry, we're just much more socially conscious than we used to be.

It may come as something of a shock to discover that the rage never really went away. It was merely dissipated and distributed. Covered up and smoothed over. A kind of 'there there – it's all going to be fine' mentality. The Government made everything better. It nannied us. Mothered us. Mollycoddled us. But the vehemence is still there under the surface; under the façade. It's bubbling away like ever before and could erupt at any time.

The fact that the country has become so weak, both socially and mentally, helps delay this eruption though. Political correctness helps stem the tide. The nastiness has been distilled somewhat by an all-pervasive niceness and fluffiness emanating from organisations such as the police. People are more aware of their rights (or what they believe to be their rights) and are much keener to exercise them. Britain is a service industry and everyone likes to be served, so the police serve the public in a way the public want and a delicate balance is maintained. Just so long as no one is nasty to anyone else. Keep the rage to a minimum. Get all the support and care you need. If it's not what you want, then complain. If someone treats you badly, complain. If the police can't sort out your affairs, complain. There will always be someone there to help you. All that anger can be shifted onto someone else. Your problems can belong to another. If you can't deal with your own existence – don't worry. There will be someone else who can take responsibility for you. Just sit back on your sofa and sip your frappe and we'll come to you. Please don't be accountable for your own life.

And if you're a criminal you can carry on committing crime. Don't worry too much about the consequences, because there aren't any. You're only accountable up to a certain point. You may end up in prison, but if you do, it won't be for very long and you can soon be out again doing what you like best – fucking other people's lives up. So even criminals can relax slightly. Even their rage can be dissipated by the lovely soft system. They don't have to concern themselves too much with their behaviour, because once they are in the hands of the system they get everything paid for and looked after. Their anger and nasty behaviour is continually dampened and smoothed over by a deferential justice process.

If criminals are constantly being arrested, released and arrested again, the Government can justify the police running around like blue-arsed flies trying to catch them. It creates for itself favourable crime figures. If you know the baddies are on the streets you can pretty much assume that crime *will* be committed, which is quite easy to measure, even if it's all crap.

An introduction of a 'standard' (NCRS) ensured that the Government could consistently measure and record crime on a national level. It could then manipulate the system, on a national level, to create for itself favourable figures. If those figures could simply not be tweaked, then it would hammer police organisations to reduce crime in certain areas. If the police were then truly able to do this, great. If not, the police would then massage the figures *themselves* in order to create the all-important illusion of crime reduction. In the end, it all boils down to statistics and the manipulation of results in order to promote Government favour. So any figures pertaining to crime reduction are based on what you've already measured, which in itself is a false indication anyway. Marry this to the fact that detections, as we have already seen, are an inherently false statistic, then you begin to get a picture of how erroneous the whole system is.[50] It is all completely and utterly false.

However, there is an even seedier side to all of this. You can't measure, in the first instance, how much crime has *not* been committed without comparing it to something else. So the Government needs to ensure that there is a certain level of crime itself. If that's the case, the police are bound to at least detect some of it. And if that crime is stuff like burglary, theft, robbery and criminal damage, then at least you don't have anybody being killed routinely as a result of it. Sure, it upsets people but it's not too drastic. They'll get over it. In which case the Government maintains a balance of locking up the most heinous of people, but allowing the mid-level criminals to walk the streets. They get arrested and detections are gained. Good job. Send them down. Let them go again. Arrest them, get more detections. Send them down. Release them again. The cycle continues. This kind of mentality leads the Home Secretary to write to judges and request that they don't send everyone to prison. Or is it because the prisons are full? There is something slightly worrying about full prisons. Perhaps it's the fact that even with full prisons, we still have a fucked up country. Perhaps there's not enough prisons. My feelings are that criminals don't spend long enough *in* prison after committing heinous crimes and, therefore, it's hardly a punishment for them. If they received decent sentences and actually got punished properly for their crimes, it might act as a deterrent for other people. Without fear of re-offending, you are always going to have full prisons. Without fear in the justice system, it's always going to be overcrowded. It's that carousel.

---

50 Therefore, if most of our detections come from trivial crap – as we have already examined – are the police actually having an impact at all? Are we truly dealing with real crime and making this country any better? There's a short answer to this, and it begins with 'N' and ends in 'O'.

It's a juggling act like no other, and the Government has to keep hundreds of balls in the air at any one time. You surely can't lock everybody up, so the Government doesn't. It wouldn't work anyway, allegedly. On a cost versus reward basis, it is better for the Government to allow criminals to commit crime – simply by letting them go, not actually encouraging them to do it – and then justify hundreds of jobs sorting out the economic, emotional and environmental damage caused by them in the first place. It's what governing and policing is all about. Serving the nation. Therefore, seeing as we are a nation of 'servers', we'd be pretty stuffed if we didn't have anyone to serve. Imagine a country where 90% of persistent criminals were locked up? Most of us would be out of a job. It would be economic chaos. So it would seem. Unfortunately, this hasn't really been put to the test. I propose that you don't need to lock everybody up anyway – you just need a system that scares the fuck out of criminals and hands out proper sentences when they do commit crime. Yet that suggestion is clearly far too severe, and tips the balance in favour of common sense and justice. It upsets the social symmetry.

So instead, the Home Office jugglers get to work and ensure that bureaucracy maintains the current equilibrium. Occasionally things get tweaked if stuff is getting a bit out of hand, which leads to amended police powers or new Acts of Parliament. Nevertheless, these new powers or Acts are never quite drastic or effective enough to tip the balance either way. They simply maintain the status quo. Terrorist threat? Introduce some terrorism legislation. There you go. Just enough to stop the pan from boiling over. Just enough to keep things on an even keel. Not so harsh as to create too much ill feeling, and just about effective enough to sound good on paper, but pretty insipid in practice. Swings and roundabouts. Maintaining a healthy balance.

Did I say healthy? What's healthy about the state of the nation at the moment? Are people happy? I'd say that a very deep and lasting rage has been brewing for quite a long time. A very significant feeling of discontent. The rage hasn't gone. The anger is being deflected, but it's still there. Britain has the second worst record of road rage in the world at present. In 2004-2005, there were 20,000 recorded instances of serious physical and verbal abuse in schools in Greater London alone.[51] I don't really need to ply you with statistics. The situation is obvious anyway. The country is in a serious social condition. Anti-social behaviour, patterns of domestic abuse, grim drink and drugs problems, social deprivation, poverty – there's malcontent, nastiness and anger in all areas of society, for many different reasons. Such rage is endemic. It's everywhere. We're not happy bunnies.

So why are we so pissed off? Could it be that Britain is in serious and terminal social decline? Perhaps we are rightfully annoyed at some things, but we are damned if we say anything at all for fear of getting into trouble. We must not rock the boat. We must be nice and kind and politically correct. Therefore, we give others short shrift over meaningless things. We are far more likely to lash out, because we are undervalued, underpaid and under the thumb and live in a culture that is weak, deferential and choked by the noxious fumes of political correctness. Furthermore, the weather is shit, the pay is crap, house prices are beyond a joke and undeserving little bastards bleed the system dry and get away with it. Anti-social behaviour is rife. The immigration system is awful, and everywhere people are demanding things that are not theirs to demand. There's so much crap happening everywhere, that we don't have any morale or motivation whatsoever. Discipline is a thing of the past and strong leadership has given way to fawning, grovelling delegation wherein it's everyone's remit to pass the buck. Everything lacks substance and clarity. No one makes any decisions. The police run ragged. Everyone runs ragged.

---

51 From a leaflet produced by Skills Development Service Ltd (SDS) www.skillsdevelopment.co.uk

The police, therefore, simply cannot cope, especially with the current obsession with recording and measuring. There's far too much to record! We really don't need to anyway. If it's about presenting the Government with information about what's going on in the country it should be completely obvious. All one has to do is walk down the street, read the news or talk to any informed person who lives and works here. The police are banging their heads against a wall. There's far too much going on and we are struggling to deal with it all. Struggling to make a dent. Not only unable to deal with effectively, but unable to deal with completely. We drive around between allegations of the lowest level social disorder and incompetence, which are in, themselves, indicative of an unrelenting social decline. Political correctness and fear of rocking the boat creates tension within all areas of the nation, and often prevents penetrating decisions being made to address the social decline and instability in the first place.

The Forces are reeling because of this state of affairs too, especially due to political correctness. Teaching used to be a good job, but now it's horrendous. Use your head, teach? No chance. Use your head and flee. Get out while you still can. And how on earth does the NHS manage to give the excellent service that it does? This isn't sarcasm. There's some awesome, hard working and dedicated people in this country, thank goodness. Still, it's no fun working for the NHS. Nobody said that life would be easy, but nobody said that they should be treated like shit, paid shit, and still expected to clean up shit without moaning about it.

Yes, dear Reader, the rage is still there. This victim culture has deflected it somewhat and tried to make it better, but in actual fact, it has fuelled an awesome fire of dissatisfaction and ill-feeling. At the end of the day, people need to be led. They need strong, firm leadership. They need sound decisions to be made and policies that protect them and care for them. They need a tough and decisive manner when it comes to crime and social incompetence, not this pathetic victim-based pandering. Over the past few years, the Government has not led this country with anything close to proficiency. Instead, it has created a climate of submission, of fear, of paranoia. It has taken away self-esteem and replaced it with self-obsession and self-satisfaction. Now people don't know what they want, but they despise what they have. We're jumping from queue to queue and not actually getting anywhere. This nation didn't stride with confidence into a new century – we followed everybody else in a kind of confused huddle.

In the midst of all of this social ineptitude, the police are constantly trying to maintain some kind of effective physical presence. We're trying to be liked. The Government wants to build bridges between the public and the police. Build and strengthen communities. Tell me, has the Government ever *been* to this country? Do they actually know what they govern and where they are? The gulf between those in their ivory towers and those who actually do anything of substance has become so large as to be almost indefinable. So much spin has created a completely disoriented nation. A nation with a deep and simmering rage.

* * *

This is where the shit really begins to hit the fan. This is where very loud warning bells should begin to sound, and the Government should take serious stock of what is happening. Owing to the current state of affairs, people begin to direct their anger in ways that are more insidious. Political parties that can only be described as dangerous get more support and credence. Parties who, on the face of it, claim they will make decisions and act in a firm, uncompromising manner, attract support and gain votes. For example, there certainly *is* a problem with the immigration system, but voting for such parties is *not* the way to sort this out. It would lead to chaos. We will discuss race and diversity again very shortly, but for the moment, the point is that people are pissed off and this is being expressed partly through the rise of unsavoury political influence.

People take a look around them and decide that their lives are being overshadowed by those who seem not to deserve the benefits of living in this country, and this creates an undercurrent of malcontent. They see people taking the piss in extraordinary ways. So they want something done about it. But what *can* be done about it? So it drives the rage even further underground and distributes it in various ways. Some of the rage emanates as verbal abuse; some realises itself in assaults, attacks and harassment. Sometimes, specific groups and gangs are formed. Certain political parties become more prominent. Other people, who are neither violent nor abusive, direct their feelings in other ways, such as voting for these unsavoury people. We mustn't think for one moment that followers of such parties are all tattooed skinheads. That would be as ill-informed as voting for them in the first place. No, there are some very clever, hard working, highly informed and well-to-do citizens who would vote in favour of them. Anger has to be directed somehow, and unfortunately, the Government has done – and is doing – such a crap job with this country that the anger is being demonstrated in a potentially disastrous way, from all corners of society.

Folks in Britain want the sovereignty, heritage and culture of the country to be maintained, but assume – wrongly – that it should be maintained by doing unpleasant things to specific groups of people. Sadly, the climate of political correctness and cringing submission has led to weak policies and ineffectual procedures. Then, when things go pear-shaped, we feel we cannot say anything for fear of being branded. A vicious circle. The Government has been trying, unsuccessfully, to keep a lid on this situation, and it is now getting to the stage where, soon enough, the cracks will become gaping crevices and the poo will really smack the fan.

Thus, the Government had anticipated various manifestations of rage and started to nanny us all. Put us in the perambulator and wheeled us back to the Victorian times. Buried their heads in the sand as to the real problems and pretended everything was fine. Fed us a diet of candyfloss and sponge cake. Sickly sweet and insubstantial. Nicey nice. Pink and fluffy. Gave us armchairs and human rights. Gave us a crutch. Treated us like victims. Turned the police into a gooey mass of syrupy sludge. Burdened them with deferential policies to try to make everyone happy. Now we're all just drowning in a bath of treacle.

To keep us on track and sufficiently covered in enough sticky gunge to ensure that we don't get ideas above our station and rock the boat too much, the Government measures our performance with threats of sanctions if we don't cut the mustard. By handing out numerous targets and performance related goals, the Government guarantees we spend most of our time scurrying around trying to meet them. It is irrelevant if the targets themselves spawn a plethora of unnecessary bureaucracies, or fly in the face of common sense, or criminalise people, or do anything else noxious – we just have to do as we are told.

So, the performance managers and number crunchers in the police keep a steady stream of information flowing to the Home Office. If the information is unfavourable, the Government frowns and the senior management panic. Heads start to roll. Chiefs quiver because their staff are not 'performing'. (Of course, they *are* performing – just not in the ridiculous ways the Government wants them to.) If the stats are down, they must be brought back up to satisfactory levels. Remember that context doesn't really come into it – so we all play the game and do our bit for the figures. In the end, it all has nothing to do with reality. It has nothing to do with true crime prevention. Nothing really to do with safe neighbourhoods or a just and tolerant society. Those are just words. It's just spin. It's all about creating an illusion of well-being and balance. The Government must remain in favour. It has to pull enough strings with exactly the right amount of force to make the puppet show look finely tuned and ready for the masses. A delusion. A fantasy. A playground game.

Unfortunately for the Government, this fantasy is showing serious and imminent signs of collapse. There is a tremendous amount of simmering discontent under the surface. Hopefully I have been general enough in some of my arguments to demonstrate that this dissatisfaction with the current state of affairs is not simply emanating from the police service. All organisations are, to a greater or lesser degree, affected by this political charade. Things simply cannot continue as they are, or the consequences will be socially, economically and politically disastrous. The fantasy has been created for many reasons, not least in an attempt to deflect attention away from issues that need serious addressing. Although maintained and perpetuated by numerous contemporary issues, the fantasy is simply in place to prevent social and cultural anarchy.

I have not mentioned any political parties by name so far in this book. I do not need to. Everyone knows who the current Government is. If that Government was to change, this book would still be valid. Proposals for policing being made on both major sides of the political fence reek of incompetence. Then there are the insidious parties waiting in the wings. We all know who they are, and we perhaps know the gist of their manifestos. If the main political parties in this country think that they would never be under threat from their smaller and less-than-savoury opponents, they need to think again. As mentioned earlier, a general feeling of malcontent will lead some people to voting away from the norm, and thus increasing the influence and prominence of the extreme right wing. Owing to an imbalanced state of affairs in this country, people will turn to drastic measures to redress the balance. These drastic measures, however, will be ultimately destructive.

Certain parties must *never, ever* be allowed to gain such prominence. It would lead to utter calamity.[52] The Government knows this. The Home Office isn't completely blind, but it might as well be. It is one of the many, many reasons why there is such a focus on diversity and racism. It has led to some of the most incredible preventative measures imaginable. It has, in part, led us right to where we are now. It has led to this victim culture. This fantasy. This Victorian playground.

* * *

To fully understand the current Governmental, social and organisational paranoia about all things diverse and race related, we need to take a brief but blunt look at history. To gain a fuller appreciation of the deferent and sycophantic nature of modern politics and organisational behaviour, and to help understand why this victim culture has been created, especially of late, we need to delve somewhat into the past.

Surely, no one can deny that throughout history, through the rise and fall of civilisations, both ancient and modern, that mankind has come across as anything but greedy, self-serving, aggressive, religiously twisted and socially ill-at-ease with anyone different. Anything but nice. When can we truly say that different nations have lived together in peace and harmony? When can we even begin to suggest that peoples of differing races have come together on a national scale and co-existed in a spirit of like-mindedness and cohesion? At the most basic and instinctive level, peoples stick together. They stick with what they know. They blend with those who are the same as them. It is the safest option. Not necessarily the right option, but the safe option.

---

52 We're in a pretty bad situation at present but nothing compared to what it would be like if certain people were in charge. Have we not learned anything from the past at all?

While there is a lot to be valued in difference, there is also a great deal that should not be valued. Quite simply, cultures clash. They clash for very good reasons, sometimes. It would be foolish of anyone to suggest that every culture is civilised, forward thinking and embracing of everyone else. This is unheard of, both historically and contemporarily. Cultures are inherently protective of what they perceive to be their own identity. They will fight to defend their beliefs, practices and historical legacies. Therefore, any mixing of cultures will undoubtedly lead to a greater sense of protectiveness, because with the diffusion of races in any one place you have a distinct distillation of cultural identity.

People then desperately try to maintain their perceived identity and this creates barriers of misunderstanding, mistrust and, quite often, anger. A difficult line is then drawn. If you have one culture that lives within the confines of another culture, how much freedom should they have with regards to their own identity? This is the crux of the matter, and one that really cannot be satisfactorily answered. It is one of the main reasons of current social unrest, and not just in Britain.

Certain countries draw the line very distinctly, however. For example, Kuwait's identity seemed to be quite clearly demarcated, and within its borders were precise boundaries, expectations and limitations on the behaviour of different cultures. It worked rather well, even though it was quite harsh. I wouldn't say Kuwait had the monopoly on democracy, but at least the boundaries were noticeable. In Britain, however, owing to the now quite obvious multicultural society that abounds, the line is blurred and indistinct. Different cultures have differing amounts of influence and expectations, which are often extremely disproportionate; wherein certain behaviours sometimes clash jarringly with perceived notions of Britishness. In very recent times, for example, there has been a greater focus on the Muslim community, especially due to world events and, tragically, events on British soil in July 2005.

Clearly the turbulence of modern day events, which are, in themselves, a reflection of what has always been – there is nothing new under the sun – has inspired a great deal of suspicion, angst and ill-feeling with many members of society. This simmering discontent emanates in various ways and creates numerous problems for the Government that has to try to keep a lid on it all. Britain has always been a nation that has evolved through the influx of peoples from elsewhere. However, in recent times, within the last forty to fifty years, there has obviously been a greater influx of various races making their home on British soil. From the 50s to the 90s, and beyond, you can clearly note a high percentage of certain races either travelling to the country, or spreading within the country. With certain cultures we are now at the second, third and even fourth generation of post-war immigrants.

This in itself creates problems, especially within some of our Asian communities. Often the new generation is at odds with their parents or grandparents due to, quite simply, a clash of cultural behaviour. This is a problem that has been highlighted to me by many of my Asian colleagues, or people I meet. Therefore, I am totally justified in saying that Britain truly does have an identity of its own. It *should* have. Our identity is what creates this clashing in the first place, and I believe it to be a good thing. Good in the sense that we still do have some identity left, albeit sidelined in favour of feckless grovelling. Sadly, the Government would prefer to distil our identity in order to try to make everyone happy, but this is simply not going to happen. It cannot happen. History teaches us that it will not. The historical behaviour of civilisations implies that people will hold on to their identity, often savagely.

The less the Government maintains a grip on the legacy of this country – its history and its cultural ideology – the more people will feel undervalued and without identity. This creates self-absorption and a general lack of respect and dignity. People start to question the whys and wherefores of other cultures, and make demands as to why other races should seem to be given credence above their own. Many people now feel that it has become almost a crime to be British. A crime to fly the flag. The solution to this problem balances on the edge of a knife, which we will examine later.

To appreciate further this delicate situation, we need to delve slightly into my past, if you can forgive me, and join me ten or so years ago in a university lecture. The context of this is a diversity lecture during my teacher training regarding the fact we would be teaching a very diverse cultural mix during our school placements. The lecturer asked the auditorium a very simple question. Perhaps you would like to have a go at answering it yourself: 'What ethnic or cultural group makes up the largest percentage of immigrants in the UK?' We all sat there for a minute or two and then suggested our answers. Suffice to say, no one got it right. Most people proposed that the answer was 'Asian' or 'black African or Caribbean'.

The answer surprised me for a number of reasons, which soon became clear. The largest percentage of immigrants in Britain comes from Ireland. It's the *Irish*. The lecturer then said something I have never forgotten: 'The reason why we don't think it's the Irish is because we can't see them.' This was an extraordinary and powerful thing to say. Entirely true, of course. The consequences are particularly interesting. For I feel we are far more likely to focus on not only visible differences, but distinct cultural differences too. Perhaps the Irish, being very close neighbours, seem to absorb within the culture with more ease than anyone else. Perhaps those who hail from far more detached cultures have a greater chance of 'standing out', not only because of their clear cultural difference, but because of their skin colour.

It's all rather basic, but then again, humans are pretty basic. We will stare at anyone who is different. We are immediately on the back foot if obvious difference presents itself in our cultural setting and appears to clash dramatically with its surroundings. It is because of this most basic of differences – the visible one – that has partly led the Government, I believe, to focussing on Asian and, by and large, black people. You very rarely hear anything about the 'Irish community'.

If you recall from the chapter on racism, there is a clear point of convergence when it comes to race issues – the Asian and black communities. Not only do these people comprise a goodly percentage of society, they are also clearly visibly demarcated. By and large, their skin colour denotes 'difference'. I wish it was not as basic as this, but as we will see further, it is a very important point. The Government is fully aware of this, and fully aware of the elementary nature of humanity, which owes itself to this somewhat lopsided racial focus. Skin colour, of course, is not the only reason, but it *is* a reason, and it is the most cardinal one.

For this reason alone, white supremacist groups, for example, are at the bottom of the evolutionary scale. They co-exist with other single cell and wholly unintelligent life forms. People who even begin to imply that skin colour alone denotes any form of superiority are worthy of the most singular disdain. History has taught us that races with a superiority complex can commit the most unbelievably horrific crimes against humanity. Any form of ethnic cleansing, in any country, and in any period of history is at its most elementary level an indication of the most basic human traits – fear of difference and warped confidence in one's own racial identity.

It also denotes that humans will naturally stick together in their own little groups, and sometimes lash out with impunity at anyone or anything that is different. It is the way of the world. It is the way of civilisations. It is the way of history. Sometimes this 'lashing out' is on a national level. Sometimes a local level. Sometimes an individual level. From the lowest level intended racist jibe through to ethnic cleansing on a national scale, we have clear demonstrations of this detrimental cultural behaviour all over the world, and throughout history. In Britain, we do not have national lashing out, but we do have plenty of individual lashing out. On certain occasions we have been witness to local lashing out, as was the case with the Brixton riots in 1981 and in very recent times, the 'Summer of Violence' – the riots in Bradford, Burnley and Oldham in 2001 (the main protagonists: white people, Asian people and black people). Racial unrest has always been with us. Cultural unease is always there. And to be quite frank, in Britain, it concerns whites, blacks and Asians. Groups and communities demarcated by colour and culture. Separated by the most basic of differences and, at times, separated by extreme cultural differences.[53]

Ironically though, often the unease and unrest isn't based on anything more sophisticated than the most elementary variances. People who throw Molotov cocktails at other cultural groups really haven't considered multicultural issues in a mature and civilised setting. These are people whose ideological beliefs and civic and national pride is wholly misplaced and skewed. The ignorance and suspicion of people will unfortunately perpetuate this issue for the rest of time. And against this backdrop of racial tension, certain political parties gain false prominence by latching on to such incongruous ideologies.

This is where any current Government steps in. Unfortunately, this is where the Government steps in rather badly! Instead of addressing the issues in a realistic and practical manner, e.g. by singling out individuals, groups or even, god forbid, *cultures,* it takes the attitude that we're *all* bastards and therefore need to be taught how to behave. This is where the nation needs to be

---

53 Of course, it's not just white, black and Asian fighting each other – there's plenty of in-fighting too. Black people fighting and killing black people, and groups of Asian males warring with themselves over religious and cultural backgrounds. Then there's the white people just fighting everybody.

educated and shown the right path. We're all racist and we all need to be brought up properly. Without the help of the Government, we're all going to kill each other. As mentioned earlier, the whole focus on race and diversity seems to presume that I'm a racist bastard. It presumes that you're a racist bastard. For it is far easier to tar us all with the same brush than single out those specific individuals or clans that promote racial unrest. Now in recent years and months – certainly within my lifetime, and of late within my professional life – we have this unique focus on race and diversity issues. Racial unrest was simmering in the very early 80s. By the mid 90s, it came to a head again. At the start of the new Millennium it erupted yet again and now, a few years later, the issue of race and diversity is here to stay. It is central to Government policy and police behaviour.

Why? To try to stop people in this country from tearing each other apart. It is nothing more than a preventative measure. Yet a preventative measure that *refuses* point blank to sufficiently address the reason why such tension may exist in the first place. Compounded by a victim-led and weak society, race and diversity issues have, unfortunately, become so out of proportion that they create more ill-feeling, paranoia and malcontent than they aim to solve. When things get out of hand, the Government appears not to address the problem. Rather, it chokes us with unworkable and extremely burdensome procedures and backs down from sorting the real predicaments out.

Shortly after the Brixton riots, we were given the Police and Criminal Evidence Act 1984 (PACE). This set a very new tone and dramatically altered the way things were in the police. After the murder of Stephen Lawrence, we had the subsequent inquiry and were all still racist, but this time *institutionally*. Clearly several years of PACE had not had the desired effect. We weren't nice enough. After the Summer of Violence and *The Secret Policeman*, it was really quite clear that the only way we were going to behave was to, quite literally, make race and diversity issues the only flavour going. And the best way to make us appreciate this flavour was to ram it down our throats. Chuck it at us from all angles and employing a variety of means, just in case we forgot what it was all about. Now it's just getting silly. Forget R&B, I think we should call it R&D and start singing about cultural issues. Oh, we already do. There's a band called The Six Strands, in case you were wondering. They play at police functions where everyone stands around drinking orange juice congratulating themselves on being so diverse. A far cry from the good old days of decent station piss-ups.

So, the Government decided that the only way to stop this country from turning into one big racially aggravated rumpus was to choke us all to death with the most single-minded focus on race and diversity you could possibly imagine. It was to permeate everything. It was to seep into every nook and cranny in every organisation, business and workplace. It was thrust with tremendous force at the police, because we were the worst. We were really, really bad. Herein was the assumption that without diversity training, the police would descend into even more heinous racist behaviour. That we would treat people's difference with impunity and discriminate without compunction. That we would jibe and poke fun and malign everyone who was different to us. That we would be bastards. Thank goodness for the training is all I can say! Otherwise, I'd have chalked up at least forty-three murders by now. In fact it's been several weeks since my last diversity input. The brainwashing is wearing off. Let me just reach for my array of barbaric weapons and take a trip into an ethnic community.

The Government feels that without this extraordinary focus on R&D, there will be widespread cultural anarchy. Rather than concentrate on the real issues of course, the Government would prefer to bury its head in the sand and pretend that all is well.

Rather than address the *serious* over population of Britain and the ever increasing migration levels, for example, it continues to perpetuate a climate of simply not saying anything about the problems at all. We have already seen that a hallmark of this victim culture is one of paranoia, and fear of putting one toe out of line. A walking on eggshells approach to life. The Government has created an environment where it is simply not possible to address pertinent topics because the very mentioning of them is heresy.

It is a self-fulfilling prophecy. A vicious circle. And the constant measuring, recording and data compiling leads to what? Important decisions being made to safeguard the welfare of the country? No, don't be ridiculous. It leads to more daft policies and burdensome procedures. More choking targets. Even more obsession with race issues. Even more deferential sidestepping. A political charade. There *is* a problem with certain cultural groups. There *is* a major population problem. There *is* an integration problem that will perhaps never go away. There *are* towns in Britain where the racial mix is so jarringly diverse and untamed that no amount of nicey-nice, all-inclusive, cohesive community focussed blah blah blah is going to make any difference whatsoever. With more and more people flooding into the country, and mainly filling up the south and south east, we are going to have tension anyway. There simply aren't enough resources to go round.

I am no mathematician (believe me, I'm crap at the subject) so I am perhaps not the best person to comment on economic financial issues. However, it is clear to me that with the current migration levels and subsequent billion or so pound employment black market, coupled with a significant hammering of the welfare state, the country must surely be losing money. Shelling out billions. Add this to the fact that a lot of tax-paying people living in Britain are now so pissed off that they are migrating themselves in quite notable numbers. We therefore have a situation that is quite unsettling. Can this country continue to support itself and safeguard the welfare of its citizens if things carry on as they are?

For this reason, I now believe that racial unrest is evolving. It is also being further affected by other events. For in very recent years we have seen in Britain a massive influx of central and eastern European people owing to the inclusion of various countries into the EU. In the town I try to police, the streets are jam packed with them. More and more flood in every day. Coaches disgorge dozens of them on a daily basis. In the past five or so years, there have been extraordinary migration levels to the country. It is not the remit of my book to present you with population statistics – a quick bit of research on the internet will present you with some quite frankly worrying information.

Britain would appear to be the land flowing with milk and honey. It would appear to be the land where you get a free house and benefits. (Did I mention the welfare state yet?) In recent months we have had peoples turn up from certain European countries, walk into the front offices of police stations and produce photographs of houses. They then point to the photograph and say, 'House, house'. They have been told to come to the country, and you'll get a free house. Ironically enough, they do. More often than not.[54]

Thus, racial tension in Britain now includes another significant cultural group – the central and eastern Europeans – lots of Polish and Romanians, as well as Lithuanians, Ukranians and Bulgarians to name a few. Ten years ago, this was not the case. Now it is a reality. But is there a problem according to the Government? Are we reaching crisis levels? No, of course not. And don't you dare say anything about the issue, or we'll brand you a racist. Don't you dare say anything about any other cultural

---

54 They also get benefits. More benefits, it turns out, than you can wag a twig at.

group either, or we'll suggest you're from one of those nasty racist parties. What we'll do instead is absolutely nothing. In fact, we *will* do something. We'll make some irrelevant changes. I fully expect the 16+1 system of ethnic self-classification to change. If you take a look back at the system, you will notice it has three main cultural groups: white, black and Asian. I'm sure it now needs to evolve slightly and include white or dark skinned European, perhaps even mentioning the specific country. In fact, I think this is a tremendous idea. It will help to eliminate any marginalisation of these cultures so that they don't feel too aggrieved. After all, we must focus on the victim!

So we'll just make some crappy, insignificant administrative alteration. It will help in the daily battle to fight crime and safeguard the cultural, historical and social identity of Britain and preserve its resources; protect its environment and economic sustainability. I mean it will help in the daily battle to compile data and provide the Government with statistics that will lead to *absolutely nothing being done about anything*. Nothing changes. Not even when things are collapsing around your ears and common sense tells you to flee. No, you will carry on doing exactly what we want you to do.

So, on a daily basis the police content themselves with scurrying around trying to maintain some form of all-inclusive presence in the community. Trying to be the bastion for equality, diversity and fairness. Trying to set the example and give everyone an impartial and consistent service. Treating each and every one of our special victims with the motherly tenderness the Government expects, irrespective of the context. Pissing against the wind. Spending thousands of pounds trying to sort out the melee that Britain has become, without anyone being allowed to even suggest there is a problem. Spending thousands on interpreters owing to the fact that a huge percentage of our most recent immigrants speak no English at all. In many cases, spending thousands dealing with, quite literally, the criminal underbelly of certain countries that have flooded, and are flooding, the streets of Britain. But dare we begin to suggest this? No, of course not. Dare we make any incisive decisions? Don't be daft. Dare we come up with any kind of solution? No, that's just racist. The answer isn't so much as blowing in the wind, but buried at the bottom of the proverbial sandpit along with the heads of Home Office ministers. A complete and utter fucking shambles.

* * *

Now I need to give a couple of examples of this shambles – this cultural melting pot. I'm not going to mention any specific culture or country here, because even *I'm* not that daft. Even though I wouldn't be referring to that country to malign it, I know that it would all get blown out of proportion. Suffice to say that we *must* recognise that certain people come to this country and behave in an abominable way *on purpose.* They take the *piss.* Some are also so ignorant of Britishness that they simply haven't a clue how to conduct their lives according to the laws and etiquette of the land.

Imagine if you will, receiving a call to deal with a female shoplifter. You make your way to the store where she is being detained by security and contemplate your options. Arrest? PND? Let her go? Clearly you're going to be thinking about things like arrest statistics and detections and other administrative shit, so your focus is completely skewed already. Bagged, tagged and sent on her way in two hours. Nice little caution. Quick turnaround. Do the business.

So you arrive at the store and walk into the office. You are greeted by a female you recognise as being from a certain country. You arrest her and take her to the police station. What you don't know, is that in the time it has taken for you to arrest her and bring her before the Sergeant, she has already wiped her hand in her private area and touched your arm. She's marked you with herself. Once in custody, she then breaks down in tears in front of the Sergeant and says that you've sexually assaulted her. Panic buttons! Victim! Tests are done and swabs are taken. Her vaginal juices are found on your arm. Explain that one away officer. Stand in the box and do your best.

This is a *true* situation. It is being conducted by a *specific* race. It has happened on a *number* of occasions. Not just some isolated incident. It is a deliberate and intended device. But dare we even bring this to anyone's attention? Dare we? However, it's not just vaginal juices and arm wipes. This same race of people also try out other stuff too. They shit and they piss in the office before you even get there. The women squirt breast milk at you. They carry knives. They beg and grovel and contaminate.

They arrive in numbers untold, and claim their benefits immediately. On the promise that they will *work*. They melt into the shadows and all but disappear, creating sub-communities and criminal gangs that exist in conspiratorial commune on the cusp of society. And what happens if a police officer tries to raise some of these issues out of work? He gets quoted in the paper by an undercover journalist. He gets investigated and referred to Professional Standards. He gets bollocked. He gets forcefully slapped for telling the truth. They say that prejudice is opinion based on little or no fact. But, what if our opinions are based on lots and lots of fact. What then? Do we dare say anything even when the facts are screaming at us?

I raise these points not to bring the issue of bodily fluid tricks to the fore. In many respects it's irrelevant. If it's not a wipe on the arm, it's some other nasty little ruse. Rather, I raise the points to give an example of the kind of cultural crap that happens, and it's recognised and observed, but we are not allowed to say anything about it. We have to skirt around the issue and not meet it head on with the necessary force. We have to wait until it's all gone completely tits up until a few weak and pathetic strategies are put in place to combat such awful behaviour. We're not allowed to say anything because it's *racist.* It's not politically correct enough to be so blunt about other cultures.

I heard a story recently where a Detective Inspector tried to mention in a meeting within the police station that a few members from a certain cultural group were persistently committing robberies. A certain group of males from a certain country were robbing people day in, day out. The Detective Inspector was told, in no uncertain terms, to *shut his mouth.* A kind of finger-in-your-ears and *la la la* approach to problem solving. The minute these issues are raised they are crushed. This weak and deferential culture lets no one speak out of turn. The Government will silence you if you dare say anything. It's all fiction anyway, apparently. There isn't really a problem. Shut your mouth and do your job.

As well as this kind of cultural behaviour that doesn't generally get reported to the press, many of us are most likely aware of some recent events in the news where the Government would appear not to have combated head on the despicable behaviour of certain cultural groups or individuals. It would seem that some people can wave placards in the middle of London saying 'British Police go to hell', or preach twisted messages of terrorism and anti-British sentiment, and simply get away with it. The sovereignty of this country is gradually being eroded by people who are taking the piss on a despicable level, and we're too weak, soft and pathetic to do anything about it. Whatever happened to maintaining the Queen's Peace? As far as I'm concerned, such deliberate and brazen attacks on the constitution do not fall under the category of 'free speech' in a democratic society, and should be treated as sedition. Unfortunately, all of us have to stand by and watch while the nation slides into rack and ruin at the hands of un-British, uncivilised and uncouth bastards.

So, in this environment of denial, and rejection of common sense, what is the role of the average shift officer? And are we allowed to have any form of opinion on the relevant issues at all? In many ways it would appear that we are not. Our role is a dispassionate one; an impartial one. A role that provides no inference on any topical subject. We are robots. Automatons. There is no room for feeling. No room to disagree with the state of affairs. Surely it is the remit of others to tell the Government where they are going desperately wrong?

I would further argue that the role of the average frontline police officer has become so de-skilled and lacking in professional impetus that we might as well abandon our uniforms and go and sit in our offices all day. The Government has already decided what is the best way of dealing with the problems of society, and that is to apply a rigid set of standards and procedures to arising incidents. What's the point of even talking to people if giving advice and reaching appropriate mutual solutions through sensible and professional discourse is no longer a valid means of police methodology? Why bother leaving the station? If it's already been decided even before attending a reported incident what has happened, how it's happened, and the method by which it will be dealt, what is the honest point of bothering to go outside?

Nevertheless, we are still given some half-baked concepts of promoting a safe and tolerant society, and pushed into creating these neighbourhood teams. Tell me, how is this possible: firstly without enough frontline staff, and secondly with staff who aren't allowed to use discretion, initiative or professionalism anyway? It's like chopping someone's arms and legs off and then demanding that they become a prize-winning basketball player. It's ludicrous. In the end, any encouraging results that we might obtain are achieved through haphazard and subjective means. A community initiative here. A popular PCSO there. A scheme.

A plan. A programme. A workshop aimed at youth. We target anti-social behaviour here and promote social responsibility there. It's all a bit disjointed and incoherent though. Our role is more concerned with recording and statistics than with anything truly substantial. So are we policing the nation? Nannying the nation? Enforcing the law? What on earth *are* we doing? As a shift officer – which is what the public most associate with 'the police' – I am at a loss as to the direction the Government is leading us, and bewildered as to the remit of my profession.

In order to appear on the ball, every now and again the Government pipes up with more disjointed plans – getting tough on crime and anti-social behaviour; giving police new powers to do this and do that; enhancing various terrorist legislation to combat the global threat. It's all completely reactive, and indicative of an administration that is clearly unable to foresee or anticipate social problems, and effectively unfit to tackle them when they arise. At present, therefore, the police operate under a subjective mishmash of cobbled together strategies, operations and knee jerk reactions to incidents, compounded by arse covering decisions and grovelling judgements. The victim culture keeps us firmly entrenched under a mountain of paperwork relating to trivial crap, and a politically correct environment prevents us from saying anything about anything anyway. I'd say we're pretty fucked. Pretty fucked indeed. Is there any hope?

* * *

Well, dear Reader, thank you for staying with me so far. If you've managed to reach this point of the book, you deserve some form of reward. I've therefore decided to treat you, in a short while, to some more input on race and diversity! However, this section is the final one on the subject and hopefully sufficient enough to leave you in a good place.

We have examined race and diversity issues from a variety of angles and considered some recent and relevant implications to the nation. We have seen how the deferent victim culture promotes lack of discourse and refusal to determine sensible solutions to current problems. We have noted that the situation is a delicate one and has created enough ill-feeling to contribute in a notable way to the undercurrents of discontent and rage that simmer away just beneath the surface.

Without mentioning specific political parties by name, we have also considered some implications of allowing far right politics to gain prominence in a society desperately struggling to make sense of its identity. We have looked at the role of the police in all of this and recognised that we are burdened by bureaucratic policies, and undermined by sycophantic strategies promoted by a weak and ineffectual Government. These serve to encourage an emotionally unstable and dependent society, and sideline those who truly do need effective police intervention.

We have also discovered that the police, and therefore many other similar professionals, have had their discretion gradually eroded away. This has been replaced by a focus on dealing with life by procedure and policy when clearly life itself is far too raw, emotional and unpredictable to be quantified as such. We have further examined how certain administrative procedures and performance related target setting has undermined the professionalism of the police service even more, creating a false image of justice and rectitude for real victims of crime. Thus, into this arena of shit, we need some kind of tangible lifeline to drag us out of the stinking quagmire. We need a basic focal point to start with, from which we can apply common sense and discretion in a nation gone mad. In which case, as it's a topic that's here to stay and certainly very, very relevant, let us consider for the last time in this book the issue of race and diversity in Britain.

* * *

The first statement I would like to make is one I truly believe in. It sounds a bit like Government spin and the sort of thing a politically correct police officer would say, but I believe that a multicultural society is entirely healthy, wonderful, exciting, challenging and essential. Diversity can be a fascinating, educational and worthy aspect of existence. It is what makes the human race the most fundamentally amazing and totally unexplainable thing in the entire universe. It can also make it the most frustrating, perplexing and distressing thing to try to appreciate.

As we have already seen, there are certain aspects of various cultures that are not so appealing. In other words, diversity *itself* is not necessarily, or inherently good. We discussed in the second chapter that the Government wants us to focus on difference for the sake of it, and I believe this is completely erroneous and ill informed. However, where you have difference that is valuable and promotes true and worthy human behaviours, then you have an excellent starting point. Clearly different cultures have very different ideas on what constitutes worthy human behaviour, so we have to start somewhere.

Any discourse on diversity then, should begin at a focal point. In this case, we begin with Britain. This is where we live and this should determine in no small way our emphasis. And because this is Britain, we should recognise that Britishness itself is a fluid and dynamic concept, affected by numerous influences and social ideologies. Your idea of Britishness will be different to mine. A British-born second generation Asian's idea of Britishness will differ greatly to that of a Polish person who has just stumbled wide-eyed into the country from a coach, clutching a suitcase and knowing very little English except, 'Me no speak English.'

This, in itself, is fascinating and exciting. It is also something to be valued and appreciated. For no one has any ownership on Britishness, whatever their cultural background. Britain does not belong to white people any more than it belongs to Asian or black people. It belongs to anyone who legitimately lives here and respects its laws, heritage, history and environment. Britishness is behaving in a manner that upholds the constitution of this country; appreciating where it has come from and what it implies. Britishness also means knowing that, while it is perfectly and worthily acceptable to practice one's own religion, the history of this country dictates that we have a Christian constitution. We have a ruling monarch who is 'head' of the Church and a wonderful ceremonial history dating back centuries. Unless such points are recognised and affirmed, we begin to lose our grasp on our own identity. For there are, I believe, certain aspects of Britishness that are immutable and unchangeable in this culture of shifting perspectives.

Unfortunately, there are some people who have ill-conceived and totally unacceptable notions of what Britishness is all about. There are people who would wish to change the constitution in favour of their own cultural background. People whose dogmas and behaviours fly in the face of traditional British sensibilities. This damaging conduct can emanate from people of any colour or culture. People who wish to promote precepts and consequences that are alien to the legal backbone of this country need to be suitably rebuffed. People who propagate acts of terrorism, or the introduction of certain religious laws that are incompatible with the constitution, a heinous breach of human rights and unquestionably un-British, need to be dealt with immediately and without political impotency. And anyone who promotes far right ideologies such as white supremacy, or anything else as shit, should be given very short shrift. This uneducated and totally ill-informed notion needs no attention save the following:

I once watched a party political broadcast presented by the leader of a particular far right wing party. Although the broadcast wasn't quite as blunt as their full manifesto, it made me frown to watch this chap standing by a Spitfire with a misty gaze in his eye, as if he was ruing the loss of Britishness in recent years since the War, and harping back to good old white British empirical rule. The implications were that in the past sixty years, certain colours of skin and specific cultures have 'ruined' the country, and the relevant people should be deported! Reading between the lines, it was quite clear that he wanted to get rid of 'Asians' and 'blacks' and put a complete block on any immigration whatsoever, as well as malign homosexuals and otherwise act in the manner expectant of the far right. This was the bottom line. No amount of spin from such parties, or from that particular leader, could really deflect from their underlying opinions.

Ignorant and unenlightened fool. By referring to World War II – owing to his inclusion of that great British symbol, the Spitfire – did he stop to think for one minute what actually happened during that War? Did he think the sacrifice of so many was solely a white British affair? Perhaps anyone of his ilk or political ideology would care to consider the facts. The fact, for example, that more than two million served in the Indian Army, making it the largest volunteer force in history. That their courage, gallantry and determination to defeat a common enemy earned them many, many awards for bravery, including thirty-one Victoria Crosses. The fact that 119,000 men from the African colonies fought in Burma. The fact that several hundred from the Caribbean also provided crucial civilian and military work.

The fact that Australia was the first of the Dominions to declare war on Germany, with more than half a million Australians serving abroad. The fact that over a million Canadians served in Europe, North Africa and Asia. The fact that one in nine of the entire population of New Zealand was in uniform.[55] Or are these last three countries acceptable because they provided predominantly white people ...?

Far right policies make me sick. Multiculturalism is a thing that should be recognised as something extremely precious. We are united not by what makes us different, but by what makes us the same. We have fought and bled and died together, in living memory; in comparatively recent times. White, black and Asian have united against a tyrant to preserve world peace and security; to safeguard the rights and freedoms of nations and stand up for justice, goodness and equity in an era plagued by vicious and depraved ideologies, at a time where the evil machine of war attacked with immeasurable barbarity the sanctity and security of free peoples.

The sacrifice of millions cannot *ever* be appreciated enough. Sadly, people forget the true cost of our freedom and treat with impunity those who gave their lives defending it. There is no one race that can lay claim to preserving this freedom. In Britain we owe a constant debt of gratitude to all of those who lost their lives in this worldwide conflict, and must pay respectful homage to those who, with incredible fortitude, survived to celebrate the glorious and boundless assuagement of victory.

The minute we place ourselves on a pedestal above any other race on the basis of some warped and twisted notion, or on the premise that our skin colour denotes superiority, we undo the bonds that bring us together and destroy the threads that unite us as common citizens in a dark and suspicious world. Such attitudes will only lead to more desperate and brutal pain.

Most humans want the same thing. We want to live in peace and security. We want to safeguard the rights, freedoms

---

55 The British Empire and the Commonwealth during the Second World War
   www.iwmcollections.co.uk

and ongoing legacy of our families by ensuring our children grow up in safe and appropriate environments. We want enough food and clean water to be healthy and be able to enjoy some luxuries and comforts. We want to be able to practice our beliefs without fear of political interference and enjoy unfettered freedom of thought, choice and action within the bounds of the law. We all want to be treated with dignity and respect, and not be crushed by evil dictatorships sustained by a love of power, greed and self-righteousness. We want to think that there is some small measure of hope left in a world that is often desperate, brutal, bewildering and full of so much anger.

It is, therefore, with a measure of humility and compassion that we must approach the issue of multiculturalism within Britain. It is recognition of our potential unity that should form the basis of any cultural dialogue and pave the way for an informed, sensible and honest examination of what is going on – what is good, what is not so good and what can be done about the situation. Honesty, above all, is paramount. Issues such as 'integration' are bandied around like they are easily measurable and attainable. In fact, integration is a misnomer. Also, is it realistic? Can people from dramatically different cultures truly integrate? I propose that in many respects, they can't, but they can certainly live side-by-side in mutual recognition of their differences, without any prejudices leading to criminal acts. Furthermore, if each culture paid full heed to the law and to the social expectations of living in Britain, then this would negate much of the tension anyway. Unfortunately, the police are unable to promote such law-abiding behaviour, and the Government has done little to safeguard such expectations, which leads to all sort of problems. Here is that vicious circle again, and Britain is spinning around within it.

For Britain is a rapidly changing society and the influences dictating its direction in the forthcoming years are numerous. In this climate of change and shifting vitality, people are clearly keen to maintain and preserve their heritage, history and cultural identity. There are many views, opinions and alternating alliances that make the issue somewhat intangible and particularly delicate, especially concerning current world events and the cultural make-up of the nation. However, preserving Britishness does *not* involve maligning particular cultural groups for the sake of it. Rather, it should involve safeguarding the welfare of the nation by at least recognising that certain aspects and behaviours of some cultures are extremely worrying, frustrating and entirely damaging to society. It must also involve clear and incisive decisions to be made regarding the current levels of people flooding into the country. This is not an issue about any specific race of people – it is a fiscal issue that bears huge relevance to protecting resources, maintaining a healthy environment and ensuring economic sustainability through the provision of suitable employment for established citizens and appropriate welfare for those who need extra assistance.

Unfortunately, the current level of migration is, in itself, quite damaging. Not only economically damaging, but also socially damaging. We are simply not equipped to deal with the amount of unfettered humanity pouring into the nation. Many such people soak away into the nooks and crannies of society, eating up resources and taking far more than they give. A welfare state hammered by an unrestrained and unrestricted 'welcome to Britain policy' that is intrinsically hazardous to the well-being of the country. In this climate, discontent is particularly rife, and malignant alliances are formed within certain groups. Ill-feeling emanates from all corners of society as people try to make sense of a rapidly changing social climate. We do not have the mental, emotional or physical capacity to adapt to such expeditious change. It leads to social unease and organisational stress – the police can't cope either!

Covering this shifting social milieu like a cloud of choking fumes, is the entirely detrimental aura of political correctness and a 'walking on eggshells' approach to dealing with issues. It would appear that the Government has allowed us to forfeit our identity as Britons in a desperate effort to please everybody. By acquiescing gracelessly to certain cultures and praising difference for the sake of it above worthy traits, the Government has poo-pooed the various hallmarks of cultural identity that certain British people hold dear. It has dismissed stalwart and worthy Britishness in favour of some mangled notion of tolerance and fairness.

Ironically enough, we have long been a tolerant nation: stoic, heroic, singularly difficult to impress and willing to pull together in the times of greatest need. We are not as uneducated as the Government implies. However, in recent times, owing to a plethora of influences, we have become weak, dependent and far too focussed on our pathetic little problems and ourselves. We have become self-absorbed and mentally unstable, wherein strength of character, chivalry and honourable resolve has given way to trivial and bitching social wretchedness. Inspiration and identity watered down to form some insipid and flavourless cultural soup. The police know this only too well – we deal with the worst of this situation every day. It would not take too much to allow us to claim back some of our identity – which in itself would be laying claim to common sense and discretion in a sycophantic environment devoid of reason.

For example, a few years ago in my police service, a chap decided to sew a Union Jack on his protective vest cover. Sadly, as you may appreciate, this meant he was a far right sympathiser, a neo-Nazi, a racist and an all-round bastard. Or did it? Of course it didn't. He wasn't anything of the sort. Nevertheless, perception, paranoia and grovelling are the order of the day when it comes to certain British things nowadays so he was hauled in front of one of the Chiefs and told, in no uncertain terms, to get rid of it. He was told that it was racist.

Since when is the Union Jack racist? It is little things like this, and a million more beside, that piss the British public off more than anything else. We do not ask for much, but what we do ask is for the opportunity and the encouragement to demonstrate our national pride in a way that will *not* be construed as racist or right wing! The Government has all but stripped us of our identity and maligns us if we try to express it. Of course, we all have different ideas as to what being British is all about, but so long as it is not evil or detrimental to anyone else, why can't we be proud of our heritage?

In these deferential days, you can walk down the street and see people from other cultures proudly demonstrating their own heritage – wearing symbols and other tokens of their ancestry, while your average British person is told off for wanting to sew the flag onto their clothes, or maligned for wearing something like a cross on their uniform. It's just plain madness. I'm not suggesting we need a revolution – we just need some common sense and discretion back. This Government has truly demonstrated the most insidious, pathetic and annoying behaviour you can imagine.

Therefore, one of my first proposals is that police officers across the country, and anyone else for that matter, should be allowed to sew a Union Jack on their uniform.[56] In fact, it should come as standard. Once that flag is in place, we then have a clear and unrestricted demonstration that we are not afraid to live in this country and that we are proud to be here. Once that flag is in place, it would then be entirely appropriate for people hailing from different cultures to attach symbols of their difference beside the flag, perhaps even their own flag. I would love to see the day when a police officer leaves the station with one or two flags sewn to his uniform. Imagine the dialogue this could inspire, especially

---

56 People should also be allowed to wear symbols of their faith, especially Christianity, without fear of being 'told off'.

if someone has two flags. Not only does this promote the fact that the person is proud to live and serve in Britain, but it would also mean, quite rightly, that they can maintain their own national pride. If I worked in another country as a police officer, I would proudly wear their own flag. I would then also wear a smaller, but no less distinct, Union Jack to pay homage to my heritage.

My second proposal is a little more brash, but I hope you can see where I am coming from. It is my final attack on political correctness in this book. It concerns a fundamental characteristic of humans, not least the British people. One of the most elementary human behaviours is to stick together and point out obvious differences in other people. The Brits are particularly good at that. We are extremely cutting and sarcastic when necessary. Our wit and wisdom has been developed by many influences through the centuries, and is really quite sophisticated. It is also quite basic. Our toilet humour is sufficient evidence of this. A well-timed fart is just as entertaining and enjoyable as an incisive political satire.

Because humans are the way they are, and because Brits are no exception to any rule, we will also always refer to certain characteristics of people when we are pissed off. As such, we will automatically allude to any peculiar or obvious characteristic, be it physical or cultural, when being disagreeable about someone. I don't need to give too many examples, but consider what would happen if a female of a rather hefty build was to cut you up on the motorway. If you were to scream abuse at her through your windscreen, you would undoubtedly make some reference to her size. This is basic human nature. It's not particularly nice or sophisticated, but to deny that we make such references would be stupid. We're all pretty obnoxious and unkind sometimes.

This kind of reference to characteristics leads some people to making allegedly racist comments. We all know certain words are unpleasant and we all know what those words are. I do not need to mention them. However, this is where we really need to slice through the gristle and get to the core of the matter.

Owing to the fact that we live in a politically correct and paranoid climate concerning all things racial and diverse, it is painfully obvious that making any reference to racial characteristics could land you in a world of shit. If I were to hurl abuse at an Asian person, for example, and call them a racist name, I would deserve some telling off, all things considered. However, what about the issue of racial remarks that do not fall under the remit of *intended* abuse? In the current political environment, anything that may be the teeniest bit racist is heresy. Racist jokes are forbidden, and any maligning of cultures though any form of sarcasm is now an extremely touchy subject. We are walking on eggshells around the issue of race.

A fallout of this is something I mentioned in an earlier chapter – that people are quite paranoid about saying certain words or phrases in case they come across as racist, especially as they don't mean to be. For example, people are sometimes scared to say the word 'black' in case it upsets someone. Furthermore, we continually update our language in order to be as deferential as possible, rejecting phrases like 'half-caste' in favour of 'mixed race'. In some cases, we then reject 'mixed race' in favour of 'mixed heritage'. It's all one big mess at the moment.

Thus, I would strongly argue that making race crime a crime of *perception* has contributed in some way to this overriding paranoia and politically correct horseplay. I struggle to comprehend how perception should override intention. It's entirely subjective and leads to completely erratic behaviour. If I call someone a racist name, or make some apparently derogatory comment about someone's culture in an attempt to harass or hurt them, this is clearly unacceptable. However, British humour and British team camaraderie has a long and glorious history of being nice and nasty at the same time. If I want to call my friend a fat bastard without meaning any nastiness at all, I believe I should reserve the right to do this. However, it clearly kind of flies in the face of this victim culture; this politically correct nightmare, this paranoid and subservient grovelling. This bogus 'niceness'.

If my friend, who is a fat bastard, does not mind me saying this and who I know would say something equally as obnoxious in return, does this mean there is a problem with this kind of behaviour? It is extremely British to be affectionately nasty to your friends and colleagues. I feel this is quite an important point, so I will repeat it. It is extremely British to be affectionately nasty to your friends and colleagues. It is something, ironically, that unites people rather than divides them. It builds character and strengthens bonds. It is what friends do. It is affection in a way that British people actually like to demonstrate. For we are not an overly exuberant or expressive nation. We are not like the Americans, for example. We are far more reserved, staid and laid back, but with a viciously and deliciously biting sense of humour beneath the surface.

It is, therefore, a travesty that the victim culture has decimated this aspect of Britishness. People are now so keen to get upset about anything, or so fearful of upsetting anyone, that we are actually driving wedges between ourselves. Teams and groups are being split apart because people cannot be realistic, caustic or honest with each other in the good old British way. People feel they cannot say anything. We have to be so bloody nice all the time. This is extraordinarily annoying, because it *is* possible to be nice and nasty! It's the British way, and it's being destroyed through sycophantic Government policies created by sycophantic Government idiots.

Thus, if I have a good friend and colleague who is Asian and they are late going out to deal with a job or something, I reserve the right to shout to him, 'Get your Punjabi arse in the car now you lazy little moron,' or make some other reference to his physical or cultural identity. I'd then probably go on about popadoms, or something. I would then fully expect him to come back with something like, 'Shut the fuck up, you lanky white git.' Neither of us should feel 'afraid' to say such things, especially considering the context. This kind of overtly nasty but affectionate humour is all but disappearing from society. Only now, between very close friends, can we say anything of the sort, and certainly not in front of people who we think might take offence, or dob us in to the bosses to be hauled over the coals for being 'racist' or 'nasty'.

I realise that the above comments completely turn the tables on what is 'acceptable' in today's fawning environment. For we have been brainwashed into thinking that the way we do things now is the favourable and agreeable method. We have been led to believe it is the preferred manner in which we should conduct our lives. So tell me, if we are supposedly doing things in the 'acceptable' way, then why is this country so fucked up, and why are people so pissed off? Surely, by now we should be leading the world with our clean, all-inclusive and politically sanitised organisational antics? However, this is clearly not the case. It's all one big fib. It's also one big Governmental edict. We're not doing it out of choice.

In other words, people are being expected to be pleasant to each other in an extremely false way, when what we really want to do as true Brits is rip the living shit out of each other and all have a laugh about it. This will, in many ways, undoubtedly contain what some may perceive to be racist, as my example above demonstrates, but I would vehemently argue back that it is *not* racist as the racist intention is not there. Sadly, the definition of race crime will not allow this to happen. It decontextualises everything. Political correctness, therefore, undermines Britishness itself, and presumes that we are all inherently racist. It suggests that the kind of behaviour, as outlined previously – irrespective of context – is wrong and, therefore, racist. To ensure that such behaviour is classified as racist, it creates a definition of racism that is entirely subjective and covers all possible angles and outcomes. Any jokes, comments or remarks concerning anything race-related at all can therefore be racist by definition. We thus *become* racist by definition – but *only* by a definition created by other people who haven't got a clue! In which case, if the definition of what is 'racist' is erroneous, then any behaviour considered to be racist in today's environment may not actually be racist at all! In fact, even writing about this is making me want to yell out loud! It's all just so fucked up.

It is my firm belief, therefore, that the current ACPO definition of racism is *wrong*. It is divisive, dangerous and creates unnecessary paranoia. It is also extremely un-British. Clearly we need to punish people who are truly being racist, or who commit crimes owing to a cultural grudge of some description, but this should be done by focussing on intention rather than perception. Sadly, a weak society prefers to look at its own feelings and perceptions rather than consider the objective nature of any so-called racist incident.

Political correctness and downright toadying around has ensured that we're all far too occupied with being weak and pathetic to consider where lies our own strength of character. If someone is nasty to us, it becomes bullying. If someone says a nasty word and it's racist, it becomes racist bullying. This is irrespective of any intention. Therefore, our perceptions become paramount, and intention – e.g. any context – is completely lost in the fog. This decontextualisation leads to driving old fashioned values underground, or driving them away completely. What used to be called 'character building' is now 'bullying'. Friendly banter is poo-pooed, especially if it is apparently 'nasty'. And God forbid if that banter should contain any racial element! You'll be burnt at the stake.

The scourge of political correctness is wholly overwhelming. It has had a carcinogenic affect on our minds. It has eroded our ability to talk honestly *to* people and *with* people. We are afraid to mention certain words or approach certain issues through paranoia. We shy away from acting in a certain way in front of certain people for fear of causing offence, even though we do not set out to be offensive. We simply assume that such behaviour will offend certain people and so say nothing at all! We dare not talk openly and honestly about apparently sensitive cultural issues in front of someone from that background, Yet, if we don't talk about the issues with our peers, how do we know if they are sensitive in the first place? We just assume we know how everyone else is feeling. We assume that other people would be upset by certain things and do our best to negate any chance of this happening. We have assumed, on behalf of other people, what offends them without ever asking them.

In the end, we do nothing more than be dishonest with ourselves and with others. Honesty and integrity? It's all false. It's all so bloody false. The Government's idea of what constitutes such worthy human behaviours is fucked up beyond all reckoning. Political correctness is an unnatural and unworthy aspect of human behaviour. Our minds have been plagued by it; our reasoning devastated by its presence. It is a deceitful and faithless affliction. For we are being forced to live and work in a false and deferential environment – one that is wheedling, cringing and speciously nice. It's a sterile climate, devoid of real and realistic human interaction. We now live a kind of automated half-life. I want to be able to talk freely and frankly with people and about people. I want to rib people and tease people and have a laugh about our foibles. I want to take the piss in a friendly way about cultural imperfections without fear of someone calling me racist.

For example, I want to joke about the 'juice' that's offered to me so regularly in Pakistani households. Juice that's come from the unknown fruit. Juice so thick and sweet and radioactively orange it would dismay a goat. Juice that makes every molecule in your body have a small seizure. I want to jest about this and ask where the hell they get it from. It's a typically cultural thing. And I want to joke about the 'cakes' I once had in a Hindu household. They were served with such grace and kindness it was a blessing to be there. The family were victims of a burglary, but were scurrying around trying to make me feel as welcome as possible. I call them 'cakes', but they were horrendous. Some cultural delicacy apparently. They were so gaggingly tasteless and dry they absorbed every drop of moisture in my body. I was on a drip for three days.

And those Indian sweets. Sweets? They call them *sweets?* What bright spark decided that the combination of flour, sugar, lard and food colouring should ever be called a *sweet?* We get given boxes and boxes of them during certain Hindu festivals and they sit on the desks at the station winking at you malignantly from their greasy cardboard containers daring you to try them. Daring you to treat them like *sweets.* What's wrong with bloody chocolate!

I want to make such jokes, and more. In fact, write a whole book about them! I want to free us from this paranoia. I want to inspire some good, honest and open dialogue between peoples in an environment that is sincere and unadorned with political obsequiousness. I want us to be honest and nice and nasty all at the same time without wanting to cause offence or be racist. I want to talk *to* people and *about* people without the veneer of false nicety that exists in every level of our organisation and throughout the country. I want to breathe the free air again and not suffer this sterile, almost carcinogenic atmosphere anymore. I want some real honesty and integrity, not some half-baked rendition of them. We've lost part of our humanness through this plague of political correctness, and it's a terrible and tragic shame.

My belief is that we have also lost so much of our common sense, reasoning and discretion in so many ways it is bewildering to try to get a handle on it all. I hope you can see my general point in the above arguments, because it was quite exhausting to write. It is time to claw back some sense and reason, and begin to demonstrate, even in small ways, that there is freedom and fresh air above the toxic fumes of political correctness.

Things like wearing a Union Jack, or revitalising realistic and friendly banter as mentioned earlier, could make a huge difference. It is a matter of applying common sense and reason in a world gone mad. I am not suggesting for one moment that such simple demonstrations would heal all the wrongs and sort the country out, but as we have already seen, such simplicity is, in itself, maligned for the sake of maintaining a false sense of cultural unity. I believe it is far better to be affectionately nasty than *un*affectionately nice. Sadly, the Government favours the latter in its quest for some unrealistic and romantic vision of society. A false and specious image of unity. For the Government demands that the police promote a fair and tolerant society. It demands that its officers are impartial, professional and extremely aware of diversity issues. All in the name of some spurious utopian notion of fairness, equity and cohesion, reminiscent of antiquated Victorian idealism. How, then, does it expect the police to remain dispassionate in this obsequious and, quite frankly, ridiculous social atmosphere?

A nation encouraged to be pathetic does not bode well for the future of this country. The police, amongst other organisations, must therefore begin to turn the tide. We must do our bit to claw back some common sense and reason. We must stop covering our arses by making grovelling and befuddling decisions, and hereby advocate that society starts to take responsibility for itself. How on earth did we manage in the post-War years? There must be more resilience and fortitude in the nation than what we see today. Surely! The police are simply *not* responsible for everyone. We can't be. It is not possible. At the moment, however, it is our fault whenever something goes wrong. It is our fault when someone is killed. It is our fault if someone is upset by two text messages they have received and we've done nuffink about it.

Responsibility must come from the bottom up. At the moment it is top down. As we discussed in the chapter concerning neighbourhood policing, any promotion of a worthy concept from the corridors of power loses its momentum by the time it hits the streets. It loses its effectiveness. What should be happening is turning the tables on promoting such worthy ideals and encouraging – and in some cases *forcing* – people to take more responsibility and acting in a decent manner, from the roots of society upwards. This can concern anything from relationships to recycling – it is irrelevant what it is, but the focus must be on citizens making informed choices for themselves, not on other people making choices for them.

If it was our responsibility to nanny the nation and prevent every social disaster from happening, then I could well accept any criticism, but how on earth can it be our remit to do this? The Government has made it our remit, and in doing so has annihilated any remaining tatters of discretion we may have had. People in this country *must* start to take more responsibility for themselves. They *must*. It is not an option. It is something that has to happen, or the consequences will be socially disastrous. We cannot continue to be such weak and pathetic victims, clinging on to half-baked concepts of human rights or civil freedoms. The Government, the police and the whole area of criminal justice *must* toughen up dramatically, or we will not be able to survive.

* * *

This victim culture is, therefore, impossible to police. We simply cannot do it. We will destroy ourselves trying. In fact, we're pretty much there already. Mind-boggling bureaucracy in all departments ensures that any police officer, whatever their role, is enslaved by oppressive procedures and perplexing red tape. Our effectiveness is continually undermined by an all-pervasive lack of clear professional direction, realism and discretion.

It is time it was appreciated that we simply cannot nanny this nation. It is neither possible nor appropriate to try. Sometimes people will just have to take responsibility for themselves, and pay the penalty when they fall foul. In which case, it should not be the fault of the police. For far too long now we have been maligned for incidents that we could never have prevented, or even been expected to prevent. Sometimes it is actually the fault of the *criminal* when bad things happen. What a thing to say! In today's police service though, you would think it is all our fault. We also need to bring back the phrase *not a police matter* and apply it to situations whereby common sense tells us that advice regarding taking some social responsibility is the best course of action.

As you can imagine, such advice is all but impossible to give. It would shock the living hell out of some of our more regular callers, and probably create more grovelling decisions when they complain, which they undoubtedly will. However, we have to get *much* tougher than we are now. The whole process has to be solidified wherein the Government accepts that not everything needs to be recorded or monitored,[57] and certain situations are simply not the remit of the police. Life cannot be quantified in the way that the Government expects, and sometimes a firm but fair word is the only effective way of resolving something. At the moment, we are not allowed to be firm and it's all rather unfair.

Furthermore, the criminal justice process needs to wake up

---

57 I'm thinking of the words 'quality' and 'quantity' here.

and smell the coffee. Our obscenely fair adversarial system is all very well until you realise that criminal justice is but a carousel that does *not* instil fear, does not indemnify victims and does not actually work at all. For example, the Crown Prosecution Service (CPS, or Criminal Protection Service) appears to have a rather strange view of what constitutes being in 'the public interest'. I think that, by-and-large, the public want to live safely and securely in their homes, earn enough money to live satisfactorily and pay the bills, with sufficient left over to enjoy some comforts; not be maligned by anti-social yobs in hoodies, plagued by terrorists on their home soil or otherwise have their cultural identity stripped from them in a climate of weak and cringing subservience. They want to be able to drive on safe roads, enjoy quiet and unassuming lives and not be robbed, burgled or have their property damaged by drug taking little skanks.

If the system was seen to deal firmly and incisively with persistent criminals and treat those who routinely offend with necessary severity, I am sure the public – especially the real victims among them – would be rather more reassured. At the moment, however, they are looking to the police to give them some form of security, but we cannot. We are not in an organisational position to do so. It is actually time that criminals were punished as opposed to the police and the victims receiving all the shit!

Frontline police *officers* also need their discretion back. We need to stop recording everything. We need to stop being performance led – in terms of unrealistic targets and unnecessary focus on irrelevant ticks in boxes, such as detections. Officers who actually leave the station and attend incidents should be recognised as having the ability to give advice, make suggestions, offer alternative solutions and leave it at that. Their role should be recognised as the professional and dignified one that it is. Civilians sitting in offices forty-five miles away sipping cappuccinos are *not* the best people to decide how to sort out a problem if they haven't even been to an incident. They can take the calls and do the admin, but should not be given the authority to override decisions or opinions of trained frontline staff. Otherwise, what is the point of having police officers in the first place?

Furthermore, we *cannot* sort out every problem and we *should* not attend every time a problem is reported. If we do attend an incident that is worthy of little or no attention, then that should be the end of the matter – stop choking us with form-filling and ticky boxes. Domestics are the epitome of this, as we examined earlier. Although domestic violence is a serious and contemporary issue, and a huge percentage of national murders are domestic related, this must not dictate that we should spend thousands of man hours dealing with incidents that have been graded as domestic by policy, but are clearly not worthy of anything further than a few words of advice or sensible suggestions.

At present, the police spend more time covering their arses with domestics than they do anything else. They are a serious and sore bone of contention with most frontline officers when it comes to paperwork and ticky boxes. Suffice to say, it is certainly a pleasure to arrest someone for beating up their partner, but not a pleasure to be expected to arrest someone for sending their ex-partner two unwanted text messages after a messy separation. Believe me, it happens. If you've been following this book in detail, you will now appreciate why.

It is a travesty beyond words what the police service has become. Note that I have tried desperately hard to call it a *service* throughout this book, and every time I do, it makes me cringe a tiny bit. To say 'police force' is obviously far too harsh and creates the wrong kind of image for what has now become an ineffectual and submissive organisation. An organisation desperately trying to be politically correct and upholding some falsely promoted concepts of unity, equality and social tolerance. An organisation battered by suffocating procedures and unattainable goals – ones that in themselves equate to nothing more than a counterfeit fight against crime and disorder. In the corridors of power, the situation is measured with statistics and figures that suggest whatever the Government want them to suggest, while on the streets, the country slides terminally into deeper social ignorance and deprivation.

* * *

It is high time for the relevant people to take a peek from the tops of their ivory towers and see what is really happening in this country and within the police service. It is high time for the development of some vertebrae, and a consolidation of the syrupy mass that the methodology of the police has become. It is time for ignorant and unenlightened dolts who have no real concept of race and diversity issues, and no real understanding of the complexities of life, to stop promoting unrealistic, irresolute and mealy-mouthed organisational behaviours. It is very high time that this victim culture dragged itself up from the pit by the scruff of its own neck – with a bit of help from yours truly, his colleagues and other social allies – and started to take far more responsibility for its own existence than at present.

It is high time that senior police officers stopped fawning around in some obsequious political charade and started getting gritty with real issues as opposed to performance related balderdash. It is time that frontline policing was recognised for the professional, serious and essential role that it is, with relevant staff being encouraged to make a real difference as opposed to chasing targets. A dramatic increase in frontline staff numbers wouldn't go amiss either.

It is high time for all of this and more, or else we will face the most unprecedented problems in the history of British society. Without some form of wake-up call, we will continue in this terminal decline, sliding ever further down the slippery slope of impotence, to further ineptitude and fruitlessness, where criminals continue to rule the roost and anti-social yobs lay claim to the streets, resulting in complete and utter social ignominy from which it will be nigh on impossible to escape.

Epilogue

8.30am. I parked my car in the train station car park and attached the sticky ticket to my windscreen. I then got out, shielded my eyes, and looked at the tiny dot in the distance that was the station. This had to be the longest and thinnest car park in the world, stretching several hundred metres from end to end – with one row of cars parked on either side. I was pretty much at the farthest end and, ironically enough, about as far away from the platform as my house. Still, it was good exercise and I wanted to pay £5 for the privilege. So park I did.

A brisk stroll to the station office took me the best part of five minutes, and I took my place in the queue directly behind a large German man wearing khaki shorts and a beige hat with green feathers in it. Outside the station were at least two dozen juveniles all wearing similar clothing. Some Bavarian scout group it looked like. Anyway, I was second in line to buy my ticket and felt confident of catching the next train.

Now, being stuck behind a large German man wearing shorts and a goofy hat was bad enough, but this was seriously compounded by the fact that I had a train to catch and he seemed intent on taking up as much time as possible at the counter. My eyes wandered to his ample waistband, and I saw that he was packing a pretty serious looking multi-tool in a leather pouch. Visions of arresting him for possessing an offensive weapon flashed through my mind, as well as various ways in which the tool could be used to inflict minor torture if he didn't hurry the fuck up, but instead I leaned closer to him and listened to his request.

'Ja, I vont return tickets to London Paddington for nineteen under sixteens and four adults. Ja, and there's two under fourteens too.'

My heart sank. He *really* was German, and I now had to wait for a machine to calculate the various costs of twenty-five tickets and, more pressingly, print the darn things out. I got my Debit Card out of my wallet in desperate time-saving anticipation, but knew that this really wouldn't make any difference. Still, one had to try. We British cling on to such tiny rays of hope. After three minutes the ticket seller said, 'That will be £176.58 please.' The big man paused and scratched his ear. He leaned back, pulled a wad of small notes and loose change out of his pocket, and then leaned forwards again. 'Ja. Last time it vos £104.33 …'

Many years of experience dealing with customers left me with little doubt whatsoever that this gentleman was here for the long haul, so I turned on my heel and descended to the platform in a huff and thought I'd try my luck with the automated ticket machine. I'd much rather have bought a ticket from a real person but, as the train approached, I had little choice left but to stuff my Debit Card into an appropriate looking slot and press several random buttons in quick succession. Remarkably, the machine gave me my card back as well as a valid ticket for travel, which surprised me as much as £176.58 surprised a big, sweaty Hun, so things were improving.

I settled down onto the train on one of those fold-down seats and contemplated the next thirty-five minutes of travel through the glorious British countryside. There's nothing quite like the view of unintelligible graffiti splattered across ramshackle walls on the arse end of industrial estates. Still, the sun was shining and I was happier than a fat kid with a cupcake.

Now you may wonder what a police officer was doing actually *buying* a rail ticket. You see, my particular police service doesn't appear to have very good negotiation skills when it comes to travel concessions, to the extent that no one seems to know whether we, as police, are allowed to 'badge' our way on various forms of public transport. Everyone says something different. We have had various emails in recent years suggesting that we *may* be permitted to use certain trains between certain stations, at certain times of the day, but it is simply not clear enough. I'm not sure if I'll ever have the need to travel between Big Knobton and Little Winkleton on the 6.12am 'Zoom-Zoom Express Service', but apparently it's free if we show our warrant cards and perform a small piece of expressive dance. We can also use the 'Buzz-Buzz Bus Company' that operates between Outer Bumblefuck and Inner Fucklebum every third Wednesday in March, but only on a leap year.

Rather, it seems that our illustrious London neighbour appears to have the monopoly on decent travel concessions, as well as several thousand pounds more a year in wages, but that's another story. (It's not a particularly long story – they get more money a year than most other police organisations on the premise that the cost of living is higher in London, or something like that. The fact that this is no longer even true appears to be irrelevant.)

So I sat there as a paying customer and would certainly *not* intervene if anything 'kicked off'. That's a very bad attitude coming from a police officer, but sometimes you just have to say 'No'. Besides, this was one of my Rest Days, and I had no intention of spoiling it by stopping a bad person from doing something bad.[58] After all, I hardly have time for that when I'm working ...

Several minutes into the journey and the mobile phone of the gentleman beside me began to ring in a jaunty tone. Well worth the £3.50. He stood up to get it out of his pocket and, simultaneously, the phone stopped ringing and his seat flipped back into the upright position. I gleefully sensed disaster. He stared at the missed number on his phone for about a second and then sat back down again. I say 'sat down' – he didn't really *sit*, per se. Instead he fell backwards in spectacular fashion where his seat should have been, spilling briefcase, coffee, phone and other personal assortments all over the floor of the carriage. I did the British thing and looked out of the window whilst pissing myself with laughter, and everyone else buried their heads further in their books or studied non-existent text messages on their phones. I even think I saw a Granny Smith's apple roll lazily underneath the seat of an unconcerned fellow passenger, but may have dreamt this. We, the British, are cruel and heartless, but we mean well.

I suppose I should have rushed to his aid and given him a CRAPPIES reference number or something (he was, after all, a victim) but I just couldn't be bothered. Sometimes life is tough, and you just have to get over it. After much cursing and mopping, the gentleman regained his composure – and his seat – and the journey continued without any more excitement. The apple, however, is probably still there.

London Marylebone approached and arrived, and I made my merry way on foot to Baker Street. I could have gone on the Tube, but fancied the quick five-minute walk through the sunlit streets.

---

58 The last time I 'intervened' on a Rest Day I ended up having a scuffle with a shoplifter in a sweetshop and buggered up my left knee. It's not worth it when they only get a caution for their sins anyway.

I ended up having a large chicken fajita baguette for breakfast, which repeated like a bitch on me all morning, but it filled a hole. I then had a quick journey from Baker Street to Westminster on the Jubilee Line.

I love London. Always have. There's something magical about the place that fills me with a sense of pent-up excitement whenever I go there. You couldn't ask for a more wonderful capital city. You also couldn't ask for a more pronounced Adam's apple than what belonged to the guy standing next to me on the Tube. It looked like he'd swallowed a door handle. I couldn't keep my eyes off him. You know how difficult it is not to stare at strange people, and this was no exception. So I looked down at the floor in an attempt not to appear rude, and then found myself aghast at what I espied down there. The guy was wearing flip flops and had the biggest gaps between his toes I had ever seen in my life. He could have fitted two more toes between each one, with plenty of space left over for a pint glass and a packet of cigarettes as well. His feet looked like inflated rubber gloves. I couldn't believe my eyes. I wanted to buy him a scarf and a pair of trainers just to cover his shame, but then he spoke and I realised he was American, so my sympathy vanished instantly.

I don't really have a problem with Americans, but they should perhaps try to encourage better dress sense when one has a variety of personal deformities that really do need concealing. We British find it all very upsetting.

Anyway, I left behind the distressing neck-and-toe man at Westminster station and emerged to more bright sunlight and a host of tourists bearing digital cameras and chatting excitedly. I love tourists. I love the melee of colour, bad hairstyles and bizarre outfits. I love the fact that they look the wrong way before they cross the road and nearly get flattened by a speeding bus. So I joined the gaudy, clicking and shrieking throng and deliberately walked in front of several people taking photographs, before

309

checking my map and walking leisurely across Parliament Square.

Several tents were anchored on the grass – one of which was bearing a weather-beaten slogan: 'Stop the War'. Hmm, *Stop the War?* Which war? I think you need to be more particular. There's plenty of wars still raging and plenty of wars that have ended but people *think* are still raging, so please specify. Nearby, a grizzled man with a matted grey beard was wearing a sandwich board that said something like, 'Truth and Justice For All'. Bless him, I thought, as I walked past. Humans have done without truth and justice since time immemorial, so why break the habit of an existence?

I headed through the crowds and finally reached my destination. It was now 10.13am and I stood outside the Home Office building seventeen minutes early for my appointment.

I was there at the behest of my police Federation to take part in a 'round table' discussion on reducing bureaucracy in the police, hosted by the police Minister. There were to be a variety of people there, including other police officers and various important people from different police authorities.

Ironically, I had written the majority of my book several weeks prior to this meeting and was looking forward to it in a subversive kind of way, especially to see if other people from other police organisations echoed anything I'd written so far. There's nothing like having your thoughts validated by other professionals doing the same job!

Ten minutes later and I was in the relevant conference room. As soon as I walked through the door I realised my first slight solecism. I was wearing jeans and a cheap sports T-shirt, with my tattoos clearly and conspicuously visible, while everyone else was smartly dressed – all the men were in shirts and ties, and the other police officers were in uniform. Still, it didn't bother me too much as I'm not that kind of person, but perhaps I *could* have made more of an effort. This clearly showed on the face of one important looking gentleman who looked at me with a mixture of disrelish and anxiety, but he soon changed his tune when he realised I wasn't about to rob him or beat him to a sticky pulp. After all, it's what's on the inside the counts. That's bollocks, by the way. It's what we *do* that matters. I've met so many arseholes who are praised by other people who say things like, 'Well, he's a really nice person inside …' Fuck that shit. If you're a decent person inside, then you'll do decent things. If you're a scumbag on the outside, you've got a pretty good chance of being a scumbag on the inside. Criminal with a heart of gold? What utter crap. That's the kind of wishy-washy attitude that fucks up a country.

Apologies. Where was I? Oh yes, so if anyone had moaned at me for wearing such casual clothing, I would have blasted them from the rooftops. So I sat down and folded my arms in a menacing fashion and looked at the opposite wall. There was a portrait of 2PAC in a thoughtful pose, staring directly at me, apparently painted by an inmate and donated to the Home Office. Things don't get any the more bizarre. I've got another great idea for inmates – how about they sell their fucking pictures and donate all the proceeds to the people they've fucked up?

Sorry, I really wasn't going to swear too much in this Epilogue, but the anger is still there. Things really grate my cheese. After all, I was at the meeting to discuss why things are so awful in the police and propose relevant solutions, so I guess that a bit of anger was quite justified. Fortunately, I didn't swear at all in the meeting and was quite surprised at myself.

On the table in front of me was a little plastic binder with note paper in it. There was the 'Home Office' emblem on the front, as well as the motto: 'Respected nationally, trusted locally; lying, obviously'. (I added the last two words, of course.) Perhaps I shouldn't be so sarcastic as they were giving them away for free. At least I hope they were, because it's now sitting on my desk at home (quick, ring the CRAPPIES hotline – there's a chance of a detection).

Anyway, the police Minister arrived forty minutes late and plonked himself down in his chair. He smelled of smoke and jammed a Danish pastry into his mouth. I liked him immediately. My mind wandered and I pictured myself leaning across the table and sniffing his suit and saying something like, 'It's OK – it's *tobacco*,' but I thought this may have been a bit inappropriate. After all, we weren't there to discuss the sins of the past. We were there to discuss the problems of the present and the expectations of the future.

For the most part the meeting went fairly predictably. It started with some useful points about police bureaucracy and I then did my best to bring the CRAPPIES issue to the fore, as well as the whole 'lack of discretion' thing, but it all sounded rather weedy and insubstantial. There was no way that such a meeting could ever really highlight what it was like to be a frontline police officer in this day and age. It seemed that words were being nodded at, but not fully comprehended.

One of the gentlemen in the room represented someone who – at the time of writing this book – was compiling a Report to be presented at the end of the year. This Report was a review of policing and was concerned, amongst other things, with reducing police bureaucracy.

If you were to read my second introduction again, you will note that I feel the problem is far deeper than simply banging on about 'bureaucracy'. If you try to reduce bureaucracy with the same political mindset with which it was created in the first place, then you are not really going to reduce bureaucracy at all. You're simply going to replace it with more bureaucracy, or distil it to the extent that what remains is worse than what was there before. Really, the meeting should have been entitled 'Removing political correctness and completely destroying spineless arse-covering in the police service', but that would be far too specific. It's much easier to simply use the word 'bureaucracy' and then spend several months compiling information about how bad it is, only to replace it with even more crap, or boil it down to even more intense and soul-destroying forms of administrative legislation.

At one point near the beginning of the meeting, someone important in a suit said that the police were very 'risk averse' and 'blame conscious'. Yes, well done. We know that already. The reasons for this are numerous, as has already been discussed in my book and many other publications. How about we all start to grow a spine and actually do something about it then? So is there a strategy you can introduce to *make* the police less blame conscious? Don't be ridiculous. This is about our mentality at the most elementary level. It's about our attitudes and our basic existence. Nothing can be improved by a top down policy or strategy. It has to come from within. It has to come from grass roots level. It has to start with all of us. We *all* need to locate our vertebrae before we start making any more decisions or implementing any more policies.

After this hopeful start, the meeting then sadly descended into a stale discussion about 'forms' and how these need to be universal; and then it focussed on 'mobile data' and how this could save so much time for the average police officer. After that, the police Minister said something about 'devolution' and someone else said the phrase 'achievable desired position', and at that point, I lost interest as well as the ability to comprehend.[59]

I can't be doing with organisational jargon. Heard far too much of it before. The problems we face are so deep and so intrinsic that they will probably need reworking from the bottom up to sort out. Top down strategies aren't cutting the mustard.

---

59 In other words, everyone was talking about the wrong things. You can change policies and processes all you like but until the mindset radically alters, Britain remains fucked.

By the time they reach grass roots level they are simply shapeless and ineffective (see neighbourhood policing). We are facing an immense crisis – nay, we are in the middle of one – and it's going to take far more than a few seemingly good strategies or a robust business-like approach to restore faith, confidence, morale, vitality and, above all, common sense and justice. If people don't start to truly listen to frontline and other operational police officers (the non-political ones) – or anyone who has a role on the front line – then all is lost. For Britain is held in the grip of something so powerful and so insidious that a few new policies aren't going to make one tiny bit of difference. We need to start at the foundation level, which means allowing frontline and operational staff to do what they were trained to do. It means allowing them to make decisions and give professional advice. And the *only* way this will happen is when it starts to happen. No policy will ever 'allow' this to take place. We simply have to start doing it. *Job be damned.*

So, with a slightly weary head, I glanced at the police Minister before I left the room. I couldn't dislike him. He was a nice guy. I wouldn't call him a sycophantic fool in an ivory tower, but I would say that he is a part of the shambles, despite his obviously good intentions on improving and reforming the police.

Thus, as I walked out of the building I knew that in a few months there would be yet another Report about the police to peruse, wherein certain recommendations would be made to improve the current situation. Perhaps all police organisations should merge – get the forty-three down to one! Perhaps officers should all carry PDA's. Perhaps we need a universal set of forms to fill in so that there is greater consistency between police organisations. Perhaps, perhaps, perhaps.

Perhaps, one day soon, someone important will wake up and realise that this country is in social and cultural chaos. Perhaps, one day soon, that person will realise that without a drastic change, the wheels are going to come off once and for all. Perhaps they will then start to allow police officers of all ranks to actually be able make decisions, and not chase pointless targets, and bring some form of stability back to this nation before all is lost.

Anyway, I'm now repeating myself again for the umpteenth time, so finally I'm going to shut up …

Thank you for reading this book and an even bigger thank you if you bought it and then read it.

* * *

If you have any comments regarding this book, please feel free to email me on the below address (all emails with attachments will be automatically deleted).

thisvictorianplayground@yahoo.co.uk